TRAJECTORIES OF JUSTICE

TRAJECTORIES OF
JUSTICE

What the Bible Says about
Slaves, Women, and Homosexuality

Robert Karl Gnuse

CASCADE *Books* · Eugene, Oregon

TRAJECTORIES OF JUSTICE
What the Bible Says about Slaves, Women, and Homosexuality

Cascade Books
An Imprint of Wipf and Stock Publishers
199 W. 8th Ave., Suite 3
Eugene, OR 97401

www.wipfandstock.com

ISBN 13: 978-1-4982-2335-5

Cataloging-in-Publication data:

Gnuse, Robert Karl, 1947–.

Trajectories of justice : what the Bible says about slaves, women, and homosexuality / Robert Karl Gnuse.

x + 194 p.; 23 cm—Includes bibliographical references and index.

ISBN 13: 978-1-4982-2335-5

1. Bible—Old Testament—Criticism, interpretation, etc. 2. Bible—New Testament—Criticism, interpretation, etc. 3. Bible—Theology. 4. Bible—Hermeneutics. 5. Women in the Bible. 6. Slavery in the Bible. 7. Bible and homosexuality. 8. Homosexuality in the Bible. I. Title.

BT19 .G4 2015

Manufactured in the USA

Dedicated to
Beth, Becky, Chris, Riley, Jake, and Adam

Contents

Abbreviations

ANET	*Ancient Near Eastern Texts Relating to the Old Testament*. 3rd ed. Edited by James B. Pritchard. Princeton: Princeton University Press, 1969
BTB	*Biblical Theology Bulletin*
CTM	*Currents in Theology and Mission*
JBL	*Journal of Biblical Literature*
JSOT	*Journal for the Study of the Old Testament*
JSOTSup	Journal for the Study of the Old Testament Supplements
NRSV	New Revised Standard Version of the Bible
OTL	Old Testament Library
SBLDS	Society of Biblical Literature Dissertation Series
WBC	Word Biblical Commentary
ZAW	*Zeitschrift für die alttestamentliche Wissenschaft*

Acknowledgments

EVERY AUTHOR IS SUPPORTED by other people. I credit my wife, Beth, with patience as I have worked on this book since 1997 at home as well as at the office. I would like to thank Loyola University New Orleans for sabbaticals in the fall 2003 semester and in the fall 2010 semester. I would like to thank the Deutscher Akademischer Austauschdienst for the research grant in fall 2005, and the Fachbereich Evangelische Theologie of Philipps Universität in Marburg Universität, where some of the research for this book was undertaken. I would like to thank the Interlibrary Loan Department of Loyola University for obtaining many volumes for me over the years, and the staff at New Orleans Baptist Theological Seminary for the use of their facilities. Finally, I would like to thank Cascade Books for their willingness to publish this work.

I would like to thank Anthony Godzieba and *Horizons* journal for permission to reprint part of my article "Breakthrough or Tyranny: Monotheism's Contested Implications," *Horizons* 34 (2007) 78–95, as a portion of chapter 1. This material is reprinted with the permission of Cambridge University Press. I would like to thank David Bossman and *Biblical Theology Bulletin* for permission to reprint my article "Seven Gay Texts: Biblical Passages Used to Condemn Homosexuality," *Biblical Theology Bulletin* 45 (2015) 68–87, which was expanded to become chapters 9 and 10.

Biblical texts that appear in this volume come from the New Revised Standard Version translation of the Bible, and specifically from *The New Oxford Annotated Bible: New Revised Standard Version*.

—Robert Gnuse
James C. Carter, SJ / Bank One Distinguished Professor of the Humanities
Loyola University New Orleans
Winter 2015.

1

Perspectives on Biblical Trajectories

Oppression in the Bible?

I HAVE TOO OFTEN heard said or seen in print that the oppression of women, the centuries-long existence of slavery, the justification for war, the pollution of our environment, and other woes of human society result from statements in the Bible as well as from the teachings of monotheistic faiths. I have had my college students say as much at the beginning of a course, usually as a prelude to a statement that explains why they have no commitment to the church. Over the years I have written several works to demonstrate the opposite—that the biblical tradition speaks a message of liberation, human freedom, egalitarianism, human dignity, and social reform.[1] Critics of the biblical tradition who attribute the source of such woes to the Bible can indeed point to the message of fundamentalist preachers, who have used the Bible in the modern age to subordinate women, attack homosexuality, attack the theory of evolution, affirm the inferiority of African Americans, and defend the notion of a just war as the solution to most international crises. In the early nineteenth century such preachers also justified the existence of slavery. But I maintain that the fundamentalist use of the Bible on these issues is a misuse of the Bible. A deeper understanding of the biblical text in its historical context reveals it to be a document that elevates

1. Gnuse, *You Shall Not Steal*; Gnuse, *No Other Gods*, 274–97; Gnuse, *Old Testament and Process Theology*, 141–57; Gnuse, "Breakthrough or Tyranny," 78–95; Gnuse, *No Tolerance for Tyrants*.

humanity, strives for human equality, and attempts to lead society forward in terms of respect for the poor, the oppressed, women, and others so often crushed by the social and economic forces in our world. It is for the purpose of reclaiming the Bible's message of liberation that I have written this volume. I shall contend that the biblical tradition, as it developed, increasingly sought to provide rights and dignity for both slaves and women, so that from our modern perspective, abolitionism and women's equality are the natural outgrowths of the biblical message. In regard to the biblical understanding of homosexuality, I shall maintain that the biblical text itself does not condemn a loving and committed relationship between two free, adult members of the same sex. Those who speak disparagingly of the biblical text as an oppressive document on these issues do not really understand its deeper message.

Critical intelligentsia who so quickly condemn the Bible and its message fail to appreciate two important realities. First, the biblical texts were generated in the first millennium BCE (for the Old Testament) and in the first century CE (for the New Testament). They were products of an era in so many ways repressive, an age of patriarchalism and imperial oppression by military empires. The biblical texts cannot help but reflect the values of that age, especially when straightforward narratives describe the everyday happenings of life. If we desire to know the values and the beliefs of the biblical authors, we are best advised not to read the stories, which, of course, reflect the mores of the common society. Rather, we should turn our attention to the laws that the authors sought to impress upon society, to the prophetic oracles spoken by those critics of religious and social values, to the classical prophets, and to the writings of the New Testament—especially to Paul. We should observe where the values of the everyday society lay, and how the values of the biblical authors stood in tension with them. We should compare the writings of the Bible with the culture of that age, and we should not compare them to our own values. We live two thousand years later, and much of our egalitarian progress, which has moved us beyond the values of the biblical authors, was inspired by those very same authors.

The second overlooked reality about the Bible is that the biblical tradition itself reflects ongoing social progress. We would acknowledge readily that in terms of democratic social values our modern society has moved beyond the social values and beliefs of the biblical text. But what is not acknowledged is that an evolutionary process occurs on several issues within the history of the biblical tradition itself. That evolutionary process or trajectory reflects how the biblical authors increasingly sought to redress the wrongs of society in the oppression of the poor and women. That evolutionary process is what has inspired us over the years. In effect, the evolving trajectory of values in the Bible encourages us to move beyond where the authors were in their own beliefs. The Bible is not to be viewed as a static and timeless work; rather, it inspires an evolutionary trajectory that begins with it and moves forward into the future. Thus, when we read a biblical text, we should ask, what was the point of the author in articulating what we read, and how would that transform itself into our values today? For example, when a biblical passage is critical of slavery in the first millennium BCE without necessarily calling for the elimination of slavery, that message should really translate into abolitionism in the modern era, as it did in nineteenth-century America. The same is true on other issues. We are called upon to go further in social reform than the biblical authors ever could have done with the limitations placed upon them by their society.

In a previous work I observed how the biblical texts inspired political thinkers in America in the eighteenth century. From 1760 to 1805 American political authors drew 34 percent of their citations from the Bible, compared to 22 percent drawn from Enlightenment thinkers, 18 percent from Whig authors, 11 percent from common law, and 9 percent from classical sources.[2] Democracy did not exist in the first millennium BCE, but biblical ideas carried to their logical conclusion ultimately resulted in the emergence of democratic thought. I observed that eighteenth-century American political thinkers quoted the biblical text more than any other resource. (They were, of course, deists, not Christians in the traditional sense.) That is what I mean by an evolving trajectory. The Bible invites us to move beyond where the biblical authors were intellectually; the Bible invites us to participate in an ongoing evolving trajectory. The evolution we can observe in the Bible is an ongoing process that has surfaced most dramatically in Western society over the past four centuries (after the interlude of the Low Middle Ages and the High Middle Ages between us and the biblical era). These intervening centuries between the biblical era and ours may have kept some radical concepts in the biblical text from surfacing.

What I will seek to explore in this short book are those aspects of biblical expression in behalf of the poor and the oppressed that appear to demonstrate development within the biblical tradition. The two issues

2. Gnuse, *No Tolerance for Tyrants*, 6–8; Lutz, "Relative Influence of European Writers," 189–97, esp. 192.

addressed by biblical texts, which appear to reflect an evolution of thought primarily, are the amelioration of the woes of slavery, along with the concomitant causes of enslavement, and the rights of women in a patriarchal culture. To me, the texts connected to these two issues reflect the dynamic nature of the biblical text as an ever-changing and evolving intellectual tradition seeking to elevate the dignity and the rights of all human beings. We should never quote the Bible as a static resource to tell where we should stand on social issues; rather, we should observe the spirit of the biblical text and ask: What is the deeper message, and where is it telling us to go with our own actions?

Intellectual Revolution in the Bible

Over two and a half thousand years ago a religious and intellectual revolution began. We still live in the midst of that ongoing, not-yet-finished revolution. Perhaps because our individual lives are so short, or because we do not readily sense the great patterns of history in our everyday lives, we fail to realize that we still live in that continuing revolution, which is changing the religious, intellectual, and social assumptions of human culture. Historians speak of the Neolithic Revolution, a period of time approximately from 9500 to 4500 BCE when agriculture spread across the Old World, and it encompassed more than four millennia in its process. But historians still call it a revolution. Analogously, we are into the third millennium of this yet unfinished revolution, and though slightly over two thousand years might seem to be a long time, it is still a revolution.

The revolution of which I speak is the emergence of monotheistic religious beliefs with their concomitant intellectual and social values. We might be tempted to refrain from applying the term *revolution* to a process that endures for millennia and appears to us to have been an established part of our worldview. But in reality, the religious and moral revolution generated by the biblical authors has been going on for a short period of time compared to the vast eons of time involved in human evolution. Human history, which has elapsed since we first settled in villages around 9500 BCE in the Near East, is but a cosmic wink, and the period of time involved in the emergence of monotheism is but a fraction of that.

The emergence of the values of justice and egalitarianism in the biblical testimony was not only revolutionary for its age, but evolutionary: that is, we may observe the stages of development within the biblical tradition, especially as we move from the Old Testament to the New Testament. An intellectual or religious breakthrough requires many years to unfold as the implications are worked out in the social-cultural arena of human existence. Thus I speak of the monotheistic process, which we can observe in the biblical text, as one that is still emerging in our own age as we continue to develop the implications of the text. For example, the Old Testament was critical of the oppressive aspects of slavery, the New Testament sought to abolish the distinction between slave and free in the Christian community, and ultimately Christianity in its liberal social manifestation gave rise to the modern abolitionist movement. For years I have used the expression "emergent monotheism" to describe the process wherein the beliefs and social values of monotheistic faith have been unfolding in society. Recognition of this process in human culture should lead us consciously to will to continue and advance the monotheistic "revolution" and "evolution" in our own age, as we advocate justice and equality in our modern world.

Modern scholars in the past generation have begun to sense that monotheism did not emerge among the Israelite people with Moses in the thirteenth century BCE, as once we assumed in the scholarship of previous generations. Rather, Israelites or Judahites did not become monotheistic in a real sense until the Babylonian exile of the sixth century BCE or even later. The religious experience of the people until then was one of polytheism. Great religious spokespersons, such as the classical prophets, and religious reform movements of Hezekiah and Josiah, provided the preliminary stages for the emergence of monotheism among the Judahites during and after the sixth-century-BCE exile.

The new scholarly view that polytheism was regnant among Israelites until the exile has been undergirded both by archaeological discoveries and by a fresh look at the various texts in the Bible that testify to the diversity of religious belief in Israel and Judah. Much of this information we had in our possession for years, especially the biblical texts. The breakthrough in our scholarly paradigms emerged as scholars were willing to look at all the information in a new way. Now scholars are more willing to speak of a development of monotheism in ancient Israel until the time of the exile, and some speak of a developmental process that continued down even into the Maccabean period of the second century BCE or even into the Christian era.

Certain assumptions and ideas in the biblical text could not be fully developed in that initial biblical age. They would be realized only in the "fullness of time," or when human culture was ready for their fuller actualization in the social arena. To put it another way, emergent monotheism creates a trajectory, an ongoing developmental process of religious beliefs and social imperatives. This process over the years would bring about greater equality and respect for all people, the abolition of slavery, concern for the poor, the affirmation of human rights for everyone, and various social reform movements. It might appear that it took a long time for the monotheistic beliefs of Judaism and Christianity to bring about these advances in western European society; but ideas and practices cannot be implemented immediately by an initial monotheistic breakthrough, nor are all the implications to be found in the minds of those initial contributors to the movement. Such values reside in the overall belief system latently, and they await the time in human history when they can become manifest. In the past few centuries, Western culture has become ready to work out the fuller implications of monotheistic faith in the social arena.

My Response to Critics

My thesis may be dramatically challenged by contemporary authors who maintain that biblical religion and monotheism do not represent a great intellectual and religious breakthrough that brings equality and justice, but rather that biblical religion and monotheism engender the repression and even violence that has plagued Western culture for those many years. My critics would postulate that monotheism has justified tyrannical governments, the institution of slavery, and the subordination of women to men in society. In part, this entire book has been written as a response to their observations.

A classic advocate of these views is Regina Schwartz, who has issued a stern challenge to the biblical tradition by declaring that monotheism produces violence and oppression.[3] She opines that belief in one God implies that God favors a group of people, gives them a unique identity, and inspires them to exclude or attack others. This attitude has been passed from the Old Testament to Christianity. Covenants in particular lead the religious community to focus its identity and thus scapegoat others outside that community. The Bible mandates love of the neighbor only until the neighbor challenges our identity, and then that "neighbor" must be resisted

3. Schwartz, *Curse of Cain.* I have responded to her arguments in the past in greater detail, "Breakthrough or Tyranny," which provides the basis for much of this chapter.

and opposed. Monotheism brings people together so they do not fight each other for scarce resources such as land and wealth, but when monotheism is combined with the "particularism" of a covenant relationship, it becomes oppressive. The gods of other peoples are idols, and if those people worship idols they become abominations.[4] Thus, Schwartz can say that God prefers some (Abel, Israelites) and excludes others (Cain, Canaanites)—hence the title of her book: *The Curse of Cain.* Since Schwartz refers to examples such as slavery and the oppression of women, reference to her thesis is appropriate for the scope of this volume.

Schwartz observes that identity is connected to owning land, which reinforces human desire to possess, defend, and conquer. Monotheism becomes political when divinely promised land is bequeathed from God and its possession is maintained by obedience to that God. For then people will defend the land militarily to prove they are obedient. After Judah's sins sent the people into the sixth-century-BCE exile, the return and renewed obedience, especially with the increased emphasis upon purity for the people, led to xenophobia. The exodus freed the slaves, which then led to the conquest of Palestine, wherein the formerly oppressed slaves became the oppressors who killed Canaanites. We have seen this same phenomenon happen again in the twentieth century; the once oppressed become the oppressors.

The biblical story of exodus, conquest, and Davidic rule created a nationalistic particularity in the form of a tradition for the later Judahites, and the narrative still influences our thinking today. Past oppression, such as slavery in Egypt, justifies violence against others. Universalism, proclaimed by a monotheism that declares that all people worship the same God, theoretically could create a toleration of others, but often it generates imperialism that seeks to conquer and absorb others.

Schwartz articulates the rebuttal to her own thesis, however, when she says that the biblical text must be interpreted differently. Ethical values are affected by scarcity of food, water, land, and other precious resources, which must be shared by people for self-survival. Monotheism proclaims that the resources are to be had by the chosen few, and others are to be excluded. Schwartz declares that the biblical text must be plumbed so that an "ethic of scarcity" may be replaced by an "ethic of plenitude," in which all humanity shares in the world's resources. I would declare that the biblical text indeed proclaims such an ethic, and monotheistic universalism may generate toleration rather than imperialism. Schwartz observes that

4. Schwartz, *The Curse of Cain,* 33.

the worship of one god does not necessarily produce a violent notion of identity, but when monotheism is combined with particularism, the combination creates a collective identity for people to set themselves apart from others.[5] I agree, but I would say that the problem is not with the Bible but with how the Bible has been used and interpreted. The greatest misuse occurs when the biblical message is taken out of its social-historical context, and especially when the message of certain biblical texts is no longer seen as part of an evolutionary trajectory that calls upon us to "move beyond" cultural values contemporary with those biblical authors. I hope to show that the biblical texts on slavery and women encourage us to move beyond the reform that those biblical authors initially envisioned and to affirm an even greater degree of equality and freedom.

What Schwartz really attacks is a misuse of biblical accounts by modern believers who use them literally to address contemporary issues and call for some form of continued subordination of other people. Old biblical narratives must be understood critically as an earlier stage in the history of religious evolution. Modern Jews and Christians view the narratives of the Old Testament through later texts: Jews use the Talmud, and Christians use the New Testament, as the hermeneutical key by which to understand and appropriate the values of those older biblical texts. Thus, some values of the older texts, such as war against one's national enemies, have been transcended by later traditions of Christianity and Judaism. Schwartz forgets, as do most believers in the Judeo-Christian tradition, that earlier and cruder values espoused by the biblical text are overturned by later revelation and human religious insight in the evolutionary trajectory, which are inspired by that very same biblical text. The problem lies with modern believers who fail to use the later biblical traditions to reinterpret the more primitive early elements in the Bible. We must view the biblical tradition-generating process as truly an organic, ever-changing, evolutionary process.

Robert Goldenberg also directs his attention to authors who declare that there is monotheistic intolerance in the Old Testament and Judaism, and his observations also can be used to respond to Schwartz's position.[6] Goldenberg admits that preexilic Israelites were largely polytheists and that only after the exile did Judahites become monotheistic. After the Judahites became truly monotheistic, they had mixed attitudes toward other religionists from the late biblical period through the rabbinic period. While some

5. Ibid., 31

6. Goldenberg, *Nations That Know Thee Not*, 1–108.

condemned the religions of the Gentiles, other Judahites believed that all people worshipped the Judahite God indirectly. This became especially true during the Hellenistic and Roman eras. Some Judean authors called for the conversion of Gentiles, while others advocated leaving them alone, as long as they did not convert Judeans to their Graeco-Roman values. With such mixed opinions expressed by Judean authors, one cannot declare that the religion of the Judeans was an intolerant religion, as Schwartz and others do. Goldenberg's thesis argues only that Judean monotheism does not give rise to intolerance; it does not discuss whether monotheism legitimates tyranny and patriarchal oppression for its own believers. Following Goldenberg, if monotheistic Judean religion is not monolithic about other religions, by inference neither does monotheistic Judean religion legitimate oppressive values on other social issues, such as slavery and women's rights.

Monotheism and Equality

Some authors and historians suspect that the rise of monotheistic religious belief elevates one deity and subsequently legitimates the elevation of one ruler on the earth. When that one ruler declares there is only one true god, and he or she worships that deity, that ruler will forcibly convert other people. Thus, a monotheistic state will conquer and absorb other peoples into its own political and religious structures. Monotheistic faith, then, lends support to the national goals of imperial conquest. Zealous monotheists create an irony in their desire to convert all people. For if you reject the religion of others, conquer and convert them, this shows that you fight for a particular religion and a particular deity, not a universal and loving God of all people. According to critics of monotheism, when a multitude of gods is present in the universe, individual believers can exhibit diverse lifestyles because each person is excused from the demands of one particular jealous god. This permits greater freedom of human actions. Monotheism, by contrast, demands submission of the will to one God and the ritual and ethical demands of that one deity. Polytheism thus permits greater diversity and human religious individuality.[7]

These observations may be true for the Achaemenid Persian Empire (550–330 BCE) and the Sassanian Persian Empire (100–600 CE) with Zoroastrianism as the imperial faith, and for the various Arabic empires

7. Marquard, "Lob des Polytheismus," 40–58; Comblin, "Monotheism and Popular Religion," 91–99; Veyne, *Roman Empire*, 216; Fowden, *Empire to Commonwealth*, 37–60.

(630–1918) with Islam. Christians likewise used religious belief to sustain empire. Constantine the Great of Rome in the fourth century CE saw the use of Christianity as a tool to rule a united Roman Empire and to marshal its energy in order to conquer Sassanian Persia.[8] This pattern of Christian imperialism may be observed throughout western European history, including Western colonial expansion into the Third World in the past five hundred years. It appears that empire and monotheism go together to produce oppression, at least historically.

On the other hand, some authors suggest that monotheistic thought may introduce both intolerance and openness into various religious communities.[9] What may be stressed for a people in a particular situation depends upon who is most responsible for articulating monotheistic faith and bringing it to the masses.

If monotheistic belief is supported by the state or an empire, it will stress the monarchical aspects of the one deity in order to legitimate kings and the institution of the monarchy. This form of monotheism articulates the analogy of one God in the heavens ruling all people as the parallel to one ruler on the earth ruling all his subjects. This is monotheism "from above," a religion imposed upon the subjects by the elite to legitimate their power. But if monotheism is generated from the people, especially poor and marginal people, such as the ancient Judahites or early Christians, the existence of one God in the heavenly realm implies that all people in the earthly realm must worship that one deity and stand as equals before that one deity. This metaphor will be critical of kings and kingship, for the ideology legitimated by "monotheism from above" puts the king into a more direct relationship with the deity, and the monotheism of the people rejects such an exaltation of a mere human being to divine or semidivine status. This is why there is so much critique of kings and kingship in the biblical tradition, as I have elsewhere sought to demonstrate.[10] The biblical tradition contains monotheism "from below," a faith system from the people. For the biblical texts were generated by people who were the underdogs and the oppressed folk of their age.

Tikva Frymer-Kensky aptly observes that the biblical narratives speak of women and honestly acknowledge their subordinate status in the

8. Fowden, *Empire to Commonwealth*; and Harris, *World of the Bible*, 164.

9. Petersen, "Israel and Monotheism," 92–107; Michaels, "Monotheismus und Fundamentalismus," 51–57; Gross, "Religious Diversity," 349–55.

10. Gnuse, *No Tolerance for Tyrants*.

patriarchal society in which they lived. However, the biblical narratives never characterize the women in a prejudicial fashion, disdaining them for their weak and subordinate status, as was common in the Hellenistic literary tradition, but rather portray them in ways very similar to how men are described. This, says Frymer-Kensky, is because the biblical authors belonged to the people of Israel or the later Judahites, who themselves were a weak and subordinate people in an age of oppressive world empires. Hence, the women in their roles were analogous to the people of God, and so no prejudicial portrayal of women is forthcoming from the biblical narratives, but instead the women often seem to be lauded for their ability to survive as "tricksters." The portrayal of women, to a certain extent, serves as a model of behavior for the biblical audience, people also trying to learn how to survive in an overwhelming world as underdogs.[11] The biblical tradition reflects the vision of the world from the perspective of the underdogs, the slaves, and the oppressed. Theirs is truly "monotheism" from below. Hence, in the legal tradition, as we shall observe later, there is special attention paid to elevating the status of slaves and women.

Critical historians recently have observed that the monotheism of the Judahites was brought to the masses due to the efforts of the scribal and priestly elite, and perhaps was abetted by the government in Jerusalem in the postexilic period after 500 BCE. Prior to the Babylonian exile in the sixth century BCE, Hezekiah's (710–700 BCE) and Josiah's (622–609 BCE) reforms in Judah used strong-arm methods to accomplish what appears to have been monotheistic reform. After the exile, the efforts of Ezra, such as the exclusion of foreign wives, appear rather abrasive and tyrannical. Nonetheless, in the great scheme of power politics of that age, the preexilic Judahite kings and postexilic Judahite priestly leadership must still be accounted as part of the oppressed, small powers in a world of gargantuan political forces, even when their religious reform was sponsored by those foreign powers (as with Ezra and Nehemiah). They are still the "underdogs." Thus, their efforts can be seen as giving rise to a "religion from below," a religion of the masses and the oppressed.

A healthy monotheism encourages freedom of the deity in the divine realm to act without the constraints of the other divine wills, but it should also affirm freedom and equality of people in the human realm as believers relate equally to that one deity. As that God is free in the divine realm, so also the devotees are free in their actions in the earthly realm. When the

---

11. Frymer-Kensky, *Reading the Women of the Bible*, xvi–xvii, xxi.

tiered class system of the gods in the heavens disappears, the tiered class system of people on earth disappears. In a polytheistic system you have high gods and the lesser divinities, who are ranked by importance and according to their function in the natural order. Gods of the sky, sun, and storm are usually supreme; gods with specialized functions, such as a deity of dreams or the seamstress goddess, hold lesser rank. Lesser deities serve in the court of those high deities, and similarly on earth you have the elite leaders and the rest of the members of society, who serve them. Often there are three classes of deities in the divine realm and correspondingly three classes of people on the earth (rulers and military elite, merchants and craftsmen, and laborers and peasants). There are high gods, who are distant in the heavens; there are the powerfully active gods below them; and, last, there are the local deities and numina, who are accessible to humans. This framework parallels the human social classes. One deity in the divine realm undercuts the notion of elites and subordinates on earth by removing those distinctions in the divine realm.[12] One God in the heavens implies that there is one single, universal basis for religious belief and human morality, which in turn becomes a standard for all men and women to adhere to, regardless of class or status. This promotes equality of all believers before one deity and one unified natural order of things.[13] Egalitarian values then surface in the literature that is produced.[14] One can observe such values in both the Old Testament and the New Testament.

Unfortunately, bad things sometimes happen in history. Constantine and others used the Christian movement for their own political purposes, even though that did not reflect the deeper spirit of Christianity. Christians contemporary with Constantine supported his actions, for it helped spread their faith. Combined political and religious imperialism often occurs in Christian history, and Christians have been willing to allow political leaders to use the Christian faith for repression in return for political favors for the institutional church. We have seen this in Nazi Germany, Communist Eastern Europe, and Latin America. We would like to believe that this is not true and pure Christian practice, but it has happened too many times in history. Christians must become aware of the frequent oppressive use of their religious beliefs against other people and learn to live the spirit of the message they preach and so oppose such regimes.

12. Gnuse, *No Other Gods*, 242–63.

13. Dever, "How Was Ancient Israel Different?," 62–67.

14. Alter, *Art of Biblical Narrative*, 129.

Biblical scholars affirm that the monotheism of the Old Testament and the Judahites, as well as the New Testament, at its heart does not legitimate political empire, but rather encourages solidarity with all humanity. The believers who generated these texts were often the oppressed and victims of political systems in their own age. For example, the prophets spoke of a universal deity who would bring a state of peace and prosperity to all people someday.[15] The following oracle is found in both Mic 4:3–4 and Isa 2:4,

> He shall judge between the nations,
>   and shall arbitrate for many peoples;
> they shall beat their swords into plowshares,
>   and their spears into pruning hooks;
> nation shall not lift up sword against nation,
>   neither shall they learn war anymore;
> but they shall all sit under their own vines and under their own fig trees,
>   and no one shall make them afraid.

This is a religious oracle that truly comes "from below," from the voice of a defeated and conquered people under the heels of the Assyrian Empire. There are monotheisms that are imperialistic, such as that used by Constantine, and then there are monotheisms of peace and human unity. There are monotheisms "from above," defined by a monarch, pharaoh, emperor, or tyrant who uses the religion for political advancement, and there are monotheisms "from below," from the people crying for dignity, toleration, and peace. This prophetic text just quoted expresses hope in overcoming war between people by the recognition that there is only one God over all humanity. This is an oracle reflecting religious faith "from below," even if the prophetic author, Isaiah or Micah, was not yet a monotheist in the fullest sense, but was evolving in that direction. In the polytheisms of the ancient Near East, the wars between peoples reflected the wars in the heavens between the gods, but according to the vision of this oracle, the emergence of one God should spell the end of wars and oppression and create a vision of all people as equals under that one deity.[16]

---

15. Lang, *Monotheism and the Prophetic Minority*, 55; Theissen, *Biblical Faith*, 71; Albertz, *History of Israelite Religion in the Old Testament Period*, 2:425; and Dietrich, "Über Werden und Wesen des biblischen Monotheismus," 25–27.

16. Theissen, *Biblical Faith*, 71.

Perhaps the spirit of this prophetic oracle has yet to permeate the consciousness of believers in those faiths. There is an evolutionary trajectory in the monotheistic process that is still seeking to come to fruition. The monotheistic breakthrough of ancient Israel is still unfolding, and we are still in the formative stages. When religion is no longer used to justify war, imperialism, conquest, and as the apology of one race of people for enslaving another race, then monotheism will have actualized one of the most significant components of its ideological matrix. Then we shall look back and see that imperialistic monotheisms were merely an evolutionary dead end. Monotheism "from below" which unites people by the power of the human spirit rather than by the sword will be seen as the true heir to the biblical tradition.

Monotheism and the Dignity of Women

Another aspect worthy of mention in this preliminary chapter is the critique that monotheism leads to the suppression of women. The assumption here is that a religion with one God will portray that deity as masculine, usually as a divine father. This excludes the feminine from the divine realm. Furthermore, if that one deity is zealous and demands that all people worship "him," then even more the feminine will be viewed with suspicion, and people who worship female deities become targets for oppression. Historically, the monotheistic faiths converted peoples who had goddesses and high priestesses and subsequently excluded the female gods and the priestesses from worship. A very critical attitude toward the presence of women in the cult was assumed by the newly ascendant monotheistic faith in postexilic Judah, for example.

Some scholars believe that the polytheistic faiths (with their inclusion of female deities) were more tolerant of women in the cult, especially given the presence of female votaries in the various polytheistic faiths. Marija Gimbutas in her study of primitive religion suggests that once religion elevated the mother goddess, but with the rise of a patriarchal religion there came the subordination of women.[17] However, it should be questioned whether polytheism or a mother-goddess-oriented religion gave women dignity in the ancient world. In the ancient Near East the cults of Inanna/Ishtar in Mesopotamia and Isis in Egypt were extremely significant, but the status of women was still very poor in both those societies, and male

17. Gimbutas, *Gods and Goddesses of Old Europe.*

leadership was the norm.[18] Polytheistic societies did not challenge the patriarchal assumptions in those cultures.

In fertility religions where a goddess was significant, it was possible
for a young woman to obtain a respectable position as a priestess. One
fortunate lady ultimately became the high priestess, but the other women
did not. Furthermore, if the role of priestess involved sexual activity in the
cult, such advancement was hardly ennobling. Most women in society did
not become priestesses; they simply remained totally subordinate wives to
their patriarchal husbands. Religions with feminine imagery did not liberate them, for not all women could become priestesses, much less the high
priestess.

Biblical archaeologists have observed that devotion to the Canaanite
goddess Asherah was a mode of pious expression. Jeremiah condemns the
actions of women who bake cakes in their homes to venerate Asherah (Jer
44:15–19). Yahwism crushed this popular piety only after many years, and
its suppression might be seen as a blow against women. The cult of Asherah
was a private, woman's religion in the home, and its status points to the
inferior status of women. That worship of Asherah was a home cult implies
that it was not worthy to become part of the official state cult. Whereas the
home cult of Asherah ostracized women, a monotheistic faith, in theory,
granted more dignity to women by including them (as Christianity did) in
public worship.

The significant question is what really caused the subordination of
women in ancient Israel. Did the religion subordinate women primarily?
Did emergent monotheism subordinate women? Or were women subordinate in a patriarchal society before Yahwism arose? I would say the
subordination of women existed before emergent monotheism, and that
monotheism helped ameliorate the low status of women by seeking to give
them more rights. A consideration of the biblical laws will bear this point
out. Preexisting patriarchalism was so strong in society long before Yahwistic monotheism that it would take years to lessen this patriarchy. In fact,
we are still attempting to do this today. The emergence of state structures
and social organization, including temple hierarchies, strengthened patriarchalism in society. Hammurabi's laws imply that in the early second millennium BCE women were the property of men, and their sexual behavior
was highly regulated by legal guidelines and social customs. Women were
precious property because of their childbearing capacity and the ability to

18. Gerstenberger, *Yahweh—the Patriarch*, 93.

create heirs who would inherit the family wealth. Do not blame monotheism for the subordination of women; it was there thousands of years before emergent Yahwistic monotheism. The rise of the Assyrian and the Babylonian empires in the eighth through the sixth centuries BCE brought great economic oppression to Israelites and Judahites, and marginal people, including women, were hurt the most in such circumstances. Finally, priestly assumptions about female impurity connected to menstruation existed before monotheism arose. The biblical tradition recalls the memory of those assumptions, which were really the generic assumptions of other cultures in the ancient world, also.[19] Once monotheism arose, old values from the prior age still endured. Monotheism cannot change society and the minds of people all at once, especially in regard to matters that affect home and the family.

Though the subordination of women continued through the emergence of Christianity, throughout the years religious articulations inspired by the biblical texts arose to stress the dignity and rights of women. The evolution of biblical values takes time to unfold, and the liberation of women takes time to develop in the hearts and minds of people. It takes longer to radically change family values than social or economic values.

I believe that the biblical tradition does not subordinate women, for when the biblical text reflects the subordination of women, it is portraying the culture of that age. To be sure, for two millennia men have quoted the biblical text to subordinate women, but they were missing the point of their religion, which declares the equality of all people before God. Too often men appealed to the masculine portrayal of God to justify their patriarchal beliefs. When the Bible characterizes God as masculine, it is because there is only one deity, and you no longer have the luxury of assigning sex to different divine beings. However, at times in the Old Testament God is metaphored as both masculine and feminine, a sign that the metaphor of gender is only symbolic. Erhard Gerstenberger said, "I find untenable an attempt to reconstruct a direct monocausal relationship between the rise of monotheism in Israel and the denigration of women . . . belief in God includes the greatest possible openness to the justified claims of equality of all people."[20] Gerda Lerner noted that it was tragic that monotheism emerged in a society with strong patriarchy, for the religious belief then

---

19. Lerner, *Creation of Patriarchy*, 88–91.

20. Gerstenberger, *Yahweh—the Patriarch*, 94, 110.

unfortunately affirmed that patriarchy in many ways.[21] I would agree, but I would respond immediately that monotheism also planted the seeds to undercut that patriarchy ultimately.

I shall direct my attention to particular themes that I believe reflect the monotheistic evolutionary trajectory as it seeks to affirm the basic equality and dignity of all people. In particular, I believe this can be demonstrated with biblical passages that speak about the economic rights of the poor, the rights of slaves, and the rights of women. Herein we may observe how the biblical tradition addressed social issues in such a way as to plant seeds of reform in human society, so that over the centuries the radical egalitarian values of the biblical tradition would unfold and make their impact upon people and society.

21. Lerner, *Creation of Patriarchy*, 198.

2

Old Testament Law Codes
and Justice for the Oppressed

Emergent Monotheism and Justice

THE GRADUAL EMERGENCE OF monotheism and egalitarian beliefs can bring forth social and religious changes for people and society. Not all of these ideas come forth into a society in completely developed form; society has to be ready for them. Monotheism plants the seeds of reform, the initial ideas about human dignity and equality, and eventually they unfold for humanity. Different insights will blossom at different times. In ancient Israel the emphasis upon devotion to only one God began to create an emphasis upon the equality of people in the presence of that solitary being in the divine realm. For if there is only one deity, then all people relate to that deity equally. As I mentioned previously, if the tiered system of gods in the heavens is replaced by one God, then gradually the assumption of equality between people will emerge among the religious intelligentsia, for there is only one corresponding class of people on earth. When the early prophets in the eighth century BCE called upon society to worship Yahweh exclusively, even without necessarily denying the existence of other gods, there also came a cry for economic justice for the poor and the oppressed. The cry of the prophets was truly a strident call for justice, but ultimately it is only with the laws that we observe a truly serious attempt to bring economic justice to society.[1] After those early voices spoke in the eighth century BCE,

1. Amit, "The Jubilee Law," 49.

18

there emerged a scribal legal tradition that articulated more guidelines and laws to promote economic justice and liberation for the oppressed.

The biblical text provides testimony to this social and religious evolutionary trajectory in its law codes. Within the law codes are commands and moral imperatives given to Israelites and Judahites over a period of several centuries, and we may observe an evolution in some of these laws that betokens a sense of increasing concern for justice and equality. The evolution of these laws parallels the emergence of monotheism partially, though many of the laws appear to have social impact before the final emergence of monotheism in its pure and radical form during and after the Babylonian exile in the sixth century BCE. Early attempts to mandate justice are found in the laws of the Book of the Covenant (Exod 20:23—23:19), which modern scholars traditionally located in the premonarchic period (1050 BCE), but that currently are dated by many critical scholars to a later era. Frank Crüsemann connects the emergence of the Book of the Covenant with the land and religious reform of King Hezekiah of Judah around 700 BCE.[2] The new direction by contemporary scholars (to date legal material later) parallels the scholarly consensus on the late development of monotheism, as well as a general later dating of other literature in the Old Testament. Deuteronomic laws (Deuteronomy 12–26) were hypothesized as being an eighth-century-BCE oral legal tradition in north Israel (possibly inspired by prophets like Hosea), and their precipitation into written form was associated with Josiah's religious and social reform in Judah after 622 BCE, supposedly resulting from his discovery of the Book of the Law in the Temple. It was believed that Deuteronomy 12–26 was that Book of the Law discovered by Josiah with editorial additions provided by the Deuteronomic Reformers around 620 BCE. Scholars more recently assume that most of the laws arose in the time of Josiah, and perhaps additions continued to be made to the Deuteronomic corpus during the Babylonian exile and beyond. The laws in Leviticus were believed to have precipitated from oral tradition to written form during the Babylonian exile, with some exilic and later postexilic additions made by the Priestly editors. The oldest laws were said to be in the Holiness Code in Leviticus 17–26, which originated in oral tradition in the eighth century BCE before their precipitation into written form by between 550 and 400 BCE.

2. Crüsemann, *Torah*, 109–200.

Sequence of the Law Codes

Newer critical theories complicate the debate and rearrange this scenario, especially with laws in Leviticus. Some suggest a well-defined Priestly legal tradition in Leviticus written as early as during the reign of Hezekiah (715–700 BCE). Some reverse the dates of the sources by suggesting that the Holiness Code may be later (exile and beyond) and more secular than some of the other Priestly laws, which then are projected back to the time of King Hezekiah.[3] I will admit that some laws in Leviticus, either the Holiness Code or the other Priestly laws, may actually be very old. But in their early and oral form these Priestly laws were not public, but rather they were the property of an elite group of priests in Jerusalem. Hence, their impact upon the Judahite populace was not felt until the exile, and therefore after the time of the other two legal codes. The narrative histories of the people of Israel and Judah show no awareness of these special laws. Therefore, I shall work with the assumption that the Priestly laws arose after both the Book of the Covenant and the Deuteronomic laws.

Another very recent scholarly paradigm suggests that the Book of the Covenant in Exodus 21–23 dates either to the Babylonian exile in the sixth century BCE or perhaps even to the postexilic era. According to this theory, the Book of the Covenant makes no reference to kings, not because the code was premonarchic, as the old theories had it, but because the laws emerged after the disappearance of the monarchy. Defenders of this paradigm point to perceived influence on the Book of the Covenant from other biblical law codes and especially Babylonian laws, made possible because the Book of the Covenant arose in Babylonian exile. This law code is thus envisioned as dating after the seventh-century BCE Deuteronomic laws. The difference between the two codes is explained by the Covenant Code being a practical set of guidelines for Judahites living in exile in simple economic conditions, whereas the Deuteronomic laws were idealistic and an attempt at reform during the time of the monarchy. Thus, the Book of the Covenant appears older than the Deuteronomic laws, when in reality the laws contained therein are simply more conservative in appearance because they are cautious and practical for Judahites living in harsh and simple conditions at a later date. Their arguments address some of the very texts I will discuss below.[4] I am highly impressed by these arguments of

---

3. Knohl, *Sanctuary of Silence.*
4. Ibid.

John Van Seters, who makes this proposal in its most cogent form, but I am not totally convinced. Laws in the Book of the Covenant other than the ones that Van Seters discussed still make me believe that the Book of the Covenant in Exodus 21–23 is prior to Deuteronomy 12–26, and that the latter is dependent upon the former.

For example, the guidelines concerning the three pilgrimage festivals appear to be older in the Book of the Covenant than the same guidelines in the Deuteronomic laws. In Exod 23:14–17 the three festivals are described by their ancient agricultural functions; they are called the festival of Unleavened Bread, the festival of Harvest or Firstfruits, and the festival of Ingathering. However, in Deut 16:1–17 they are referred to by names that recall historical memories to be celebrated or recalled at each of these three respective festivals. They are called the festival of Passover, the festival of Weeks, and the festival of Booths or Tabernacles. Passover commemorates the exodus out of Egypt, the festival of Booths or Tabernacles recalls the wandering in the wilderness, and the festival of Weeks may recall the entrance of Joshua's people into the land of Palestine. This historicizing of the old agrarian festival celebrations betokens a later reinterpretation of the old festivals that were probably pre-Israelite in origin. Rooting the festival celebrations in the pentateuchal traditions appears to be a distinctly Israelite interpretation that might be connected to the rise of early monotheistic faith and emergence of literary traditions that recall Yahweh's guidance of the people in the historical past. This, for me, is one cardinal piece of evidence for an earlier date for the Book of the Covenant. Furthermore, as we reflect on the laws concerning debt, interest, and slavery, I still feel that the laws in Exodus precede and are further elaborated upon by the laws in Deuteronomy. I will acknowledge, however, that there is a complex debate concerning the relationship of the laws in the Book of the Covenant and the Deuteronomic laws that renders any presentation of the history of the legal tradition subjective. Perhaps the ultimate answer may lie in a gradual evolution of the Book of the Covenant before and after the emergence of the Deuteronomic laws. However, to reconstruct such an evolution may be impossible. So for the purposes of this study I shall continue to use the traditional scholarly sequence, and I will make reference to the interpretive possibilities that are suggested by the research of Van Seters. I assume that laws in the Book of the Covenant are the oldest, Deuteronomic laws come later, and Priestly laws in Leviticus are the youngest.

A significant relationship between the Book of the Covenant in Exodus, the Deuteronomic laws, and the Levitical laws exists. An initial affirmation of human rights occurs with some of the laws in the Book of the Covenant, but a fuller expansion of the same laws appears in Deuteronomy, which was produced by the reform movement in Judah under Josiah around 622 BCE. Traditionally, scholars have listed comparisons of the two law codes that demonstrate how Deuteronomy 12–26 shares many parallels with Exod 20:23—23:19, and these scholars assume that Deuteronomy 12–26 contains a revised version of the laws from Exodus, updated in response to social and economic change.[5] Those reformers who expanded the laws were inspired by prophetic preaching and other protomonotheistic reform tendencies (which did not exclude the existence of other deities), for the Deuteronomic revision attempts to provide more rights for poor and marginalized people. Repeatedly readers of Deuteronomy 12–26 see the refrain to care for the poor, the widow, the orphan, and the sojourner in the land because of what Yahweh has done for the people in the exodus and in subsequent years. In addition to these social imperatives, there is increased legislation to undergird exclusive worship of Yahweh. The call for social justice and monotheism appears to be organically connected in the laws and sermons of Deuteronomy and in the Deuteronomistic History of Joshua, Judges, Samuel, and Kings.

The Actual Use of Law Codes

A final point is worthy of mention. Contemporary scholars suspect that biblical law codes were written by scribal intelligentsia for the purposes of instruction and exhortation, but these codes actually may not have been used in everyday legal deliberations by elders in the villages or by formal judges in urban courts. Rather, the actual courtroom situation may have continued to rely upon an oral tradition that could evolve over the years as social-historical circumstances changed. We are best advised to distinguish between "Israelite law" and "biblical law." "Israelite law" is what elders in the villages and judges in more formal courtroom situations used, and these guidelines probably remained in oral tradition throughout the centuries and probably evolved over time. "Biblical law" is what was written in our biblical text by theologians who sought to inspire legal reform, affirm

---

5. Patrick, *Old Testament Law*, 97–98, provides a good summary chart for comparison of the law codes.

Israelite identity, and seek justice for all people. Biblical law codes are literary creations that might best be called theological expressions. They are selective, addressing particular issues of theological concern and calling for change in the actual legal tradition at those points where the monotheistic reformers believed change was necessary. A perusal of the law codes, especially Deuteronomy 12–26, will reveal that there is much preaching and exhortatory rhetoric interspersed in these laws, so that one will sense that these law codes are sermons. Also, many laws are enjoined upon the readers with statements to the effect that this is the will of God, or that God will punish those who break these laws. Deuteronomy 12–26 especially calls for obedience to these laws by an appeal to the exodus experience and the grace of God in electing Israel. Such "law" cannot be enforced in a court of law. Hence, the "law codes" in the Bible are sermons, not really collections of actual law. They are revelation from God with an unchanging message for all time.[6]

To be sure, there probably was much similarity between actual "Israelite law" as it was practiced and the "biblical law" as set forth by the biblical authors, but we will never be able to sort out the differences, for the oral legal traditions are lost forever. Also, it is very likely that over the years the biblical tradition influenced the way that actual law was practiced, especially after Judahite exiles began to return from Babylon after 539 BCE, until eventually for the Judahite tradition their biblical law became their actual everyday customs for living. That phenomenon probably occurred somewhat gradually after the return from Babylonian exile, but even more dramatically after the destruction of Jerusalem in 70 CE and the rise of the rabbis, who focused upon the interpretation of biblical law to provide guidelines for everyday life.

In a comprehensive evaluation of the social and economic settings of preexilic Israel, Douglas Knight presents a challenging thesis to the traditional understanding of the biblical law codes. He concludes that the biblical laws were postexilic literary creations generated by scribal intelligentsia in response to the demand of the Persian rulers in the later sixth and fifth centuries BCE for local leaders in the various satrapies to organize their laws and their customs in written form. In particular, Darius I of Persia made this demand, and we have evidence that such activity occurred in Egypt. Knight's detailed evaluation of the legal, social, and economic environment of preexilic Israel leads him to conclude that there was no need for

6. Knight, *Law, Power, and Justice in Ancient Israel*, 9–16.

people in the villages or the royal court to create written laws in the preexilic era, when their oral traditions and customs sufficed. Written laws were generated only at the behest of Persian rulers, and then only some of the laws reflected actual juridical practice; the majority were literary creations.[7]

Knight observes that according to modern scholars the Book of the Covenant in Exodus 21–23 appears as though it emerged from rural villages in preexilic Israel, and the Deuteronomic laws in Deuteronomy 12–26 appear to have a court origin under King Josiah around 620 BCE. However, an evaluation of the social context of both the villages and the royal court indicates to Knight that neither of those codes really reflects the actual legal needs and practices that logically would have belonged to those environments.[8] For example, Jer 34:8–22 and Neh 5:1–13 indicate that the Deuteronomic laws on slave release were not really observed, for the laws were simply idealistic literary statements by the scribes. In Jer 34:8–22, King Zedekiah's emancipation edict to release Hebrew slaves, male and female, appears to have been a one-time proclamation and a one-time occurrence, and even then the people took back their slaves after initially freeing them. The prophet Jeremiah implies that there was a law behind this emancipation (probably Deuteronomy 15), but that the law had not been kept in years past (vv. 14–15). In Neh 5:1–13 Nehemiah excoriates the nobles in Jerusalem for charging interest and reducing poor Judahites to debt-slaves, and no reference is made to any laws that condemned such activity, as if guidelines in Exodus and Deuteronomy had been forgotten. Apparently Israel and the postexilic Judahites had as many slaves proportionately as any other ancient Near Eastern society.[9] Knight's study reinforces what other scholars have suspected about the literary and theological nature of the law codes in the biblical world, which were not really used in legal practice.

At this point let me observe that this does not affect my thesis. Whether the laws were observed or not is irrelevant to me. What is important is that scribal intelligentsia or theologians, if you please, had a vision of hope, justice, and change that they cast into a literary form that has lasted for over two thousand years. Their vision has become part of our biblical text, which is meant to inspire and guide us today. I theologize off of the text, not history; I theologize off of vision of hope, not the heartbreak of historical reality. Furthermore, although Knight observes that the codes are postexilic

7. Ibid., 97–112.
8. Ibid., 118–224.
9. Ibid., 210.

literary creations, he does not attempt to sequence them in terms of their development. If I were to accept Knight's theoretical model, I would still maintain that there is a developmental process, in which the Book of the Covenant appears to be early and the Deuteronomic laws and the Priestly laws appear to be later and build upon the ideas in the Book of the Covenant. Someone in the biblical era appears to be thinking out the implications of these laws and furthering their development, even if the reflection and further development of laws does not arise as a result of actual practice in village courts. It is this process of reflection that draws my attention, for it betokens a mindset that is concerned with justice.

These observations about biblical law codes as ideal literary creations are borne out by comparable studies of Mesopotamian law codes. Those codes also appear to be literary and political creations by kings, and not really guidelines for legal practice in the law courts. Thus, the Law Code of Hammurabi, for example, was in the possession of the scribal schools but not really used in the courtroom. Hammurabi promulgated it for purposes of declaring the justice of his rule. This would explain why no Mesopotamian legal decision ever refers to Hammurabi's Code, or any law code for that matter.[10] We have discovered copies of Hammurabi's Code in royal archives but never in court settings, even though we have thousands of court dockets from those archaeological sites. In fact, these Mesopotamian dockets never refer to any law code, even when they address issues that are clearly covered by Mesopotamian law codes, especially by guidelines of Hammurabi's law.[11] Furthermore, Hammurabi's laws were incomplete; they did not cover the bulk of the economic issues that needed to be addressed. Perhaps, Hammurabi's laws were limited to those laws that the king sought to change or standardize, but if so, they did not attempt to change the greater legal tradition significantly.[12]

The scribal intelligentsia produced these fixed, written codes to be used for writing exercises in scribal schools, but, more important, the codes also inspired the scribal class and other literate intelligentsia with a sense of justice. Some of these intelligentsia may have become judges, and their scribal education and familiarity with the written law codes may have

---

10. Bottéro, "Le 'Code' de Hammurabi," 409–44; Watson, *Evolution of Law*; Fishbane, *Biblical Interpretation in Ancient Israel*, 95–96; Jackson, "Ideas of Law and Legal Administration," 185–202.

11. Berman, "History of Legal Theory and the Study of Biblical Law," 24.

12. Greengus, "Legal and Social Institutions of Ancient Mesopotamia," 471–72.

influenced the decisions that they rendered. In this way the written law codes ultimately may have exerted a gradual influence upon the actual legal decisions handed down in the law courts. Thus, after many years, the laws of Hammurabi's Code may have become actual practice in the law courts. We have found fragments of Hammurabi's Code in many archaeological sites (probably school exercises), and the frequency of these finds testifies to the widespread knowledge of the code.

The same might be true for biblical law codes. Generated by intelligentsia, they may never have been used directly in law courts, but over the years they influenced Judahite practice. Especially after the Babylonian exile (586–539 BCE), Judahites may have turned to these codes for direction in how to reconstruct their society and live their everyday lives. Even though they were a province in the Persian Empire (539–330 BCE), in various Greek kingdoms (330–164 BCE), and in the Roman Empire (63 BCE–70 CE), they followed the guidelines of these codes, often with the consent of the foreign rulers, who saw the codes as providing stability and order in one of the provinces of their empire.

Biblical law codes were indeed reformist in their outlook, with an ideal sense of how society should function. These written law codes evolved, to be sure, in the hands of religious intellectuals, for the laws became rhetorical tools, perhaps used in public proclamation, to inspire a society to commit itself to justice. Such appears to be the dynamics underlying the public reading of the Deuteronomic laws during the reform of Josiah in late seventh-century-BCE Judah. Judahite scribes may have been well aware of the law codes of other peoples, including the Law Code of Hammurabi, for the diverse law codes would have circulated among the scribal classes in various societies, and these other codes may have given Israelite and Judahite scribes inspiration for their own formulations. The influence of these law codes upon literate people eventually led to the actual change of legal practice in society. Among the Judahites this may have happened gradually in the postexilic era, perhaps beginning with the leadership of Ezra and others who found it necessary to re-create (or create for the first time) the social and political institutions of the Judahites. These written legal corpora ultimately did become the working norms by which Judahite society would function.[13]

<hr>

13. Davies, *Scribes and Schools*, 91–92; Fitzpatrick-McKinley, *Transformation of Torah*, 11–182, who develops this argument most thoroughly and suggests comparison with the teaching Dharma of India, idealistic laws and ethics promulgated by a scribal Brahmin class.

Connected to this is another concept we must bear in mind. The biblical legislators did not have a coherent concept of social justice as we have today. The biblical legislators had a vision of reforming society for the sake of aiding the poor, widows, orphans, sojourners, and other victims of economic distress and injustice. They did not consistently provide a social vision for the total reconstruction of society. Nor were all of their laws thoroughly consistent with this notion of an egalitarian society. Social justice was not an abstract principle for them. Justice did not mean the creation of a just and egalitarian society; it meant ameliorating the woes of those marginalized people whom Yahweh loved. Like any people or any society, postexilic Judahite society evolved in stages. Thus, when we read their laws, some laws, in our opinion, will promote a sense of justice greatly, while other laws may still reflect the oppressive actions of that age. The laws come from different segments of society with different interests and agendas (from priests, prophets, and others). The postexilic Judahites were a first-millennium-BCE society with a strong sense of patriarchalism, and they were incapable of conceiving of a society without kings or slaves, one in which everyone had totally equal rights.[14] Laws evolve unevenly, as do societies. The implications of certain laws will unfold when the society to which they speak becomes more developed. That, of course, is the point of this book: we are the product of an unfolding monotheistic process, and even today we have not consistently worked out the implications of the Judeo-Christian monotheistic message.

14. Habel, "Future of Social Justice Research in the Hebrew Scriptures."

3

Loans, Interest, and Debt That Leads to Slavery

Ancient Near Eastern Antecedents

THE EARLIEST BIBLICAL LEGISLATION that provides rights for economically disadvantaged people appears to be in the Book of the Covenant in Exodus 21–23. Deuteronomy's social and religious imperatives further develop the trajectory established by the older legislation in Exodus. Prime examples are laws concerning interest on loans, debt-slaves, and the status of women. Here we may perceive the evolutionary development in the biblical tradition that continues into our own, modern age. There are no universal and timeless laws in the Old Testament but rather several law codes from different eras and social settings, which continue to develop a legal response to particular issues. The literal definition provided by each particular law or set of laws is not what is binding upon the listeners and readers of a later age, especially Christians. Instead, the spirit of the laws or the direction in which the legal tradition is evolving should be the source of inspiration for the audience. These laws evolved in order to provide justice for all, protection and hope for the poor, equality for all people before God, and a society that lives with dignity. Such a society provides praise and honor to God by its very existence. For modern believers to keep the spirit of the biblical laws, we must heed the message of the evolving trajectory to which they testify. Reflection upon selected laws in these corpora will demonstrate the nature of this trajectory.

Biblical interest laws protected highland peasants and the poor; our modern equivalent would be the middle and lower classes of society. The laws attempted to prevent the rich from seizing the land and possessions of those who were economically marginal. Earlier royal edicts in the ancient Near East likewise attempted to protect debtors and those at potential financial risk. Already in the Sumerian cities of third-millennium-BCE Mesopotamia there was an interest in social justice for the poor. Enmetana of Lagash (2404–2375 BCE) removed interest and debt and restored household property for the poor. Urukagina of Lagash (2351–2342 BCE) undertook significant reforms to protect the poor, the orphans, and widows in general by freeing people from debts and taxes. Manishtushu of Akkad (2200 BCE) bragged about releasing thirty-eight cities from corvee and debt. The first Mesopotamian king to promulgate a law code was Ur-Nammu (2113–2096 BCE) or his successor, Shulgi (2095–2048 BCE), of the Sumerian Ur III Dynasty, who explicitly stated that his laws were designed to protect the poor, women, orphans, and widows against the rich and powerful. (Language similar to the texts of these kings is found in Deuteronomy.) In the next century the Amorite king of Isin, Lipit-Ishtar (1934–1924 BCE), also issued a law code to create justice and to protect the poor from the powerful, and it included provisions for the release of debts that forced people into slavery and state labor projects (especially in the cities of Nippur, Ur, Isin, and Akkad). Likewise, comparable rhetoric may be found in Law Code of Hammurabi (1792–1750 BCE) and the Edict of Ammi-saduqa (1646–1626) BCE), both rulers in Amorite Babylon who claimed they sought equity for all people. The later Kassite king, Kurigalzu (1345–1324 BCE), released the poor from state labor.[1]

Hammurabi especially maintains that he established justice for both Sumer in the south of Mesopotamia and Akkad in the north. In his law code he declares that the gods commanded him "to cause justice to prevail in the land, to destroy the wicked and the evil, that the strong might not oppress the weak . . . I sheltered them in my wisdom. In order that the strong might not oppress the weak, that justice might be dealt the orphan and the widow . . . to give justice to the oppressed."[2]

Parallel concerns may be observed in Egypt during the First Intermediate Period (2400–2100 BCE) and the Middle Kingdom (2100–1800

---

1. *ANET*, 16–17, 48–64, 78–92; Saggs, *Babylonians*, 87–88, 97, 101–106; Sperling, *Original Torah*, 48–49; Lowery, *Sabbath and Jubilee*, 16, 29, 38.

2. *ANET*, 164, 178.

BCE), particularly in Egyptian wisdom literature, which reflected the values of the scribal intelligentsia.[3] Wisdom-literature collections of Merikare, Amenenhet, Amenemope, and Ipuwer contain moral imperatives to help the poor.[4] Throughout Egypt's history the imagery associated with pharaoh implies that his duty was to protect the weak and the poor from oppression. In the Early Kingdom, Pharaoh Pepi II (2284–2216 BCE), and in the New Kingdom, Pharaoh Seti (1294–1279 BCE), both boasted of their release of people who owed service to the gods. The overarching religiophilosophical principle of *Ma'at* (justice or order) defined a universe in which justice demanded the poor be protected from oppression.[5] Outside the river valleys of Egypt and Mesopotamia, with their complex economies that so often created poverty, we can also observe this same concern with justice in Hittite and Canaanite texts from the second millennium BCE. The Hittite ruler Hattushilis I (1650–1621 BCE) reportedly freed slaves. In Ugaritic literature kings were admonished to judge properly the cases of the widow, the poor, and the orphan.[6] We can observe many such imperatives in the literature of the ancient Near East, and therefore we should not place the biblical authors in dialectical contrast with the ancient Near East in regard to the issue of social justice.[7]

The biblical literature especially sought to alleviate the difficulties faced by the poor with the release of debts. Debt release has precedents in the ancient Near East, and some of the terminology of ancient Mesopotamia surfaces in the biblical text. Noteworthy examples of debt release in ancient Mesopotamia include those of Enmetana of Lagash (2404–2375 BCE) and Urukagina of Uruk (2351–2342 BCE), who released the debts of poor farmers, which probably arose due to the economic hardships created by the long war between Uruk and Lagash. They called their debt releases an *amargi*, a "return to the mother" or "release." It also included the return of some property. Arrears in taxes owed to the palace were also remitted. Later debt releases were granted by Gudea of Lagash (2144–2124 BCE), Ur-Nammu of Ur (2113–2096 BCE), and Shulgi of Ur (2095–2048 BCE),

3. Malchow, *Social Justice*, 1–6.

4. *ANET*, 407–10, 414–19, 422–24, 441–44.

5. Weinfeld, *Social Justice*, 16–17; Lowery, *Sabbath and Jubilee*, 29; Lehner, "Absolutism and Reciprocity in Ancient Egypt," 84–87.

6. *ANET*, 149, 151.

7. Rankin, *Israel's Wisdom Literature*, 13–15; Fensham, "Widow, Orphan, and the Poor"; von Waldow, "Social Responsibility and Social Structure," 184–85.

but they did not use the term *amargi*.[8] In the years thereafter Amorite kings in Babylon proclaimed similar edicts and issued law codes with legal guidelines to protect the poor, and their language can be recognized in Leviticus 25 and Deuteronomy 15.

The Amorite law code from Eshnunna (nineteenth century BCE) and the later Amorite Law Code of Hammurabi (eighteenth century BCE) both mandated fixed interest rates to protect debtors and lessen debt enslavement. Rates were fixed at 20 percent for money loans and 33 percent for grain investments. Assyrian laws fixed rates at 25 percent for money loans and 50 percent for grain investments.[9] However, bankruptcy and debt enslavement could occur for borrowers, since these rates were still fairly steep. Laws also protected the widows and orphans of debtors who had died. They occur in the law code that originated with Ur-Nammu (2113–2096 BCE) or his successor, Shulgi (2095–2048 BCE), two kings of Ur III, both of whom ruled a vast Mesopotamian empire with well-developed economic concerns.[10]

Scholars often pay attention to the Mesopotamian debt-release edicts issued by second-millennium-BCE kings of Amorite Babylonian and Assyria. The Amorite kings Lipit-Ishtar of Isin (1934–1924 BCE) and Ishme-Dagan of Assyria (1781–1742 BCE) released debts and tax obligations from several cities under their rule. The best-known edicts of release came from Hammurabi (1792–1750 BCE), Samsu-iluna (1749–1712 BCE), and Ammi-saduqa (1646–1626 BCE) in the Amorite Babylonian Empire. These royal proclamations were called *misharum* and *anduraru* edicts, words that recall terminology in Leviticus 25 and Deuteronomy 15 (*deror*, which means "release"). These edicts were issued irregularly by the kings to release both debts and slaves. Debt-slaves were released and returned to their families, but not prisoners of war; farmlands were returned to their owners unless they were in the towns or commercial properties; and personal debts

8. *ANET*, 526; Lambert, "Les 'Reforms' d'Urukagina," 169–84; Charpin, "Les Decrets Royaux," 36–44; Jacobsen, *Harps That Once*, 440; Weinfeld, *Social Justice*, 49, 78–79; Hudson, "Proclaim Liberty," 28–29; Lowery, *Sabbath and Jubilee*, 16, 29, 38; Greengus, "Legal and Social Institutions," 471.

9. Weber, *Ancient Judaism*, 63–64; Mendelsohn, *Slavery in the Ancient Near East*, 26; de Vaux, *Ancient Israel*, 171; Gamoran, "Biblical Law against Interest," 127; Maloney, "Usury and Restrictions on Interest-Taking," 1–20; Varso, "Interest (Usury)," 324–26.

10. Mendelsohn, *Slavery in the Ancient Near East*, 26; Weber, *Ancient Judaism*, 63–64; Gamoran, "Biblical Law against Interest," 127; Maloney, "Usury and Restrictions on Interest-Taking," 1–20; Greengus, "Legal and Social Institutions," 477.

of individuals (usually farmers) were released, but not commercial loans to merchants. Most of the debts actually were owed to the palace. The goal was to restore agrarian families to the land but not to disrupt business. Such actions also reinvigorated that class of people who provided soldiers for the armies, and debt releases often came from kings in the beginning of their reign when it was necessary to stabilize their city-state or empire militarily. The Amorite king Lipit-Ishtar of Isin (1934–1924 BCE) issued a release early in the Amorite period. But later Hammurabi (1792–1750 BCE) declared such a release four times during his reign, in his first, twelfth, twenty-first, and thirtieth years of rule. He, of course, built an empire in Mesopotamia during his reign, so that debt release was part of this process also.[11]

Needless to say, the rich and powerful in society could be hurt by these sudden and arbitrary royal edicts. But sometimes those rich and powerful people were the potential opponents or rivals to the king, so that debt release served the political needs of the king. Often Babylonian temples lost wealth by this process, for they had accumulated a large amount of wealth by offerings. In turn, they would extend loans to merchants at high interest rates and garner even more wealth. Defaulted loans from merchants, and even more frequently from simple farmers, then provided the temples with debt-slaves and property. The royal edict would then weaken the tremendous wealth and power of the temples and obviously make the king more popular in the eyes of the people, thus strengthening the king's position in society. Hammurabi issued several of these edicts during his long reign in Babylon, and several of his successors followed in this custom. Even later Nebuchadrezzar I of Babylon (1126–1105 BCE) issued such a release.

Implementation of this custom by kings strengthened their economies by freeing many people with deep indebtedness. Wealth was released from the control of temples and returned to the people, or to the private sector (in modern economic categories). However, the ancient Near Eastern kings had no sense of economics; they released debts and debt-slaves periodically because it brought them great esteem in the eyes of their people and hurt their potential opponents by eroding their wealth. These kings spoke of how they brought "freedom" (*anduraru*) and "justice" or "equity" (*misharum*) for their people.[12] Of course, this was pious political rhetoric. In

11. Grayson, *Assyrian Rulers*, 15; Weinfeld, *Social Justice*, 82–83; Hudson, "Economic Roots of Jubilee," 29; Lowery, *Sabbath and Jubilee*, 38; Greengus, "Legal and Social Institutions of Ancient Mesopotamia," 471.

12. Lamberg-Karlovsky, "Near Eastern 'Breakout,'" 12–23; Willey, "Ancient Chinese, New World, and Near Eastern Ideological Traditions," 28. Both scholars believe that the

Mesopotamia tensions always existed between the temple and the palace over who truly functioned as the supreme leaders. This may have been true in Israel, even though the scale of power and wealth in both the temple and royal palace was much smaller. In small states there is often political conflict between "factionalized elites," and a king might undercut the wealth of opponents with debt-release laws, as we find in the biblical text.[13] However, even if this is true for Israel, we must admire the idealistic vision of those scribes who articulated the laws, regardless of other reasons underlying the royal motivation to implement them. Israelite laws connected to debt easement appear far more developed and capable of regular implementation in society than do the occasional ancient Near Eastern economic decrees. If enforced, the Israelite laws pertaining to debt easement would have helped their poor people much more.

Israelite Society

Israelite laws perhaps developed out of previous comparable ancient Near Eastern legislation on interest and debt release. Israelite laws, however, attempted to protect the poor even more significantly by a total condemnation of interest. Because ancient Near Eastern laws were designed for the more developed economic systems of river-valley societies, they had to legitimate some form of interest for the sake of economic development. Loans were often for commercial purposes, such as to trade caravans on their way to foreign lands. All the reforms undertaken by Mesopotamian rulers essentially sought to maintain the existing economic system, not to totally change it, so that these reforms ultimately helped the rich and the powerful, and especially the king.[14] Since most Israelites were simple highland villagers in a pastoral economy where barter was the mode of economic exchange, most loans were given by individuals to others to assist in times of economic difficulties. Loans were designed to help others, for in a kinship society there is the assumption that all people are members of a larger family (Lev 25:35–38). There may have been commercial loans in the urban centers, such as Samaria and Jerusalem, extended to merchants and craftsmen. But even here the complex economic structures of Mesopotamia

---

Mesopotamian kings actually took their responsibility to bring freedom and equity seriously, and that this ideology significantly influenced later Judahite tradition.

13. Chaney, "Debt Easement," 127–39.

14. Varso, "Interest (Usury)," 327.

or Egypt were lacking. In the large river-valley civilizations, lending institutions were the temples and the palaces of the various city-states, institutions that had tremendous capital from the great offerings of religious devotees and royal taxation. Israel's institutions were not comparable, and most loans in the urban centers were probably provided by affluent individuals. Thus, throughout Israel the bulk of the loans were given by more affluent people to the less fortunate. (Ironically, Israelite law imitated Babylonian practices, which were addressed to a different economic setting. Most of the debt in Amorite Babylon was owed to the palace or temple and not to affluent individuals, as in Israel and postexilic Judah. Hence, one suspects the biblical legislation may have been more idealistic than historical, especially with Jubilee land restoration.)

Israelite villages and communities were predicated upon a kinship model found throughout the West-Semitic villages of Syria-Palestine. In such communities the neighbor was seen as part of one's extended family. Loans were intended to assist in the reduction of poverty and to keep the extended family from experiencing complete loss of land, possessions, and status. But with the economic development that came to both Israel and Judah in the eighth century BCE with the expansive trade caused by the rise of the Assyrian Empire to the north, many people attempted to become rich at their neighbor's expense. After the rich and powerful began to victimize the poor highland peasants and seize their land, the prophetic critics and legal reformers proclaimed traditional beliefs about the nature of loans and interest. These beliefs were formalized subsequently in legal imperatives, which were written down by idealistic reform-oriented scribes. Loan and interest laws emerged with a novel concept: the outlawing of interest altogether. Israel may have been unique in outlawing interest in an attempt to protect the poor.[15]

Rejection of Interest

Interest was condemned because it eventually turned many borrowers and their families into debt-slaves. In a pastoral and agrarian society, such as Israel and Judah, most of the debtors were simple peasants, whereas in a more complex economy, such as in Egypt and Mesopotamia, debtors would have included a higher percentage of businessmen and merchants, who could potentially turn great profit from their economic activity. The chances for

---

15. Marshall, *Israel and the Book of the Covenant*, 144.

a simple peasant repaying a loan with interest was significantly less than that of a merchant who might receive profit from successful caravan ventures. Interest rates of 20 percent to 33 percent on loans could be repaid by peasant farmers, if the crop yield in a year was significant. A very good agricultural year could bring a thirty-five-fold to fortyfold return, in which case the interest owed would amount to only 1 percent of the yield. But when drought or insects (or occasional war with foreign invading armies) brought disastrous harvests, the likelihood of loan default was great. The possibility of loan default by numerous debtors was greatest in areas subject to small amounts of rainfall, which included Palestine.[16]

The oldest condemnation of interest is found in the Book of the Covenant, which has been dated from the premonarchic period down to the late eighth century BCE by different scholars. If the lower date is to be correct, then the Book of the Covenant is an early attempt to mandate economic reform in the face of the economic changes wrought by eighth-century-BCE economic and political developments in Israel. The law of loans and interest reads in Exod 22:25: "If you lend money to my people, to the poor among you, you shall not deal with them as a creditor; you shall not exact interest from them."

This passage uses expressions, such as "my people" and "the poor," which are common vocabulary used in the first part of the book of Exodus to describe the experience of the Israelites as slaves in Egypt. Subtly the biblical author compares the creditor to pharaoh, someone who oppresses the poor and turns them into slaves, so that the collection of interest is an act that undoes the liberation brought about by the exodus.[17]

In addition, the Book of the Covenant laid limitations upon the taking of pledges in return for loans extended to a poor person. Exodus 22:26 states that if a neighbor's cloak was taken in pawn as a pledge, it had to be returned to him every night so that he could sleep in it. Presumably, this law implied that other possessions necessary for life had to be returned temporarily or perhaps not borrowed at all. If the pawned item had to be returned consistently, the creditor probably would seek to borrow another item not so necessary for life.

People circumvented these laws with subtle redefinitions of interest. A loan could be extended and a select amount taken out of the sum before the creditor even obtained it. Upon repayment the debtor had to return the full

16. Ibid.

17. Varso, "Interest (Usury)," 329–31.

amount, including the initial sum or "bite" taken out by the creditor who extended the loan. This "bite" or *neshek* was not defined as interest by the creditor, but it forced the debtor pay back the loan with profit to the creditor. A later law in Deuteronomy condemned this subtle form of interest. We read in Deut 23:19–20,

> 19You shall not charge interest on loans to another Israelite, interest (*neshek)* on money, interest (*neshek*) on provisions, interest (*neshek*) on anything that is lent. 20On loans to a foreigner you may charge interest, but on loans to another Israelite you may not charge interest, so that the LORD your God may bless you in all your undertakings in the land that you are about to enter and possess.

Israelite creditors were permitted to charge interest on a loan to a foreigner (*nokhri*), since he was probably a merchant from a distant land who operated by the appropriate guidelines for loans and interest in his own country, and he probably was making a good profit margin as a merchant anyway. Such an imposition would not reduce a profit-seeking merchant to poverty, as interest on a loan would do to a poor peasant farmer.[18]

What is also impressive about the guidelines in Deuteronomy 15 is the strong encouragement for Israelites to make loans to poor people so that they do not suffer. We observe the rhetorical appeal made in Deut 15:7–8,

> 7If there is among you anyone in need, a member of your community in any of your towns within the land that the LORD your God is giving you, do not be hard-hearted or tight-fisted toward your needy neighbor. 8You should rather open your hand, willingly lending enough to meet the need, whatever it may be.

This is clearly not a law, but encouragement, a type of discourse commonly found throughout Deuteronomy, and language such as this makes us reluctant to define Deuteronomy strictly as a law code, for it is more of a sermon with laws contained within it.

In reference to items pawned for the sake of a loan, Deut 24:6, 10–13, 17 elaborates upon the earlier references in the Book of the Covenant,

> 6No one shall take a millstone or an upper millstone in pledge, for that would be taking a life in pledge . . . 10When you make your neighbor a loan of any kind, you shall not go into the house

---

18. Neufeld, "Prohibitions against Loans at Interest," 359–62, 375–410; Phillips, *Deuteronomy*, 25; Craigie, *Book of Deuteronomy*, 302.

to take the pledge. ¹¹You shall wait outside, while the person to whom you are making the loan brings the pledge out to you. ¹²If the person is poor, you shall not sleep in the garment given you as the pledge. ¹³You shall give the pledge back by sunset, so that your neighbor may sleep in the cloak and bless you; and it will be to your credit before the LORD your God . . . ¹⁷You shall not deprive a resident alien or an orphan of justice; you shall not take a widow's garment in pledge.

The millstone and the upper millstone in v. 6 refer to the two stones used in grinding grain into flour so as to bake bread. If either of these two stones were taken, the woman would not be able to bake bread for her family, and the family members would be forced to buy or barter for grain at a much more expensive rate than if they were to make the bread. Taking away a family's capacity to make bread would drive them deeper into debt, perhaps to the very creditor who took their millstone as a pledge. This would be a dirty tactic used by the creditor to turn a poor family into his debt-slaves. By inference the law probably implied that other essentials for life should not be taken from a poor family as a way of manipulating them into further debt. Verse 6 adds the rhetorical flourish that taking the millstone would be depriving a person of the object so important that it "would be taking a life in pledge."

Deuteronomy 24:10–13, 17 reiterates the example of returning a cloak at night, but it also adds the stipulation that the creditor may not go into the poor person's house to choose a pledge but must instead wait outside until the poor person brings an object acceptable as a pledge for the loan. Thus, the dignity of the poor person is protected as well with the choice of object placed in pledge. Again, as is the case with the millstone, it prevents the creditor from taking an object necessary for the well-being and financial security of the family. Verse 17 explicitly says that the cloak of a widow is not to be taken at all. Perhaps, she would not have the courage of the poor man who might go to the creditor and request his cloak back at night, as was permitted by the law. So Deuteronomic laws find it necessary to emphasize the limitations on pledges taken for loans. The little phrase in v. 13 of how the poor person will bless you and it will be a credit for you before the Lord, indicates to us that these laws in Deuteronomy are found not really in a law code but rather in a theological sermon cast in the format of a law code.

However, creditors still might demand an unspecified added amount, not called interest, on a loan. Such an added amount might have been called a *tarbith* (or *marbith*). (There is scholarly debate concerning the difference between *neshek* and *tarbith*. Perhaps the word was fictitiously defined as a "gift" according to the creditor and thus not truly a form of interest.) Regardless, if *tarbith* is another way to sidestep the laws against interest, then Leviticus subsequently seeks to close this loophole also.[19] For in Levitical legislation condemning interest, both the *neshek* and the *tarbith/marbith* are condemned. When fellow Israelites fall into economic difficulty and require loans, the following guidelines are given in Lev 25:36–37: "Do not take interest (*neshek*) in advance or otherwise make a profit (*tarbith*) from them, but fear your God; let them live with you. You shall not lend them your money at interest (*neshek*) taken in advance, or provide them food at a profit (*marbith*)."

There is a clear developmental trajectory through these three texts. Idealistic scribal lawgivers legislated in behalf of the poor and oppressed, and in each generation new laws were articulated to cover new loopholes that arose. Though this reflects the simple process that many laws go through over the years, we can observe that the spirit behind these three laws is one designed to protect the poor and not just to provide for mere stability in the economic order.

Some believe that the *neshek* is interest on money while the *tarbith* may be interest on food, since the latter is mentioned in reference to grain in this passage.[20] If so, the law is still a development upon earlier law, for it distinguishes a type of interest on grain that some Israelites may have felt was not really *neshek*. This law then expands the prohibition on interest to include loans of grain and not simply monetary loans.

An important question to ask is whether the Israelites and the Judahites attempted to keep these guidelines in any serious fashion. We can never be sure whether the answer is that these biblical texts were idealistic scribal creations, which the average person did not know about, or whether these were moral guidelines that people were aware of but did not keep, or whether these were guidelines that Judahites did keep as best they could at

19. Driver, *Deuteronomy*, 266; North, *Sociology of the Biblical Jubilee*, 177; Neufeld, "Prohibitions against Loans at Interest," 357–74; Gamoran, "Biblical Law against Interest," 129–32; Loewenstamm, "*Neshek* and *m/tarbith*," 79–80, Stein, "Laws on Interest in the Old Testament," 163; Snaith, *Leviticus and Numbers*, 166; Hyatt, *Exodus*, 243; Porter, *Leviticus*, 205.

20. De Vaux, *Ancient Israel*, 170.

times. Papyrus records from the Judahite communities in Egypt indicate that interest was charged on loans from 456 BCE to 221 BCE, but that after 182 BCE loans were interest free.[21] Other references to debt remission exist from the time of Nehemiah in the fifth century BCE down to the second century CE.[22] This indicates that at least some Judahites may have been observing this law. To me it also indicates that increasingly in the later postexilic era Judahites may have kept Judahite guidelines for living to preserve their Judahite identity.

Additional Laws for the Poor

Additional texts deserve mention. These are laws that were designed to prevent poor people from falling into such as abject state of deep poverty that they would be forced to take out loans and ultimately become debt-slaves. We are not sure how faithfully these laws were observed, but at least, they were articulated by scribal theologians who had a vision of how society should function in order to protect the poor and marginalized people of their age.

In the Book of the Covenant we find guidelines for a custom called Fallow Year in Exod 23:10–11,

> [10]For six years you shall sow your land and gather in its yield; [11]but the seventh year you shall let it rest and lie fallow, so that the poor of your people may eat; and what they leave the wild animals may eat. You shall do the same with your vineyard and with your olive orchard.

What is described here are "volunteer crops," a phenomenon that modern farmers understand rather well. Accidental seeding by the previous year's crop will cause a partial crop to grow in an uncultivated field the next year; perhaps as much as one-tenth of a full crop yield can grow nowadays. Modern farmers plow it under or leave it in an uncultivated field for their livestock to graze on it. In this biblical law "volunteer crop" in an uncultivated field is to be left for the poor or the wild animals and not to be used for the farmer's livestock. Also, scholars ask the question of how Fallow Year worked. Were all fields nationwide left fallow for a year? Probably not! The law may have applied to individual fields on a rotating basis, and the land

21. Gamoran, "Biblical Law against Interest," 133–34.
22. Kessler, "Das Erlassjahrgesetz Dtn 15,1–11," 15–30.

parcels may have been left fallow only for one growing season, either the fall or the spring crop, but not both seasons. This actually sounds like what might have been normal farming practices in ancient Israel.[23] What is then important about this legislation is that the poor people have access to the "volunteer crop."

In Deuteronomy we see a number of new laws or guidelines designed to help the poor, and this indicates that Deuteronomy more seriously takes action to help the plight of the poor because it comes from a later era and builds upon the earlier legislation in Exodus. Or at least we might say that the author of Deuteronomy 12–26 was inspired by Exodus 21–23 and wove a more comprehensive vision of ideal legislation designed to help the poor.

In Deut 14:28–29 we have a poor person's tithe for the Levites and the poor people of the land,

> [28]Every third year you shall bring out the full tithe of your pro-
> duce for that year, and store it within your towns; [29]the Levites,
> because they have no allotment or inheritance with you, as well
> as the resident aliens, the orphans, and the widows in your towns,
> may come and eat their fill so that the LORD our God may bless
> you in all the work that you undertake.

We have no evidence in the biblical text that this custom was ever under-taken. Scholars have assumed that since the Deuteronomic laws came from the time of King Josiah of Judah (622 BCE), and since Josiah centralized worship in the temple of Jerusalem and closed local shrines, thus putting many local Levites out of work, legislation had to be generated to care for them and their families. Not all scholars, however, concur with that theory. Nevertheless, we observe that the tithe every third year is to go to poor people in general and not to the temple in Jerusalem. This is a generous piece of legislation that would help people from falling into even more ab-ject poverty, if it were to be practiced on a regular basis.

Another law in Deuteronomy, which helps the poor greatly, is also found elsewhere in the ancient world, including in the Code of Manu in In-dia. This law requires that employees who use day laborers, what we would call migrant workers, must pay these workers at the end of each day so that they might have food for their families. We read in Deut 24:14–15: "You shall not withhold the wages of the poor and needy laborers, whether other Israelites or aliens who reside in your land in one of your towns. You shall

23. Hopkins, *Highlands of Canaan*, 192–202.

pay them their wages daily before sunset, because they are poor and their livelihood depends on them."

The imperative is also found in Lev 19:13, "you shall not keep for yourself the wages of a laborer until morning." The guideline applies to both native and foreign people who are poor, and the most likely workers would be those helping with harvest in either the spring or fall growing season. The law may indicate that these workers are to be paid in grain or produce, and their wages would be used immediately as food for their poor families. The law also prevents employees from shortchanging the workers. If a worker was paid at the end of the week, the employer could claim that the worker only worked four days when he actually was present for six days. This cruel shortchanging often occurs even today. This law provides for equitable payment and may have prevented exceptionally poor people from failing into debt-slavery.

The ancient world produced many widows, often because of war, and also because women married men older than themselves. Biblical law often sounded the call for special attention to be given to widows, along with the poor, orphans, and resident aliens. Gleaning customs, in particular, helped widows, as well as other poor people in general. The poor were permitted to follow behind the reapers and bundlers of the grain and pick up the fragments left behind, so that they might be able to make bread for their families.

In Deuteronomy an additional twist is given to these gleaning guidelines. If an entire sheaf is left behind in the field, the good fortune of that mistake goes to the poor. With high yield cash crops like grapes and olives, one should deliberately leave some of the produce behind for the poor. In Deut 24:19–21 we read,

> 19When you reap your harvest in your field and forget a sheaf in the field, you shall not go back to get it; it shall be left for the alien, the orphan, and the widow, so that the LORD your God may bless you in all your undertakings. 20When you beat your olive trees, do not strip what is left; it shall be for the alien, the orphan, and the widow. 21When you gather the grapes of your vineyard, do not glean what is left; it shall be for the alien, the orphan, and the widow.

The concept of deliberately leaving something in the fields for the poor is also voiced in Lev 19:9–10,

9When you reap the harvest of your land, you shall not reap to the very edges of your field, or gather the gleanings of your harvest. 10You shall not strip your vineyard bare, or gather the fallen grapes of your vineyards; you shall leave them for the poor and the alien.

The command is repeated again in Lev 23:22,

When you reap the harvest of your land, you shall not reap to the very edges of your field, or gather the gleanings of your harvest; you shall leave them for the poor and for the alien.

Presumably the word "poor" in both these texts would have included widows. Leaving remnants of your crop for the poor to scavenge may not sound very generous to us today. However, in the subsistence economy of the ancient world, even more successful agriculturalists struggled to stay alive. Leaving something behind in the field was truly a sacrifice. Considering the impossibility of enforcing these laws, we must acknowledge that much of the legal material in the biblical text is really rhetorical moral encouragement.

These law codes often appear to be literary and theological creations seeking to create of vision of hope for society. But we today should be inspired by these texts, for we are part of an evolving trajectory created by these texts and we continue the process of bringing justice for the poor and the dispossessed of our world.

4

Freedom for the Oppressed Debt-slaves

Debt-slaves

WITH THE EVOLUTION OF slave laws an even better example of the Israelite urge for social reform may be observed. Interest laws changed in order to stop different ways of charging interest, but slave laws evolved in a process that gave increased rights to slaves with each successive legal code. One may observe a steady progression of debt-slave and slave-release laws from the Book of the Covenant to the Deuteronomic laws and finally to Levitical legislation so that guidelines for the release of debt-slaves developed significantly. However, not all scholars feel this was an evolutionary process. Some suggest that the laws functioned to cover different situations and so were applied simultaneously. According to these scholars, the laws may have arisen in separate eras, but there was no evolutionary trajectory in them.[1] In spite of such observations, most scholars prefer to interpret the texts in terms of a historical development that responds to the changing social circumstances of Israelite and Judahite society. This would be true whether you consider the law codes to be used directly in courtroom

---

1. Chirichigno, *Debt-Slavery in Israel and the Ancient Near East,* 17–357, who believes that the earliest code in Exodus 21 refers only to dependents, "chattel slaves," and Israelite debt-slaves; Leviticus 25 covers the head of the household (and hence land ownership also); and the latest laws in Deuteronomy 15 cover only dependents. His arguments are brilliant, but they depend too often upon his very nuanced reading of the text and a strong appeal to comparable Amorite Babylonian laws from the early second millennium BCE.

situations or whether you think they were scribal creations by idealistic reformers inspired by the prophets. Ultimately the slave-release laws were grounded in the belief that Yahweh had delivered the Israelites from slavery in Egypt (Exod 22:21; 23:9; Lev 25:42, 55; Deut 15:15).

Jeffries Hamilton, in particular, believes that there is an evolutionary development in these slave-release laws, and he uses language similar to mine. From his initial consideration of Deuteronomy 15, he describes the biblical manumission slaves laws as being a "trajectory" or a "thrust" in history. The earlier laws permit "subsequent interpreters of the law to build a case for a broader condemnation of slavery." Within Deuteronomy 15, for example, there is a "submerged condemnation" of slavery that will force an audience someday "to pose justice questions which even the text is not willing to pose" to its original audience.[2] Indeed, my thesis, like his, would be that each of these laws leads to the next legal articulation, and ultimately the total condemnation of slavery will unfold in the minds of the religious readers of the text, who eventually will realize that this was the ultimate implication of the biblical message. The monotheistic undergirding behind this legislation leads to such insights.

In the ancient world slaves arose in two ways: by becoming prisoners of war and by falling into severe debt. Needless to say, in Israel the latter category accounts for the majority of slaves. In particular, Israelites could become slaves in the following ways: children might be sold voluntarily for debts (Exod 21:7–11) or seized for debts (2 Kgs 4:1; Neh 5:5), and likewise adults could be enslaved for debts involuntarily (1 Sam 22:2; Isa 50:1; Amos 2:6) or voluntarily (Exod 21:5–6; Deut 15:16–17).

Debt-slavery and interest were very closely connected, for the inability to repay loans due to high interest rates forced many people into debt-slavery. Sometimes a debtor would lose certain members of his family into debt-slavery, and then eventually he would be forced into it also. This occurred universally in the ancient world, but it was especially frequent in Mesopotamia, where economic stagnation or collapse resulted from the large numbers of people who fell into debt-slavery and lost their land. As I mentioned previously, Amorite Babylonian kings, including Hammurabi, issued irregular *misharum* and *anduraru* proclamations to release debts and debt-slaves in order to reinvigorate an ailing economy and diffuse social

---

2. Hamilton, *Social Justice and Deuteronomy*, 120–21, who believes that Deuteronomy 15 is part of a sequence in Deuteronomic laws paralleling the Ten Commandments, and that this law assumes a Sabbath Rest theme, for the release of slaves brings true rest to an entire society (1–158).

unrest. Biblical authors may have been inspired by some of these Mesopotamian traditions in their own articulations of ideal reform, especially with the institutions of Sabbath Year in Deuteronomy and Jubilee Year in Leviticus.[3] Perhaps, scribal intelligentsia in Israel may have learned to write by copying legal corpora from other countries, including Hammurabi's Law Code in particular, and this would have prompted them to use similar laws in the construction of law codes in the Bible.

In comparison with the rest of the ancient Near East, biblical authors attempted to provide greater protection and mandate more situations under which slaves could be released. This was inspired by prophets and early reformers who reminded the people with vivid rhetoric that their ancestors had been slaves in Egypt. In Mesopotamia, for example, slaves had no legal protection against abuse. If a slave were hurt or killed, the criminal offense was committed against the slave owner for loss of property, not against the slave as a person.[4] Practically speaking, however, the simpler economy in Israel produced fewer debts slaves than Mesopotamia. Nonetheless, debt-slavery was a social problem in certain eras of Israelite history, such as the eighth century BCE, when classical prophets vehemently condemned debt-slavery and the conditions that caused it. Amos declared that debt-slaves became so common in his age that one could purchase a slave for the cost of a pair of sandals (Amos 2:6).

The scribes who generated the biblical laws challenged the assumptions of debt-slavery and slavery in general, and the Bible appears to be the first document in the ancient world to contain such stern critique.[5] Slaves were to be treated respectfully; they were permitted to share in the family religious life: Sabbath (Exod 20:10; 23:12), sacrificial meals (Deut 12:12, 18; Lev 22:11), festivals (Deut 16:11, 14), and Passover (Exod 12:44). One cannot stress enough the significance of the provision that enables slaves to rest on the Sabbath, for throughout the ancient world slaves would have been forced to work continually; only the rich owners would have been granted leisure time. Sabbath rest may be the greatest provision made for the rights

---

3. Chiricigno, *Debt-Slavery*, 30–100, elaborates upon biblical use of Amorite laws in great detail.

4. Saggs, *Babylonians*, 56.

5. Mendelsohn, *Slavery in the Ancient Near East*, 123; Weber, *Ancient Judaism*, 64; Croatto, *Exodus*, 36.

of slaves, especially due to the frequency of this rest, which obviously could hurt the profit of the master.[6]

Under certain circumstances slaves would be released contrary to the owner's desires. Provisions were made to release the slave, if the master brutally beat the slave (Exod 21:20, 26–27). If the master struck a male or female slave, and the slave died during the beating, the owner could be punished (Exod 21:20). If the master struck the eye or knocked out a tooth of a male or female slave, the slave went free (Exod 21:26–27). In an age with no toothbrushes or dental floss, it was very easy to knock out a tooth. This last law set a very strong limitation upon the power of a master to punish, for it prevented him from hitting the slave in the face altogether. Such protection for slaves could not be found elsewhere in the ancient world. Provisions were made for release if young slave girls were not treated appropriately by becoming full wives when they reached adulthood (Exod 21:7–11). Especially significant is the law that demands the death penalty for whoever kidnaps people to sell them into slavery (Exod 21:16; Deut 24:7). A similar law, which demanded capital punishment for kidnapping, is found in the Law Code of Hammurabi (Law #14), but it applied only to the young male children (minors) of free citizens of Babylon.[7] The Israelite law applied to all people. All these protections appeared already in Israel's earliest legal traditions, the Book of the Covenant.

Subsequent legislation in Deuteronomy proposes more radical guidelines. Deuteronomy 23:15–16 declares that a slave who escapes from a foreign country should not be returned to his master or land of origin, but he should be permitted to live in the land of Israel wherever he wishes. Israelites thus violated universally recognized international laws promulgating the return of escaped slaves across national borders.[8] Similar legislation cannot be found elsewhere in the ancient world. Ancient Near Eastern fugitive-slave laws were extremely stern on issues of slave escape. Sumerian law fined a person twenty-five shekels of silver for hiding a fugitive slave, Nuzi laws in the late second millennium BCE in northern Mesopotamia also imposed fines. In the Law Code of Hammurabi the penalty for hiding or assisting an escaped slave was death. In LH 15–16, 19 we read,

> [15]If a man should enable a palace slave, a palace slave woman, a commoner's slave, or a commoner's slave woman to leave through

6. Wright, *Deuteronomy*, 76.

7. Edwards, *Hammurabi Code and Sinaitic Legislation*, 30.

8. Loewenstamm, "Law," 252; Craigie, *Book of Deuteronomy*, 300–301.

the main city-gate, he shall be killed. [16]If a man should harbor a fugitive slave or slave woman of either the palace or of a commoner in his house and not bring him out at the herald's public proclamation, that householder shall be killed. [16]If a man seizes a fugitive slave or slave woman in the open country and leads him back to his owner, the slave owner shall give him 2 shekels of silver . . . [19]If he should detain that slave in his own house and afterward the slave is discovered in his possession, that man shall be killed.[9]

Hittite laws from the Old Kingdom (1650–1500 BCE) also contain laws about escaped slaves. We read laws 22–23 in the Old Kingdom Law Code,

> [22a]If a male slave runs away, and someone brings him back, if he seizes him nearby, his owner shall give shoes to the finder. [22b]If he seizes him on the near side of the river, he shall pay 2 shekels of silver. If on the far side of the river, he shall pay him 3 shekels of silver. [23a]If a male slave runs away and goes to the land of Luwiya, his owner shall pay 6 shekels of silver to whomever brings him back. [23b]If a male slave runs away and goes into an enemy country, whoever brings him back shall keep him for himself.[10]

In addition to these laws, the owner of a slave who had escaped could appeal to the state authorities to help him find and return that slave.[11]

The biblical law in Deut 23:15–16 stands forth in vivid contrast. I believe that this is the most dramatic guideline to demonstrate the attitude of biblical authors toward slavery. The text reads,

> [15]Slaves who have escaped to you from their owners shall not be given back to them. [16]They shall reside with you, in your midst, in any place they choose in any one of your towns, wherever they please; you shall not oppress them.

Upon reading the first verse, we suspect that this guideline might apply to all escaped slaves, including those who might have escaped from other Israelites. However, after reading the second verse, we believe that the reference to dwelling in any one of the various villages in Israel indicates that the law refers to foreign slaves who have escaped to Israel. This is an incredible law, totally unique in the ancient world. All other nations had legal provisions for the return of escaped slaves, and such provisions were often

---

9. Roth, *Law Collections*, 84–85.

10. Ibid., 220.

11. Mendelsohn, *Slavery in the Ancient Near East*, 58–63.

an important part of covenants made between nations. The actual implementation of this guideline, if indeed it were the practice of Judah under Josiah after 622 BCE, would have made Judah into a rogue state defying international law.[12] What an incredible law, clearly designed to recall the memory that the ancestors of the Israelites were slaves who escaped from Egypt! The radical nature of this law leads many to assume that it was an idealistic projection by the biblical authors and not real political practice. But who knows? Maybe Josiah did try to enforce this guideline for several years.

In the ancient world, people who helped slaves escape could receive the death penalty, and those who returned escaped slaves would receive a reward. But the Deuteronomic authors, defying ancient law and custom, declared that their practice would be that which others considered worthy of the death penalty. This is an awesome law to place in a collection of laws, whether or not it was actually practiced. Herein we glimpse one of those seeds that would give rise to modern abolitionism.

In general, the biblical laws concerning slavery mount an attack upon the assumptions of the institution of slavery in the ancient Near East. Israelites envisioned themselves as a people born as escaped slaves from Egypt, and this rhetoric ultimately led their prophetically inspired legal authors to declare it a crime to return a foreign slave to his foreign master.

Debt-Slave Release

Truly important legislation for us to reflect upon from our modern vantage point are those slave-release laws that evolved throughout the history of the Israelite legal tradition. Exodus 21:2–6 provides perhaps the earliest guidelines for debt-slave release. Scholars have observed that already with this law the biblical authors were really crafting ethical guidelines in the form of legal formulations.[13] The text reads as follows,

> 2When you buy a male Hebrew slave, he shall serve six years, but in the seventh he shall go out a free person, without debt 3If he comes in single, he shall go out single; if he comes in married, then his wife shall go out with him. 4If his master gives him a wife and she bears him sons or daughters, the wife and her children shall be her master's and he shall go out alone. 5But if his master gives

12. Loewenstamm, "Law," 252; Craigie, *Book of Deuteronomy*, 300–301.
13. Arneth, "Der Exodus der Sklaven."

him a wife and she bears him sons or daughters, the wife and her children shall be her master's and he shall go out alone. [6]But if the slave declares, "I love my master, my wife, and my children; I will not go out a free person."

The male slave must be released in his seventh year of service, for the law assumes that no debt is greater than six years of bonded service to a creditor. There appears to be no provision for the release of female slaves in this initial legal statement. She was to eventually become the wife of her owner or to be married to someone else by her owner.[14] If the slave owner did not wish to marry her, and no other spouse could be found for her, then at that time he had to make provision for her redemption or release (Exod 21:7–11). The male slave may leave with his family if they fell into slavery with him. But if the slave married and had children after becoming a slave, his family belonged to the master. Modern scholars suggest that crafty masters paired slave girls with their male debt-slaves so that the resulting wedded couples with their children would become permanent slaves. What wonderful matchmakers they were! The slave would supposedly say that he wished to remain a slave because he loved his master, but probably more often male slaves loved their families and remained in slavery for their sake.

Furthermore, the debt-slave release law could be circumvented by slave masters who simply failed to count the six years, and the male debt-slave was forever in year four or five of his servitude with no channel of appeal. If the family of the male debt-slave made legal appeal to the local village elders or to a more formally organized court in a larger walled city, they might discover that the judge was a relative of the affluent slave master or at least someone susceptible to a bribe from a rich or powerful person. In these ways clever slave masters could create a large number of permanent slaves.

Because of such legal loopholes, later scribal legislators had to develop and expand the protective laws for debt-slaves. In the Deuteronomic laws an institution called the Sabbath Year Release was created by the biblical authors: this combined debt release, which led to debt-slavery, and a broader set of guidelines for debt-slave emancipation. The Sabbath Year is described in Deut 15:1–18, and selected verses read as follows,

> [1]Every seventh year you shall grant a remission of debts. [2]And this is the manner of the remission: every creditor shall remit the claim that is held against a neighbor, not exacting it of a neighbor who

14. Lowery, *Sabbath and Jubilee*, 26.

is a member of the community, because the LORD's remission has
been proclaimed. 3Of a foreigner you may exact it, but you must
remit your claim on whatever any member of your community
owes you . . . 12If a member of your community, whether a Hebrew
man or a Hebrew woman, is sold to you and works for you six
years, in the seventh year you shall set that person free. 13And
when you send a male slave out from you a free person, you shall
not send him out empty-handed. 14Provide liberally out of your
flock, your threshing floor, and your wine press, thus giving to him
some of the bounty with which the Lord your God has blessed
you.

There is perhaps a reference to the observance of this custom in the
time of Nehemiah, which would be around 444 BCE. The people of Judah
promised, "we will forego the crops of the seventh year and the exaction
of every debt" (Neh 10:31). Not growing crops on the seventh year is the
observance of Fallow Year, a custom legislated in Exod 23:10–11. If the release of debts is connected to this Fallow Year custom in the seventh year,
then the people were referring to the debt-release law in Deut 15:1–2. This
would indicate that the Sabbath Year debt release may have been taken seriously by people in the late fifth century BCE. (The reference to debt-slave
release, however, is lacking in Neh 10:31.) In a negative sense Lev 26:34–35,
43 indicates that Sabbath Year was not observed in the preexilic era, and
this text may also indicate why a further reiteration of the customs was
required in the text of Leviticus 25.

There appear to be allusions to the practice of Sabbath Year in some
ways in various texts and by historians. These include allusions to land rest
(Fallow Year) and debt remission (Sabbath Year), which appear to have
been synchronized according to the few references that we possess. 1) According to the Judean historian Josephus, in 330 BCE Alexander the Great
exempted Judeans from taxes during their Sabbath Year. 2) 1 Macc 6:49–54
states that Judas Maccabeus lost the fortress of Beth-Zur in 163–162 BCE
due to famine caused by the Sabbath Year's lack of grain production. 3)
According to Josephus, in 135–134 BCE John Hyrcanus failed to avenge the
death of Simon Maccabeus because it was a Sabbath Year. 4) According to
Josephus, in 37–36 BCE Herod and his general, Sossius, took Jerusalem by
siege due to a food shortage in the city caused by Sabbath Year. 5) A papyrus
note in 55–56 CE under Nero's reign speaks of indebtedness being remitted
for a Judean. 6) *Seder Olam*, a rabbinic tract, implies that Jerusalem was
destroyed after the Sabbath Year in 68–69 CE. 7) Contracts at Murabba'at

in Palestine in 132–133 CE imply the existence of a Sabbath Year at the beginning of the Bar-Kochba revolt. 8) Jewish tombstone inscriptions refer to a Sabbath Year in 433–434 CE and 440–441 CE. 9) The Roman historian Tacitus refers to the Judean custom of abstaining from work every seventh year.[15] If we check the math on all these dates, it must be noted that they all fit somewhat into a centuries-long seven-year cycle. That cannot be a coincidence. It thus appears that Judahites, at least in the later postexilic era, sought to keep the guidelines of Fallow Year and Sabbath Year.

One must acknowledge initially that the concept of a debt release is a great reforming law for the poor. If every seven years debts were forgiven for poor people, the likelihood of poor people falling into debt-slavery is greatly diminished. Whether the debt release forgave all the debt owed by a poor person, or simply the portion of the debt that had not been repaid is sometimes debated. However, that debate may be somewhat irrelevant, because it would seem certain that if the poor person had repaid some of the loan, the creditor would not refund that portion that had already been paid. Thus, we can assume that it was the outstanding loan debt that was forgiven, whatever the status of the original loan might have been.

This Deuteronomic law attempts to address several problems that had arisen, according to prophetic critics and legal reformers in Israel. The dishonest counting of years for an individual debt-slave is eliminated by making the year of slave release a universal seventh year of release for slaves in the entire country. Scholars suggest that the Deuteronomic law did this by a literary trick. The law of slave release in Deuteronomy 15 is connected to the law of debt release, which clearly was a debt release designed to occur every seven years all over the country. The slave-release law follows directly after the debt-release law, giving the impression that a seven-year universal cycle is still assumed. So instead of a slave being released in the seventh year of his own personal servitude, the new law makes it appear that the debt-slave is to be released at the same time that all debts are forgiven. The reference to the six years of debt-slavery in Deut 15:12 as a result becomes a reference to the fixed cycle of six years of national release, mentioned in the previous passages concerning debt release.[16] If all slaves were released at

15. North, *Sociology of the Biblical Jubilee*; de Vaux, *Ancient Israel*, 174; Wacholder, "Calendar of Sabbatical Cycles," 158–84; and Wacholder, "Sabbatical Year"; Pruitt, "The Sabbath Year of Release."

16. North, *Sociology of Biblical Jubilee*, 33; Morgenstern, "Sabbatical Year," 4:142; Wacholder, "Sabbatical Year." Also see the annotated footnote in Coogan, *New Oxford Annotated Bible*, 269.

the same time, no dishonest counting could keep debt-slaves permanently in servitude to their masters.

It must be admitted, however, that some commentators believe that the law still refers to six years of an individual slave's service, so that the year is not universal. According to some authors, a universal release of all debt-slaves would cause economic chaos.[17] However, Roland de Vaux points out the compelling argument that if you release debts you also release the debt-slave, who no longer owes a debt: therefore debts and debt-slaves logically should be released at the same time.[18] The prophet Jeremiah alludes to slave release (Jer 34:8–11) in which all the debt-slaves are released simultaneously, which appears to be in accordance with the Deuteronomic law. However, it could be that each slave should have been released after his own personal six years of service, and since this had not been done in Jeremiah's day, all those slaves were finally released at the same time, thus giving the appearance of a universal release.[19] I suspect ultimately that the purpose of the law is to call for the release of debts and debt-slaves simultaneously every seven years, for why else would the laws be placed in proximity? Reading the debt-slave release law after the debt-release law would naturally incline readers to assume that debt-slave release is on a seven-year national cycle, like debt remission. This is a radical law articulated in behalf of slaves, even if it was not observed over the years.

The Deuteronomic legislation also addresses women slaves as well as men. Women debt-slaves also are released in the seventh year of universal debt and slave release, according this new law. We infer that the law in Deut 15:1–18 covered the wives of male debt-slaves who became married during the debt servitude, in contrast to the law in Exod 21:2–6. Under the law in Exodus the wife and children of a debt-slave remained with the master if the debt-slave obtained them during his service, and then the debt-slave would be tempted to remain with his family and his master in permanent slavery. Now, thanks to the Deuteronomic law, the family of the debt-slave could leave with him. Such women released from debt-slavery also might have included the wives and daughters of householders who fell into deep financial

17. Phillips, *Ancient Israel's Criminal Law*, 76–77; and Phillips, *Deuteronomy*, 106; Craigie, *Book of Deuteronomy*, 238; Wright, *Deuteronomy*, 192–94; Leuchter, "Manumission Laws in Leviticus and Deuteronomy," 637.

18. De Vaux, *Ancient Israel*, 173–74.

19. Leuchter, "Manumission Laws in Leviticus and Deuteronomy," 641, who suggests that this oracle by Jeremiah inspired the evolution of the Jubilee Law of slave release by virtue of being a general amnesty (649–50).

distress, while the husbands and fathers of these women still retained their freedom. Or some of the women might have been in debt-slavery before their husbands and fathers fell into debt-slavery, so that technically they were seen as not covered when the man fulfilled his six years of servitude. Perhaps their husbands or fathers died in debt-slavery, and now the law was seen not to apply to them. At any rate, they were not previously covered by the laws in Exodus 21, and now Deuteronomy 15 seeks to rectify that.

The slave master also must give provisions to the newly freed male slave, so that the former slave will not fall back quickly into debt and debt-slavery. Previously a slave master might have extended a loan immediately to a former debt-slave, knowing that the ex–debt-slave soon would be his once more. Hence, Deuteronomic laws greatly developed debt-slave legislation in light of the previous two centuries of economic development and social abuse. This legislation is more than simple law with the presence of these additional stipulations; it is truly a humanitarian move to reform society.[20]

However, it has also been suggested that since hiring free workers in some labor markets is cheaper than supporting slaves on your farm (which includes feeding and lodging costs), that slave release may be an economically feasible move to improve the profit in farming.[21] However, I do not believe that the ancient Judahites understood economics that well, and as is so often the case in human history, the greed of the rich to make a profit often causes them to engage in activity that harms the economic well-being of the community. One slave owner will not release his slaves because he thinks it will be cheaper to pay them a daily wage in the overall market of the national economy rather than feed and lodge them and make them work for no wages. He will keep his slaves, for people are motivated more by greed than by foresight. This is the greatest flaw of modern economic theories that argue for a completely free market; they overlook human greed and the lack of common sense that accompanies such greed. People seek short-term profit not long-term economic development.

A different interpretation of these slave-release laws in Exodus and Deuteronomy is provided in careful detail by John Van Seters. He suggests the laws in Exodus are later than the three laws on slave release in Deuteronomy and Leviticus, and that they speak of purchasing Hebrew slaves from foreigners in exile whereas the earlier laws speak of debt-slaves who

20. Nicholson, "Deuteronomy's Vision of Israel."
21. Glass, "Land, Slave Labor and Law."

have to sell themselves to Israelites. Exodus 21:2 states, "when you buy a Hebrew slave," whereas Deut 15:12 states the Hebrew slave "sells himself" or "is sold." Van Seters assumes that you "buy a Hebrew slave" or "acquire a Hebrew slave" from a foreigner ("acquire" is the more literal meaning of the verb). He also points out that Neh 5:8 refers to buying Judahites out of slavery from foreigners, and the Exodus guideline probably arose shortly before the time of Nehemiah.[22] I believe Van Seters may be stretching the meaning of the text a little bit, for I am not sure that there is a difference between "buying" or "acquiring" and the image of the slave "selling himself." Furthermore, the Exodus law lacks any reference to a foreigner, which I feel is a crucial weakness in Van Seters's theory. In response to the late dating of the Exodus law, Benjamin Kilchör marshals an argument that Deuteronomy 15:12–18 is the latest and combines the concepts from slave laws in Exodus and Leviticus for the sake of social protection.[23] This, indeed, seems to me what those guidelines in Deuteronomy 15 are doing: providing greater social protection for slaves at several levels.

Van Seters further believes the Exodus guidelines are later because they take into account a more practical approach to slave release. He believes that Deuteronomy does not really suggest that women debt-slaves should be released, but rather he thinks that Deuteronomy is simply speaking idealistically when it says "Hebrew man" or "Hebrew woman." Women would not be released alone into a harsh world. The Book of the Covenant guideline provides the humanitarian advice that the debt-slave male should stay with his wife instead of assuming his freedom and leaving her (Exod 21:4–6). Further, the guideline in Exod 21:7–11 that directs a slave master to either marry his slave girl when she comes of age or marry her to his son indicates a practical approach to young slave girls, since they certainly cannot be released like men can. Exodus thus proposes that better care can be provided for daughters rather than having them simply released. Since the laws in Deuteronomy and Leviticus fail to mention these guidelines, Van Seters assumes that they are prior to the guideline in Exodus.[24] The weakness in Van Seters's argument is that the guidelines in Exod 21:7–11 actually do provide an option for the release of the slave girl. If neither the owner nor

22. Van Seters, "Law of the Hebrew Slave"; and Van Seters, "Law of the Hebrew Slave: A Continuing Debate," esp. 169–72, 179.

23. Kilchör, "Frei aber arm?," 381–97.

24. Van Seters, "Law of the Hebrew Slave: A Continuing Debate," 169, 182; and Van Seters, *Law Book for the Diaspora*, 85–86, 90.

his son desires the girl, the slave owner must allow her to be "redeemed," or to have her freedom purchased for her (Exod 21:8). If real freedom is an option in Exodus, then the Exodus laws are not more humanitarian in providing an alternative for a young girl rather than releasing her into the cruel world. It would seem to me instead that Deuteronomy has moved beyond the occasional possible option of redemption in Exod 21:8 and has made release of young girls into a universal release like the men experience. Thus, Deuteronomy omits the obligatory marriage a young slave girl might have had to undergo, which was likely not a pleasant experience for her. (With her release we would assume, of course, that someone would either marry her or assume responsibility for her, who was not chosen by her former master.) Van Seters suggests that Deuteronomy would not have overlooked the legal guidelines for slave-girl marriage to her master in Exod 21:7–11; therefore, for Van Seters, Deuteronomic guidelines are earlier than those laws in Exodus.[25] I believe the author of Deuteronomy did not overlook the law in Exodus; he simply ignored it because he moved beyond it with a more sweeping guideline of liberation for women than having female slaves simply marry their owners. Van Seters's observation that the Exodus law is more practical and more like a judicial text while the Deuteronomic Law is exhortation and may be too idealistic is probably correct, but it does not mean that the Exodus law necessarily comes later.[26] The bottom line is that the law in Deuteronomy comes after the law in Exodus. Finally, the expression in the debt-slave release law of Exod 21:1–6 which says that the slave who decides on being a permanent slave should be brought "before the deity" to have his ear pierced (v. 6) is an old expression that reflects an age when an image of God was acceptable. Such a reference is not possible by the time the laws in Deuteronomy are formulated. This expression alone indicates that the law in Exodus is older than the one in Deuteronomy. Van Seters believes that this is merely an expression meant to sanctify the act; it does not literally refer to an image of God.[27] I think that is a weak excuse. The guidelines in Exodus are older, and thus there is a reference to an old religious practice involving an image of God.

25. Van Seters, "Law of the Hebrew Slave: A Continuing Debate," 169, 182; and Van Seters, *Law Book for the Diaspora*, 86.

26. Van Seters, *Law Book for the Diaspora*, 88.

27. Ibid., 90.

Jubilee Year

Perhaps the most idealistic and dramatic legislation in the biblical law codes
are the guidelines in connection with Jubilee Year, a custom proclaimed in
Leviticus 25. Every forty-nine or fifty years the land was to be restored to
the original family that owned it. Thus, if a family fell upon hard times,
fell into debt-slavery, and lost their farm, this guideline provided for the
return of that land so that they might once more have the chance of living a reasonable life of freedom and self-dependency. This custom moves
beyond earlier biblical legislation and seeks to be even more humanitarian
with the addition of land restoration than did those earlier guidelines of
land rest, debt release, and slave release.[28] This law may be inspired by the
Mesopotamian customs of periodic debt and slave release proclaimed by
kings, but it moves well beyond them by adding the concept of land restoration and the concept of regular, periodic implementation, which means it is
not tied to the whim of a monarch or dependent upon a sufficiently strong
monarch who can initiate it.[29] To the best of our knowledge Judahites never
practiced this custom, but it remained in the text as a vision of hope for
poor people. The most dramatic reform, even today, is land redistribution,
and this biblical custom attempts to undertake that activity by restoring
land to the poor peasants who once lived on it. This law builds upon the old
custom of Fallow Year, a seven-year cycle, and speaks of Jubilee Year as a
cycle of seven cycles of seven years. So first, let us observe the guidelines for
the seven-year cycle of Fallow Year. Guidelines for land rest, the old Fallow
Year, already mentioned in Exodus, are found in Lev 25:2–7,

> 2When you enter the land that I am giving you, the land shall ob-
> serve a Sabbath for the LORD. 3Six years you shall sow your field,
> and six years you shall prune your vineyard, and gather in their
> yield; 4but in the seventh year there shall be a Sabbath of complete
> rest for the land, a Sabbath for the LORD: you shall not sow your
> field or prune your vineyard. 5You shall not reap the aftergrowth
> of your harvest or gather the grapes of your unpruned vine: it
> shall be a year of complete rest for the land. 6You may eat what the
> land yields during its Sabbath—you, your male and female slaves,
> your hired and your bound laborers who live with you; 7for your

28. Stackert, "Sabbath of the Land in the Holiness Legislation," 242–43.

29. Milgrom, "Sweet Land and Liberty," 8, 54; Hudson, "Economic Roots of the Jubilee," 26–33, 44.

livestock also, and for the wild animals in your land all its yield
shall be for food.

Ultimately this seven-year cycle of land rest will be tied into the fifty-year
cycle of Jubilee as the Jubilee Year follows after the seventh seven-year rest.
It is worth noting that the text clearly says that some of the wild volunteer-
crop growth, which will naturally grow on fallow land, is to be given to
slaves. Clearly the author of Leviticus 25 wishes to retain the old custom of
Fallow Year in the context of social economic reform for the poor and for
slaves in particular.

Debt-slave release and land-restoration guidelines appear in Lev
25:39–55, and selected passages read as follows in vv. 10 and 39–41,

> 10And you shall hallow the fiftieth year and you shall proclaim lib-
> erty throughout the land to all its inhabitants. It shall be a jubilee
> for you: you shall return, every one of you, to your property and
> every one of you to your family . . . 39If any who are dependent
> on you become so impoverished that they sell themselves to you,
> you shall not make them serve as slaves. 40They shall remain with
> you as hired or bound laborers. They shall serve with you until the
> year of the Jubilee. 41Then they and their children with them shall
> be free from your authority; they shall go back to their own family
> and return to their ancestral property.

According to this text, the entire family of debt-slaves, particularly children, who would have been born while their parents were debt-slaves, may
come out of servitude. This new legislation yet again attempts to end the
practice of matchmaking by masters who sought to tempt their debt-slaves
into permanent slavery. The Judahite tradition and some critical scholars
suggest that perhaps this legislation freed those debt-slaves who chose voluntarily to remain in debt-slavery according to the guidelines in Exodus
21 and perhaps also foreign slaves.[30] Others suggest that the Deuteronomic
Sabbath applies to landless poor while Jubilee Year addresses landowning
Israelites. Another possible approach to this legislation would be to suggest
that the Deuteronomic Sabbath year was not being kept, so the Priestly
legislators attempted to undertake their own variation on the issue of slave
release, combining ideas from laws in the Book of the Covenant and the
Deuteronomic Code, thus making it more comprehensive. Some believe
that Sabbath was observed, but Jubilee was too idealistic to be implemented, especially when you realize that the forty-ninth and the fiftieth years

30. Mendelsohn, "Slavery in the Old Testament," 4:389.

should have been theoretically land-fallow years, and two consecutive years of no crop harvest would have been devastating.[31] Still others observe that all the slave-release laws were idealistic suggestions by biblical authors, and none of them were seriously kept in those early centuries before and after the exile.

Whatever the case may be, I observe that this text still articulates an incredible vision of hope for poor people and is boldly crafted by the biblical author. It was a guideline that reminded the rich that someday the poor would stand before them as equals in the community. This vision of slave release and land restoration would still be a radical form of economic revival today. We have still not caught up to the imagery of hope found in the Old Testament.

The Jubilee Year release outlined in Lev 25:1–55 was to occur every forty-nine or fifty years. There has been debate among scholars as to the actual mechanics of that process and whether Jubilee release was actually practiced or whether it remained a literary and theological ideal of the scribal authors of the biblical text that could not really be applied in real life.[32] It was a very comprehensive attempt to restore economic equilibrium to society by canceling debts, freeing slaves, and restoring land to the original family owners. It has been called the most visionary and vigorous attempt in the laws of Israel to ameliorate the woes of the poor peasants.[33] Reform involving the transfer of land to poor people has been a radical form of economic change at any time in human history.

Jubilee imperatives thus surpass the Book of the Covenant and Deuteronomic laws by including land restoration in the process of economic reform. If former debt-slaves can be resettled upon their original farmland, they have an economic future far more substantial than if they merely received provisions, as Deuteronomic laws suggested. Perhaps the

31. De Vaux, *Ancient Israel*, 176–77; Fager, "Land Tenure in the Biblical Jubilee," 59–68; Amit, "Jubilee Law—an Attempt at Instituting Social Justice," 47–59, especially 53–56.

32. Gnuse, "Jubilee Legislation in Leviticus," 43–48, summarizes the debate on the aspects of historicity. Lowery, *Sabbath and Jubilee*, 57–77, provides a good summary of more recent sources and likewise concludes that the practice was idealistic and never really practiced, unless it was used in the sixth or fifth centuries BCE to give land back to the exiles returning from Babylon. Leuchter, "Manumission Laws in Leviticus and Deuteronomy," 638–40, views it as an idealistic priestly vision and calls it a "near mythic concept of law" and a "mytho-sacral law" that reacts against the Deuteronomic release law.

33. Brueggemann, *Old Testament Theology*, 80.

Deuteronomic provisions were seen to be insufficient to give former debt-slaves a new head start in self-sufficiency. Of course, such drastic measures then threaten the greater economic security of society, so the land restoration cannot come as frequently as earlier legislation proposed (every seven years). Thus, Levitical Jubilee Year compromises for a longer period of time.[34] In return for the longer period of time proposed for Jubilee Year, legislators in Leviticus sought to make slavery less degrading by also increasing the quality of treatment received by debt-slaves. Levitical guidelines provide idealistic rhetoric to demand that slaves be given honorable treatment during the period of their debt servitude and not be treated with harshness. We read in Lev 25:42–43, 46,

> [42]For they are my servants, whom I brought out of the land of Egypt; they shall not be sold as slaves are sold. [43]You shall not rule over them with harshness, but shall fear your God . . . [46]But as for your fellow Israelites, no one shall rule over the other with harshness.

It must be admitted at this point that the treatment of Israelite debt-slaves in Leviticus 25 is more generous than the guidelines provided for the treatment of foreign slaves (Lev 25:44–46a). But the evolving trajectory in the biblical tradition will address this issue in later years, when the dignity of all slaves will be respected. Leviticus 25 is seen by some authors to lay the foundation for the Western European development of universal human abolitionism.[35]

In summation, the evolving legal tradition in the Old Testament attempts to eliminate the oppression in the institution of slavery, especially debt-slavery, which was the most common form of enslavement in the ancient world. Progressively through the years more expanded and drastic legislation was provided not only to restore the slave's freedom but to give to the slave the opportunity to return to some form of financial independence. This was, in effect, an attempt to create a stable middle-class society of free and self-sufficient peasants. Though the biblical authors may not have understood economics in the way we do, we can recognize here a wisdom that understands that the strength of a society resides in its ability to maintain a healthy middle class capable of production and contribution to

---

34. Mitchell, *Ethics of the Old Testament*, 263; North, *Sociology of the Biblical Jubilee*, 135, 153; and Porter, *Leviticus*, 205.

35. Lowery, *Sabbath and Jubilee*, 70.

the society as a whole. (Even today many leaders in our world still have not grasped the importance of that insight.)

Jubilee Year was a utopian vision of hope generated by the priests seeking economic egalitarianism: that is, it was an attempt to prevent the rich from accumulating too much wealth at the expense of the poor in the struggling postexilic community and so to forestall serious economic injustice. At a deep level the Jubilee laws embody a egalitarian vision of humanity, espouse a high view of the family unit as the cornerstone of society, and see the land less as an economic commodity to be bought and sold and more as a gift from God. The gift of the land is to foster an ability to live honorably, free from the fear of poverty and oppression, and thereby to bring divine justice to society. The custom was not so much an economic vision of reality as it was a moral vision.[36] This vision of hope would continue to inspire postexilic prophets, the New Testament, and the later Jewish and Christian traditions.[37] Truly, in these biblical laws concerning debt and slave release we can sense a definite evolutionary trajectory in the legal tradition of ancient Israel.[38]

It took Western society until the nineteenth century to realize that slavery was an evil institution that needed to be abolished. Until that time defenders of slavery would simply quote biblical passages that recognized the existence of slavery as a permanent institution in society in that ancient age. Those who quoted biblical texts failed to appreciate the laws that attempted to ameliorate the woes and suffering of slaves. Not until the last two centuries, when we understood that there was an evolution in the legal tradition of ancient Israel and that the biblical text was composed of sources that developed and were woven together over the years, did we appreciate that there was an evolution in these laws. Once we could observe that developmental process, we could see that increasingly biblical authors with their idealistic legal articulations sought to lessen the extent of slavery,

36. Fager, "Land Tenure in the Biblical Jubilee," esp. 66–67; Amit, "Jubilee Law—an Attempt at Instituting Social Justice," esp. 51.

37. Gerstenberger, "In der Schuldenfalle."

38. Carmichael, "Three Laws on the Release of Slaves," creatively and poetically observes how the three laws relate to narratives in the Pentateuch by endeavoring to correct the abuses described in those accounts: the Exodus rule describes Jacob's situation with Laban in Genesis 29–31, the Levitical rule characterizes Jacob and his sons in Egypt in Genesis 47, and the Deuteronomic rule applies to both Laban and Jacob again and to Israel in Egypt in Exodus 1–12.

and in so doing, they came as close to abolitionism as they could for their own age.

Evolution of Laws

The laws of Deuteronomy expanded upon the laws from the old Book of the Covenant. They sought to plug the loopholes in those older laws about economic rights for the poor, which had originated in a much simpler society. Deficiencies in the older customs became evident in Israel and Judah during the economic and political development of the late eighth century BCE when new economic growth created a new class of rich. The greed of these new rich and powerful people victimized many poor highland peasants and led to debt enslavement and seizure of peasant lands. Deuteronomic reformers and the scribes who wrote down our biblical text in Deuteronomy 12–26 were inspired by the critique of the eighth-century-BCE classical prophets and thus elaborated upon the older laws. The common themes in their new laws were the exclusive worship of one God and the defense of the poor and marginal elements of society. It would seem from the rhetoric of Deuteronomy that these two elements—monotheism and social justice—are closely intertwined. Important for the argument of this book is the recognition of this salient point. With the emergence of the Yahweh-alone movement and early monotheism there also appeared a cry for justice and an attempt to legislate guidelines for the poor and marginal people of the society.

What we also observe here is a simultaneous evolutionary development and a revolutionary breakthrough in the legal traditions of that age stimulated by social, political, and economic forces. The development of Deuteronomic laws is an unfolding of latent ideas found already in the earlier laws of the Book of the Covenant, but their fuller manifestation would come only in the later evolution of human cultural experience. The cultural and historical experience of Israel further developed the concepts of monotheism and social reform over the years prior to the exile.[39] These ideas then paved the way for the breakthrough to the radical monotheistic faith of the exile and beyond. But even then this would not be the conclusion to the unfolding of the "monotheistic revolution." For the latent implications of these religious, social, and legal insights would continue to unfold in the Christian movement.

39. Albertz, *History of Israelite Religion in the Old Testament Period*, 1:1–242.

In conclusion, the new scholarly view of ancient Israel and Judah may inspire us with a comparable vision for social reform. Our contemporary theories speak of the later evolutionary emergence of monotheism and the concomitant notion that Israelites and Judahites shared much in common with their ancient Near Eastern predecessors. In our pedagogy we now stress continuity rather than dialectical contrast between Israel and the ancient world. If we acknowledge that Israel's monotheism emerged late in the biblical period, we may be led to see that the evolving process in ancient Israel is a process of growth that continues to unfold in our own age. This will affect our rhetoric in how we appeal to the Bible to inspire action in the modern church and society.

5

Rights for Slaves in the New Testament

Jesus and the Kingdom

JESUS PROCLAIMED THAT EVERYONE should prepare for the coming kingdom of God in which such temporal and physical distinctions as race,
gender, age, class, purity status, and free or slave status would be ended.
Jesus thereby affirmed all of humanity, but to declare that all people would
be equal in the coming kingdom was a radical affirmation of the poor and
the oppressed in that age, especially slaves and prisoners of war, who by
definition in the Roman Empire were no longer considered to be human.
In the Jesus sayings recalled by the Gospels, no specific traditions are remembered concerning slavery, but one might intuit that the Jesus tradition
speaks of how God would look more favorably upon the slave than the
oppressive master. For much of the rhetoric in the Jesus tradition speaks of
how when the kingdom of God comes, the tables will be turned: the poor
will be lifted up, and the rich will be cast down. Whether this rhetoric refers
to a reversal destined to happen in material and economic categories, or
whether it refers to a reality that occurs in the spiritual dimension or in the
life of a community of disciples is difficult for us to discern. At any rate, in
the later Christian communities such a reversal did happen as possessions
were shared, to some degree, by ancient Christians, and in the two thousand years of church history that followed, Christians of good conscience
have attempted to implement the ideal rhetoric of Jesus in the economic

realities of the everyday world. This has been particularly true with social movements led by committed Christians in the past two centuries.

New Testament Advice to Slaves

In regard to the institution of slavery, the later writings of the New Testament refer to slaves and the nature of their relationship to owners. An initial reading of these texts appears to demonstrate that early Christians supported or at least accepted the institution of slavery. Most notably, there is the saying in Ephesians 6:5–9,

> 5Slaves, obey your earthly masters with fear and trembling, in singleness of heart, as you obey Christ; 6not only while being watched, and in order to please them, but as slaves of Christ, doing the will of God from the heart. 7Render service with enthusiasm, as to the Lord and not to men and women, 8knowing that whatever good we do, we will receive the same again from the Lord, whether we are slaves or free. 9And, masters, do the same to them. Stop threatening them, for you know that both of you have the same Master in heaven, and with him there is no partiality.

Upon first reading this text, we would say that the New Testament has compromised the reform rhetoric and the evolutionary trajectory of the Old Testament concerning the rights and dignity of slaves. However, the New Testament passage must not be taken out of its social context in the Graeco-Roman world, especially in a political realm that was under the heel of the Roman Empire. In the barbaric age of cruelty spawned by Rome, slaves were simply things—the property of their masters—who could be killed whimsically and indiscriminately by their masters or even used to provide entertainment in the gladiatorial displays of the arena. Though in the early years of Paul's mission there was a strong emphasis upon abolishing the distinction between slave and free people among Christians, it seems that the second generation of Christians cautiously had to become more like their neighbors to avoid drawing the attention of the authorities and perhaps to make a broad-based appeal in society.[1] Christians did not wish to appear dedicated to violent revolution in the name of abolition, which is certainly how they would have been perceived if they dramatically reiterated Paul's language that declared there was no difference between slaves and free people. That would have brought the Roman Empire down

1. Glancy, *Slavery in Early Christianity*, 145.

upon them in a violent military fashion. Thus, Christians gradually had to accept the existence of the institution in order to survive in Graeco-Roman society, and this acceptance appears in the virtue lists of the later New Testament writings.

We read the imperative for slaves to be obedient to their masters, and this offends our modern sensitivities. But we must not overlook the second half of the imperative, beginning in v. 9, which addresses the masters. It is most revolutionary for that age. To call upon masters to be kind to their slaves would have been completely offensive to many Roman authorities and slave masters, who maintained absolute control over slaves lest a slave uprising destroy all of them. The rebellion of Spartacus in Italy, as well as other uprisings, were not forgotten by the Romans. From our perspective we fail to appreciate how radical such biblical statements to masters would have sounded in that era, and how dangerous it was for the author of Ephesians, who was probably a colleague of Paul, perhaps Apollos, to encourage such respect and kindness from masters toward slaves in an age of absolute rule by Rome. Most Romans believed that to show kindness to slaves was a to demonstrate weakness and would bring a violent response from slaves.

In that age of oppression, slaves were not considered to be human beings. To address slaves, as our biblical author does, and to call upon them in their own free will to submit to their masters, would have been viewed as offensive by Roman slave owners. One should not ask slaves to be obedient to their masters; one would simply expect it of them. The biblical author considers slaves to be people worth addressing, thus treating them as human beings, and by requesting them to give obedience to their masters, actually gives them dignity by making their submission the result of their own free decision. There is no other literature in the ancient Roman Empire wherein an author speaks to slaves as though they are rational human beings. We cannot appreciate how radical the language of the biblical author is in this regard. It is easy for us to misunderstand the biblical text in this passage unless we really recognize the cultural values of that age. This passage does not accept Graeco-Roman beliefs about the institution of slavery.

Another passage worth mentioning is one that calls upon Christian slaves to be respectful to their masters, especially their Christian masters. A quick reading of this text would make us think that here is an example of Christian authors supporting the horrid institution of slavery. But it actually tells us much about real Christian attitudes toward slavery in a subtle fashion. In one of the Pastoral Epistles, a letter written after Paul's death by one of his colleagues, we read in 1 Tim 6:1–2a,

> [1] Let all who are under the yoke of slavery regard their masters as worthy of all honor, so that the name of God and the teaching may not be blasphemed. [2A] Those who have believing masters must not be disrespectful to them on the ground that they are members of the church; rather they must serve them all the more, since those who benefit by their service are believers and beloved.

The passage begins with advice to slaves that they should be respectful to their owners, but this should alert us initially that something is unusual. In the Roman Empire household slaves were not advised to be obedient to their owners; they did so because they feared death. One of Nero's household slaves tasted some leftover food that was destined to be discarded, and when Nero observed his behavior, he had the slave executed. The mere fact that the author of this pastoral letter encourages Christian slaves to be respectful to their Christian masters implies immediately that there was a far more lenient attitude toward slaves in Christian households. In addition, our author continues by observing that slaves should not take advantage of the attitude of their Christian masters toward Christian slaves by behaving inappropriately. Our author would not have said this unless it was happening. Thus, this passage indirectly testifies to a decidedly different mode of relationship between masters and their slaves in Christian households. Slaves did not live in abject fear of their owners as was the case in so many other Roman and Greek households of the first century CE; in fact, they may have acted a little too bold at times because of the newfound equality provided by the spiritual relationships in the Christian community.[2]

It must be remembered that those early Christians, including Paul and the other biblical authors, lived with the expectation of Jesus's imminent return. They did not see it necessary to reform society, for this age with its evil and tyranny soon was to pass away. We should not condemn them for the failure to call for the abolition of slavery, as much as we might wish that they had. For those ancient Christians were some of the weakest members of society, and they simply had no power to oppose the institution. Such an attempt might have brought tremendous destruction to the early Christian communities. (They got thrown into the arena for enough other reasons, anyway!)

2. Kelly, *Commentary on the Pastoral Epistles*, 130–32.

Value of Slaves in Christian Communities

What we must recognize is that in those early Christian communities they sought to eliminate distinctions between slaves and free persons in their worship experience and Christian life. This clarion cry was heralded by Paul in Gal 3:27–28,

> [27]As many of you as were baptized into Christ have clothed your-
> selves with Christ. [28]There is no longer Jew or Greek; there is no
> longer slave or free, there is no longer male and female; for all of
> you are one in Christ Jesus.

Some popular, pious interpretations of this passage attempt to say that Paul is describing what relationships will be like in heaven. But if we read the text closely, it is obvious that Paul is describing real life in the Christian commu-nity. These class distinctions are meant to be abolished in the relationship that Christians have with each other. Though they could not change life in the world, wherein masters ruled slaves brutally, their relationship in the worshiping Christian community was different.

Even though Christians had to accept the institution of slavery, it is amazing that slaves could become clergy, and in the second century CE there were slaves who served as bishops. One such bishop is even said to have excommunicated his master over a moral issue, and the master re-lented. Around 115 CE the Roman governor Pliny wrote to the Roman emperor Trajan that in his investigation of Christians in Bithynia, northern Turkey, he questioned by torture two Christian leaders, both of whom were deacons. He describes them as midwives, which is a lowly profession, and it probably indicates that both women were slaves. Yet they were deacons, and their testimony was important to Pliny. In the past, scholars viewed these women as merely servants in the church, but now we suspect that they were actually bishops (since the word *deacon* can mean both "servant" and "overseer"). At least they held some significant clergy status, for Pliny felt that their testimony was the most convincing evidence that he obtained.[3]

Even though compromise with Graeco-Roman values had to occur, Christians did not capitulate completely to the values of their society. The true early Christian understanding of slavery is best articulated by Paul's statement in Gal 3:28. We cannot underestimate the radical nature of the Christian movement's acceptance of slaves into the worship setting with free people. Bringing slaves and free people together in a single worship

3. Glancy, *Slavery in Early Christianity*, 130.

context was scandalous to the sensitivities of people in the Graeco–Roman world. On this point alone Christianity was a revolutionary movement.[4] Is it worth pointing out that in early nineteenth-century America, Southern slaves and free people would not worship in the same church? We had not yet caught up to the values of the first-century CE Christian movement in nineteenth-century America, yet we prided ourselves on being a so-called democratic nation.

In their spiritual relationships to each other, and in the life of the church, slavery was abolished in their minds and hearts. One might assume that they felt they were powerless to change society and eliminate slavery, so they believed they had to wait until Jesus came. How disappointed they would have been had they known that Christianity would ultimately become the religion of the Roman Empire in the fourth century CE and that slavery was not abolished! How shocked and ashamed they would have been were they to have known that it would not be until the nineteenth century that significant abolitionist movements would arise. But then, as I noted earlier, the message of the biblical text sometimes has to await an age when people are ready to hear it, and only then do the full implications of the biblical, monotheistic revolution unfold in the social arena.

Paul's Views of Slavery as an Institution

Paul, in particular, is criticized by some modern intellectuals for being a supporter of the institution of slavery. This appears to be the case in 1 Cor 7:21 where Paul says,

> Were you a slave when called? Do not be concerned about it. Even if you can gain your freedom, make use of your present condition now more than ever.

"Make use of your present condition" more literally might mean, "take advantage of it." At first glance Paul appears to encourage slaves to stay slaves, so that they "take advantage" of their condition as slaves. Certainly early nineteenth-century pro-slavery commentators interpreted the passage this way.[5] Other authors have suggested that Paul is telling the Corinthian slaves to "take advantage" of the opportunity to gain their freedom.

---

4. L. T. Johnson, *1 Timothy, 2 Timothy, Titus*, 104.

5. Braxton, *Tyranny of Resolution*, 235–74.

Modern commentators, however, suggest that what Paul really says is that Christians who were slaves should not fear that their slave status makes them second-class Christians; rather, they are spiritually equal to free people. Their slave status should not prevent them from living out their Christian calling. Paul refers to himself as a slave of Christ and a slave to all (1 Cor 9:19–23). He does this, in part, to deconstruct the mindset of the powerful and the rich who think themselves to be superior to slaves, and he also emphasizes humility and equality in his service to others.[6] He thus says to Christians who are slaves that their calling to be Christian is more important than their low social status as slaves.

Furthermore, the urban slaves who were likely to belong to the Corinthian community actually had a good chance of receiving manumission from their masters after some years of faithful service, and this freedom did not always mean a better economic status, since they often remained obligated to their former masters in certain ways. Hence, even if Paul were critical of the institution of slavery, he is somewhat indifferent to the issue of whether these Christians should seek manumission from their masters. Rather, it was more important that they feel an inner sense of freedom brought by Christian belief, and that they should act as Christians in the world.

When Paul states that they "should make use of their present condition" or "take advantage of it," it might be possible that Paul means that slaves should take advantage of manumission. Increasingly some scholars are suggesting that this indeed is what Paul meant. Paul would have considered slavery to be in tension with the status of brotherhood and sisterhood that all Christians share with each other. Paul would have felt that if we are liberated and redeemed by Christ's salvific activity in the life of the church, this should also apply to life in the world. Practically speaking, if a slave were to be freed, he or she could then contribute to the mission of Christ, both through mission service, and through the ability to earn more income and contribute to the community fund.[7]

Other commentators still suggest that Paul more likely means that slaves "make use" of their calling as Christians, for previously in vv. 17–20 Paul refers to the Christian calling in reference to circumcision. Since Paul says that circumcision is irrelevant in terms of the Christian calling, so also in v. 21 he may imply the same thing: all Christians are equal regardless of

6. Martin, *Slavery as Salvation*, 117–49.
7. Dawes, "'But If You Can Gain Your Freedom'"; Harrill, "Paul and Slavery."

their status of circumcision or slave identity.[8] Thus, seeking freedom is not really that important in the light of one's Christian calling.

It has also been suggested that Paul discreetly speaks in deliberately ambiguous fashion when he says, "take advantage of it," thus seeking not to take a hard stand on a sensitive issue in the Corinthian congregation, where both slaves and owners worshiped together.[9] He may be subtly saying that a slave might seek manumission, but he does not wish to express this opinion directly or too loudly. Paul may not be recommending wholesale manumission here; nonetheless, to say that a slave is equal to an owner in the Christian faith is a very revolutionary (and potentially dangerous) statement to make under the watchful eyes of the Roman Empire.

It must also be acknowledged that a slave owner could manumit a slave against the slave's desires simply to be rid of him or her. If a slave could not refuse manumission, Paul may also be referring to situations in which a slave might obtain freedom unwillingly, in which case Paul may be saying that the slave needs to make the best of this situation, too.[10] So even if Paul is not advocating manumission in this particular passage, his understanding of the equality between slave and master in the Christian community is extremely radical for his age.

Paul's Letter to Philemon

Paul sometimes receives criticism from modern individuals because as he wrote the letter to Philemon, he sent a slave back to his master. Defenders of slavery in the nineteenth century gleefully appealed to the Letter to Philemon as they acerbically attacked the Underground Railroad. Paul appears to contradict the spirit of the law in Deuteronomy, which commands Judahites not to send slaves back to their masters, especially if they are foreign. But Paul is sending Onesimus back to Philemon, a Christian, and this made a difference for Paul. Both Onesimus and Philemon would live and function with Christian moral guidelines. These guidelines would differentiate their relationship from the common master-slave relationship in the Roman Empire. A Christian master's treatment of slaves should be humanitarian, similar to the treatment to which Judahite masters are called

8. Bartchy, *First-Century Slavery and 1 Corinthians 7:21*, 1–183; N. Elliott, *Liberating Paul*, 32–40; Briggs, "Paul on Bondage and Freedom."

9. Braxton, *Tyranny of Resolution*, 7–67, 220–34.

10. Dawes, "'But If You Can Gain Your Freedom,'" 693.

in Leviticus 25. It should go beyond the mere humanitarian spirit that some idealists, such as the Stoics, might exhibit in their relationships with others, including slaves.[11] Pliny the Younger interceded with Sabinianus on behalf of a slave for the sake of clemency, which Pliny described as a virtue. But Paul calls for love, not just a virtuous response. Christian slaves and masters were expected to work with each other and treat each other with love and dignity. That would have been condemned by governmental authorities in the Roman Empire and certainly disdained by slave owners in general.

Since Paul expected Jesus to return within his lifetime, he saw no need to encourage the abolition of slavery. Furthermore, those early churches were composed primarily of the poor (with occasional rich benefactors), and most of these were slaves, or women and children (equally powerless groups in the Roman Empire). They were powerless to change their society, and any serious opposition to social norms on slavery would have gotten them quickly killed. Paul really encouraged a practical abolition of slavery and the distinction between slave and free in the church, as the passage in Gal 3:28 indicates, and for him that was sufficient.[12] Perhaps more dramatically, Paul may be encouraging Philemon to manumit Onesimus, but of that we cannot be sure, since we do not know of the spoken conversion that might have occurred between Paul and Onesimus over the years.[13]

There is a significant aspect of Paul's advice to Philemon that we totally fail to appreciate. Slave masters in the ancient Graeco-Roman world had the power to punish their escaped slaves indiscriminately, and often did so.[14] Roman law mandated that escaped slaves had to be punished upon their restoration to their masters, usually by whipping, or in some parts of the empire the penalty was death.[15] In Philemon 16–18 Paul implores Philemon not to punish Onesimus but to receive him as Philemon would receive Paul himself (v. 17).

Paul tells Philemon that not only should he receive Onesimus back, but he should have him "no longer as a slave, but more than a slave, a beloved brother . . . both in the flesh and in the Lord" (v. 16). This indeed sounds

11. Lohse, *Colossians and Philemon*, 187, 196–99.

12. Cousar, *Galatians*, 86–87.

13. N. Elliott, *Liberating Paul*, 40–52.

14. Lohse, *Colossians and Philemon*, 196; Dunn, *Epistles to the Colossians and to Philemon*, 306.

15. Wall, *Colossians & Philemon*, 183; Dunn, *The Epistles to the Colossians and to Philemon*, 306.

like Paul is asking Philemon to grant Onesimus his freedom. The phrases "in the "flesh" and "in the "Lord" may refer to everyday society ("the flesh") and the Christian community ("in the Lord") respectively, and the former phrase might imply real manumission. Onesimus was free in Christ in that he had equality with other Christians in the community of faith that met in Philemon's home, but now he would be free in the "flesh," in the actual social world outside the church community. Furthermore, Paul also implies that he would like to have Onesimus come back and work for him, most likely as a free person (vv. 13–14). Although some commentators believe that Paul merely means that Onesimus should have a new relationship with his master, as a Christian brother, most commentators now suspect that Paul is hinting strongly that Philemon should manumit Onesimus. The term *manumission*, of course, refers to the custom wherein some Greek and Roman slave masters did release individual slaves as a reward for faithful years of service, and Paul may be requesting that favor as a third-party intercessor between a slave and his master.[16] This is rather bold of Paul in that world of slavery, where Romans were exceptionally paranoid about anyone encouraging folk to free slaves. But Paul is doing that. He cannot directly demand that Philemon free Onesimus, but he comes pretty close with his persuasive rhetoric.

Paul reminds Philemon that his salvation came as a result of Paul's activity, thus appealing to his sense of honor to treat Onesimus kindly because Paul has saved him. This letter might have been read publicly in a home church where Philemon worshiped (vv. 2, 22), and so the demand for honorable treatment of Onesimus would have been greatly encouraged by Paul's rhetoric. Paul implies that Philemon needs to do the honorable thing as an example to his fellow Christians that meet in his home (vv. 6, 8–9, 13–14, 22). We need to appreciate the issue of honor in east Mediterranean society, for Paul is pressuring Philemon to act with honor and Christian values in the presence of his Christian community. It is a matter of honor for Philemon to repay Paul for bringing him the Christian message, and now Paul perhaps implies that Philemon show that indebtedness by manumitting Onesimus.[17] Paul knows how to really lay guilt on Philemon! But this is an extremely radical statement by Paul for his age. He is telling Phi-

16. Getty, *Philippians and Philemon*, 78–80; Bruce, *Epistles to the Colossians, to Philemon, and to the Ephesians*, 217; Bartchy, "Philemon, Epistle to," 308–9; and Bartchy, "Slavery (Graeco-Roman)," 71–72; Wall, *Colossians & Philemon*, 210–13; Fitzmyer, *Letter to Philemon*, 12–24.

17. Petersen, *Rediscovering Paul*, 86–78, 99–109, 261–70.

lemon to not punish Onesimus, and thereby to engage in a visual act of civil disobedience against Roman law and custom. This is not the socially conservative Paul that some modern people never tire of criticizing.

If this reading of the Letter to Philemon is correct, then Paul's rhetoric against slavery is to be viewed by us as even more revolutionary for its age. Paul may be asking Philemon to treat Onesimus in a new fashion as a Christian brother, or he may be hinting that Philemon manumit Onesimus. Either way, Paul's advice runs counter to prevailing social attitudes about the treatment of slaves.

Early Christianity and Slavery

The degree to which later Christians may have been inspired by Paul and Christian values in general to oppose the evilness of the institution of slavery is difficult to gauge. Some New Testament commentators believe that Christians tried to mollify the severity of the institution, and that better treatment of slaves resulted from the rise of Christianity. Others suspect that Christians pretty well accepted the guidelines by which the institution operated because it was beyond their conceptual ability to so radically transcend the social values of their age, and though they may have paid lip service to better treatment of their fellow humanity, their actions were not too radically different from other non-Christians in their treatment of slaves.[18] Perhaps the best answer is that Christians fell on both sides of the fence in this regard. A telling example comes from the early first-century-CE correspondence of Ignatius, who complains that Christians ought not use their church funds to manumit slaves who are members of the Christian communities. That he has to remonstrate against this activity clearly indicates that Christians were doing this because they felt compelled to do so by conscience. Their actions may have helped many Christians move up into more of a free, middle-class status, which would have enabled the recipients of such generosity to give more money to the Christian community for the potential liberation of other slaves. Ignatius's opinion probably reflects the feelings of other Christians, including leaders, such as himself, who believed this would draw individuals into the Christian movement for the wrong reasons and seriously deplete the resources of Christian churches.[19] His insights were probably correct, but I believe that over the

18. Glancy, *Slavery in Early Christianity*, 3–156.

19. Ibid., 96, 151.

years this liberality in the use of funds to free slaves actually may have pro-
moted Christian growth in a significant fashion, as slaves were drawn to
the movement and many of them became valued members of the various
Christian communities. Ignatius's advice indicates to us that indeed many
Christians did practice a rather liberal ethos in regard to slavery by freeing
many slaves.

From our modern vantage point we fail to appreciate how revolutionary Paul's advice was. One cannot say, in the light of this advice by Paul, that
Paul supported or tolerated the institution of slavery as it was practiced in
the Roman Empire. He may appear conservative to us because it simply
was not part of his "mission agenda" to instigate an abolitionist movement
in the first century CE. That would be the responsibility of Christians in
a later era. Had he been alive in another era, when Christians were not
the weak and oppressed members of Roman society, as they were in his
age, Paul might have said things differently. He probably would be very
angry had he known that people would quote him at a future date in order
to legitimate the institution of slavery in America. He probably would be
disappointed that it took Christians so many centuries before they finally
abolished slavery.

In the nineteenth century some preachers and theologians appealed
to the biblical text and its apparent acceptance of slavery in an attempt to
justify the institution. To appeal to laws in the Old Testament or to the writings of Paul in order to justify the institution of slavery, merely because the
laws and Paul recognize the institution as an existing and common practice
in their age, is most incorrect. This misunderstands the spirit of the biblical laws, which were created to lessen the impact of this evil institution by
providing slaves with some rights and by enabling their emancipation at
some point. Such interpretations additionally overlook the nature of the
evolutionary trajectory in the Bible, which attempts to lessen the evil impact of slavery with each new law code. Laws in the Old Testament sought
to alleviate the oppression of the debt-slaves, provide them with dignity
and rights, and make their access to freedom more possible. In the New
Testament age Paul lived with the hope that Jesus would return shortly and
end all evil institutions, including slavery, so there was no need to seek
the abolition of the institution. Reading Philemon in its proper historical
context gives us the deeper understanding that Paul had concerning slavery
as an oppressive institution.

As we read the Bible today, we must perceive that these biblical laws
tell us that slavery ought to be abolished in all forms—physical, financial,

or psychological; for such abolition would be the culmination of the evolutionary and revolutionary trajectory set in motion by those biblical authors thousands of years ago. Ancient Christians could not affect the greater institutions of their society. But if they could have seen what so-called Christian Western society has done with slaves and slavery, they would weep. For they would see Christians with the power to change their societies, and too many of those Christian leaders and spokespersons did nothing. Not only did they not seek to abolish slavery, but they prospered from it and justified their actions by referring to texts from a bygone age when early Christians were powerless to change those forces that beat people into submission.

Charles Cousar said it so well while speaking of Paul's understanding of slavery in Galatians,

> Unfortunately the later history of the church is not universally commendable. At times individuals discovered Paul's revolutionary insights and engaged heroically in the struggle to abolish slavery. At too many other times, however, the church claimed it had only a spiritual responsibility to slaves and either defended the owners of washed its hands of the whole issue.[20]

Before we say, "thank goodness slavery was finally abolished in the nineteenth century in America!," we must ask ourselves if slavery still exists in our world today. Yes, it does. Many people in our country and vast numbers of folk overseas are trapped in menial-wage jobs that make them virtual slaves. Many sweatshops in Asia employ people at miserably low wages to manufacture the goods sold cheaply in our country. We in America especially live off slave labor of people in other countries. We, as Christians, need to speak up on behalf of such workers. Then there is the even more insidious sex slavery that exists in our world: young girls are forced into prostitution in order to survive. We recognize that this happens extensively in countries around the world, especially to young girls from poverty-stricken countries. But it shocks many to discover that sex slavery exists here in our own country too. The message of the Bible that speaks for justice and seeks the ultimate elimination of slavery is still an important message we need to hear. We need to condemn and seek to eliminate those insidious forms of slavery that still exist in the modern world. The evolving trajectory of biblical values that seeks to eliminate slavery still proclaims a message to society, which has much work to do.

20. Cousar, *Galatians*, 86–87.

The Biblical Revolution

Christians confess that Jesus took religious and social teachings of the Old Testament, especially Deuteronomy, and developed them in his radical ethic of love and total obedience to God the Father that then entailed a new community of love and equality among believers. His message was not totally new, was very Judean at its core, and built upon and further developed the Israelite and Judahite intellectual values he had inherited. With the teachings of Jesus, the "biblical revolution," or the evolutionary process, advanced significantly. Jesus's imperative to go beyond the requirements of the law was certainly in full accord with the message of the classical prophets and the Deuteronomic Reformers, but he expressed these radical insights of love and nonviolence with a pungent clarity that assured his sayings would inspire millions of people for thousands of years. Jesus was the "one through whom the insights and vision of Jewish prophetism transformed the West and now the East as well."[21] His prophetic call to love one's enemies, to eschew violence, and to embrace a common humanity in its pain and suffering was in itself a breakthrough in the human cultural experience.[22] It was a significant early move toward a common humanity that transcends the particularity of families, groups, tribes, and nations.

Those early Christians, who heeded the imperatives of Jesus, were a minority movement of primarily poor and powerless people. Their quiet but deliberate protest against the barbarism of that age slowly made itself felt. They brought a minority report against brutal customs (such as the exposure of unwanted babies, when they adapted such children as their own, or the callous disregard for human life, when they fed the poor and hungry. Even the roar of the crowds for the spectacle of gladiatorial conflict waned with the gradual emergence of a Christian majority in the empire. Christians heeded the call of Jesus even when they were powerless, and they prevailed. Christians have been called to follow and fulfill these imperatives of Jesus to attain the liberation of all humanity in some fashion for two thousand years. It is a goal toward which we still painfully aspire today.[23]

---

21. Cobb, *Christ in a Pluralistic Age*, 98.

22. Brueggemann, *Prophetic Imagination*, 81–113; Theissen, *Biblical Faith*, 82–128.

23. Theissen, *Biblical Faith*, 170, likewise declares that we have a moral responsibility for continuing this cultural evolutionary process, which includes the further actualization of religious values.

6

Women's Rights in the Old Testament

Women in the Ancient World

IT IS AN ASSUMPTION among modern intellectuals that biblical religion, as well as the biblical text, is patriarchal and has been, in part, responsible for the suppression of women in the history of western Europe and the Middle East. Such were the implications drawn by Erika Schwartz, whose views were discussed earlier in this volume. I maintain that much of that suppression of women resulted from the cultural assumptions of the era in which the biblical texts were created (from 600 BCE to 100 CE). The biblical texts arose in a rather rough-hewn age, and many of the sexist assumptions of that era impinged upon the value system of the biblical authors. It was a very patriarchal age, and patriarchalism was intertwined with many social values in the culture.[1] Patriarchalism existed in the culture long before our biblical traditions were generated, and the religion often inherited and carried those patterns of behavior unconsciously through the years. Only in time were those practices challenged by critics who dared to appeal to the heart and core of biblical teachings.

We should not judge the value of any religion by the cultural accretions that come from the era of that religion's origin; rather, we should evaluate a religion by the core of its teachings in its sacred texts. For instance, I do not want Christian theology to be evaluated on the basis of what some Christians have done in the name of the religion. Too often religionists do things

1. Gerstenberger, *Yahweh—the Patriarch*, 88–94.

quite inconsistent with the core of their religious beliefs. Religionists need to return to their central sacred texts to continually reform their practices. Every religion needs continual reform and growth in its religious practice. Some Christians in particular have articulated this belief with the motto *ecclesia reformanda est,* according to which the "church must be reformed continually," and often the call to reform has been occasioned by a return to teachings in the biblical text. A return to the message of the sacred texts from the past can enable religionists to move progressively into the future, when those texts are understood in their fullest sense.

In the monotheistic faiths of the Middle East and Europe we can observe the historical subordination of women, but both regions were exceedingly patriarchal before monotheism arose. So deeply embedded was patriarchalism that religious leaders were unconscious of it or unaware that it was a problem to be addressed. That recognition is a modern realization. In reference to the Jewish and Christian Bible, a return to the deeper message of the sacred text can help to overcome the patriarchalism bequeathed to the text by the ancient cultural environment; that is, a deeper understanding of the biblical text can critique the literal message of the biblical text.

Before we accuse monotheism or the biblical texts of creating the modern subordination of women, we must acknowledge that the subordination of women may be observed in the nonmonotheistic, pagan religions of the ancient world, both before the emergence of monotheism, and in the pagan religions that endured contemporaneously with emerging monotheisms. The oppression of women is not something that monotheisms invented or uniquely preserved. The fact that women could become high priestesses in some of the pagan religions of the ancient Near East or the Graeco-Roman world did not ameliorate the suppression experienced by the vast majority of women. So to appeal, as some modern intellectuals have done, to the elevation of a handful of women intermediaries in the pagan religions as examples of equal treatment for women and men is rather shortsighted.

In general, the monotheistic faiths elevated the status of women beyond the status women experienced in the prior pagan religions. Though women may not have attained the kind of equality and dignity to which women aspire today (and sometimes receive), their lot in life was improved by the advance of monotheistic faiths. In Israelite laws rights were given to women in the earliest law codes, and in Christianity women were given equal status together with men in an age when the two sexes often had to belong to separate religions. None of the religions achieved what some modern critics today might wish they would have accomplished, but then to meet our modern standards would have been impossible in the early years when those religions were born. What they did accomplish should be recognized by us as significant. We must admit furthermore that the modern reformer's expectations of the rights of women have been made possible today because a monotheistic faith centuries ago made the first early moves to protect the dignity and rights of women. Each monotheistic faith contains within it the seeds of potential growth that ultimately will seek equality for women.

Women in the Judeo-Christian Tradition

This is especially true of the Judeo-Christian tradition that has as its core formulations the Torah and the teachings of both Jesus and Paul. These core formulations provide rhetoric for the improved status of women in society. When we heed these core messages of the Torah or the New Testament, we encounter an imperative to change our lives and improve our society. Often these imperatives stand in tension with the actual descriptions of the society of that age provided by the biblical authors. Of course, this is deliberate by the biblical authors. They sought to contrast human sin, disobedience, and past human failures at all levels with that vision of a better life willed by God. Thus, there will be a contrast between the narratives that describe human sin and the brutal life of that age and the vision of a more faithful humanity and a healthier community envisioned by the inspired authors.

Too often when we read the biblical texts, we fail to appreciate this. We read the narratives, which reflect the social historical phenomena of that age and thus reflect the sad experiences of women who are brutalized. We read stories of rape and abuse and are offended.[2] We read other accounts where women are routinely forced into submission to men. But the biblical authors are not commending these narratives to us for our emulation; rather, these stories simply reflect the events and culture of that age. How could the accounts recall otherwise if they were a true reflection of those people and their lives? The extremely violent accounts are provided by the final editors as examples of the evil and violence of the age. The story of the Levite's concubine in Judges 19, who is raped and killed, is ultimately

2. Trible, *Texts of Terror.*

a testimony for the need to have a stable government, a king, so that such behavior will no longer occur.

Hence, we should not look to such stories and say, this is what the Bible teaches us about women. Rather, we should look to other texts, especially laws and prophetic imperatives, which seek a higher moral ground, the protection of the weak, and better living opportunities for marginal people. Within that material we will discern the message of the biblical authors concerning what the status of women should be. This is the message of the biblical text, and this is what the biblical authors want us to emulate. We should not read the narratives but rather heed the moral imperatives of legal and prophetic texts.

Not to more fully realize this at those times when we actually were ready as a society for such reform constitutes a failure on the part of the Christian church in the past two thousand years. Too often the religious leaders have been content to accept the social and religious status quo and to legitimate it by an appeal to the biblical narratives. Thus, slavery, the suppression of women, and other woes were accepted and legitimated by the clergy simply because those phenomena existed in the biblical world. They failed to read those biblical texts that either demanded or implied that we move beyond such conditions. The sin of Christendom was that too often it read the stories and not the moral imperatives; it contented itself with the sinful human condition testified to by the narratives and failed to see the vision in the laws.

With this in mind we need to turn to some of those texts wherein the biblical authors actually appear to be speaking about what the status of women should be. We should heed these texts, and not those texts that merely describe what the status of women was. We heed the message of what should be, not what "is" or "was." For we are farther along on the monotheistic trajectory, and we need to know where we should be going, not where we once were.

Though we cannot touch upon all the texts that would be germane to a discussion of women's rights in the Bible, we may consider some of the more significant passages. The biblical tradition was making significantly new observations about the status of women. It is simply a misfortune in the history of Christian interpretation that we have failed to clearly see and theologize from these texts until the modern era. But perhaps now we are truly ready to hear the stories and actualize the deeper message that lies within the text.

Laws and Women's Rights

In the Old Testament one may discern an evolving trajectory in the legal tradition toward greater rights for women. Laws seeking to adjudicate the injustice of oppressed people in general include those that speak to the rights of women also, but specific laws address the status of women. The earliest laws arose in the Book of the Covenant, but later laws expanded upon these.

The Book of the Covenant initially sought to provide dignity and rights for women with legislation that protected female slaves. Young women sold as debt-slaves by their families had to be married to their owners or to the sons of their owners as full wives when they reached the age of adulthood. If this did not occur, then the women had to be redeemed by their families or released as free women. If married to their owners or their owners' sons, their marital rights could not be diminished, even if their husbands took additional wives. Above all, female slaves could not be treated like property and certainly could not be sold to a foreign people. We read in Exod 21:7–11,

> 7When a man sells his daughter as a slave, she shall not go out as the male slaves do. 8If she does not please her master, who designated her for himself, then he shall let her be redeemed; he shall have no right to sell her to a foreign people, since he has dealt unfairly with her. 9If he designates her for his son, he shall deal with her as a daughter. 10If he takes another wife to himself, he shall not diminish the food, clothing, or marital rights of the first wife. 11And if he does not do these three things for her, she shall go out without debt, without payment of money.

Notice that the text says that either she can be redeemed (that is, paid for with a monetary price [v. 8]), or she can go out completely free without payment if he has not faithfully discharged his responsibilities to her in later years (v. 11).

As I mentioned previously, provisions were made for slave release under special circumstances: if the master brutally beat a slave (Exod 21:20) or knocked out either an eye or a tooth of a slave, the slave went free (Exod 21:26–27). This prevented masters from striking slaves on the head or face. These biblical laws cover women as well as men. References to a "slave," without mention of the slave's gender, were understood as references to male slaves. Female slaves likely did not experience the release that came with enduring an owner's abuse. Such is often the case with human culture worldwide; women are not covered by the legal protection that is sometimes provided for marginal men.

Deuteronomy provides even more protection for women than the Book of the Covenant gave. Deuteronomy introduces the custom of giving divorce papers to a woman who is divorced by her husband. We read in Deut 24:1–4,

> ¹Suppose a man enters into marriage with a woman, but she does not please him because he finds something objectionable about her, and so he writes her a certificate of divorce, puts it in her hand, and sends her out of his house; she then leaves his house ²and goes off to become another man's wife. ³Then suppose the second man dislikes her, writes her a bill of divorce, puts it in her hand, and sends her out of his house (or the second man who married her dies); ⁴her first husband, who sent her away, is not permitted to take her again to be his wife after she has been defiled; for that would be abhorrent to the LORD, and you shall not bring guilt on the land that the LORD your God is giving you as a possession.

To us it may seem unfair that women may be divorced by their husbands but cannot divorce them in return. But we must recognize that the lawgivers were ameliorating the plight of women within the parameters of the social customs of their age. Giving the right of divorce to women would have been impossible in that age and perhaps beyond even the conceptualization of the most progressively minded reformer. What was done with the divorce papers was a significant accomplishment.

By demanding that husbands give papers to their divorced wives, the lawgivers actually were giving a significant form of protection to women. Otherwise a man could expel his wife, and if another man took her in, the first husband could accuse her of adultery and have her stoned to death. So the divorce papers provided proof that the woman was clearly divorced and could remarry and thus avoid a quick trip to the rock pile. Without the possibility of remarriage, difficult though that may have been, she either would have to go back and live with her father's family or would become a homeless person (or worse). Additional guidelines prohibited the woman from remarrying her first husband if she had married another. This cautioned the first husband against a hasty divorce or may have prevented some shady activity that involved the movement of women for immoral purposes under the guise of divorces. Rather than criticizing the text because it does not provide women with the equal opportunity to divorce their husbands, we ought to acknowledge the breakthrough that was provided to protect women in this legislation.

Widows also receive increased attention in Deuteronomy. A general imperative in the Book of the Covenant to protect the rights of widows in general (Exod 22:21–24) is expanded to explicitly protect a widow from injustice in court and to prevent her garment from being taken in pledge for a loan (Deut 24:17–18). There was a tradition in the ancient Near East to provide special protection for widows.[3] But special effort is provided by Israelite legal corpora to articulate rhetoric for the well-being of widows as well as other marginal peoples.[4]

An interesting law designed to protect widows is the Levirite Law. If a man dies and leaves his widow without a son, the brother or the appropriate next of kin becomes responsible for impregnating the widow until she gives birth to a son who will bear the deceased husband's name. We read in Deut 25:5–10,

> 5When brothers reside together, and one of them dies and has no son, the wife of the deceased shall not be married outside the family to a stranger. Her husband's brother shall go in to her, taking her in marriage, and performing the duty of a husband's brother to her, 6and the firstborn whom she bears shall succeed to the name of the deceased brother, so that his name may not be blotted out of Israel. 7But if the man has no desire to marry his brother's widow, then his brother's widow shall go up to the elders at the gate and say, "My husband's brother refuses to perpetuate his brother's name in Israel; he will not perform the duty of a brother's husband to me." 8Then the elders of his town shall summon him and speak to him. If he persists, saying, 'I have no desire to marry her,' 9then his brother's wife shall go up to him in the presence of the elders, pull his sandal off his foot, spit in his face, and declare, "This is what is done to the man who does not build up his brother's house." 10Throughout Israel his family shall be known as "the house of him whose sandal was pulled off."

This custom ensures the widow, and the community in general, of a son who will carry on the father's name, and more importantly for the woman, a son who can inherit the family property legally so that the woman is not displaced. He also can care for his mother when she gets old. The custom not only provides for widows, but it also keeps specific families alive as

3. Fensham, "Widow, Orphan and the Poor."
4. Gowan, "Wealth and Poverty in the Old Testament."

integral parts of greater clans and tribes, and it ensures that individual families will continue to hold their land in the highlands. This, in turn, provides for a strong middle-class society of peasant farmers. The book of Ruth adds insight about the process whereby apparently there was a sequence of kinsmen responsible for the woman if the first individual, the brother or whomever, could not or would not assume the responsibility. However, we do not know whether the book of Ruth reflects customs of the postexilic age or has romantically told the tale and represented the law poorly.

According to Deuteronomic legislation, foreign women who are taken as prisoners in war are now given protection. Such women must become full wives of their captors and not be treated as slaves or sold. But before marriage the women must have their heads shaved, and leading into the marriage, their captors must refrain from sex with them for a full year. This is to protect the women from the immediate sexual gratification of the men. Then after a year the men may take them as wives or give them their freedom. We read in Deut 21:10–14,

> [10]When you go out to war against our enemies, and the LORD your God hands them over to you and you take them captive, [11]suppose you see among the captives a beautiful woman whom you desire and want to marry, [12]and so you bring her home to your house; she shall shave her head, pare her nails, [13]discard her captive's garb, and shall remain in your house a full month, mourning for her father and mother; after that you may go in to her and be her husband, and she shall be your wife. [14]But if you are not satisfied with her, you shall let her go free and not sell her for money. You must not treat her as a slave, since you have dishonored her.

Of this law Eckart Otto said, "Compared with the average and usual treatment of captive women in antiquity this provision in Deut 21:10–14 was a moral revolution on the long road towards equal dignity and rights of men and women."[5]

Gleaning rights for poor people is legislation designed to help the truly marginal folk in society, but since special attention is paid to widows, we should consider these guidelines to be special provisions for women's rights. In Deut 24:19–21 we read,

> [19]When you reap your harvest in your field and forget a sheaf in the field, you shall not go back to get it; it shall be left for the alien, the orphan, and the widow, so that the LORD your God may bless

5. Otto, "False Weights in the Scales of Biblical Justice," 145.

you in all your undertakings. ²⁰When you beat your olive trees, do not strip what is left; it shall be for the alien, the orphan, and the widow. ²¹When you gather the grapes of your vineyard, do not glean what is left; it shall be for the alien, the orphan, and the widow.

Realistically, one would suggest that the larger number of folks in the fields gleaning the remnants of the grain or produce would be the widows, so that this particular guideline falls into the category of legal rights for women.

Worthy of mention is the revision of the Decalogue proposed by Deuteronomy. In Deut 5:21 the Deuteronomic legislators changed the coveting command so that coveting of the neighbor's wife is mentioned before coveting of the neighbor's house. In the earlier version of the Decalogue in Exod 20:17 the same command placed house before wife. The word for house (*bayit* or *beth-*) can mean "family," "dynasty," or "home." Thus, the word can refer to people or property, depending on the context. In the Exodus version of the Decalogue "house" most likely means the family, and hence it is logical to refer to coveting of the house before coveting of the wife, since the wife is part of the family. That sequence is probably the original form, and it comes from an early period in Israel's history when there was not a developed concept of tangible private property. By the time of the late seventh century BCE when the version in Deuteronomy 5 was generated, Israelites had developed a more advanced economic system, in which the possession of land and property was a significant aspect of society. The word "house" was understood more in terms of property. Placing the reference to woman after house would have implied that the wife was part of the husband's "property." The Deuteronomy version reflects the later values of the Deuteronomic movement, which has been influenced by the prophetic call for justice. Hence, Deuteronomy seeks to elevate the rights of women by changing the sequence of the commands to clearly indicate that women are not property and therefore should not be included under the "house" of the man. Thus, changing the Decalogue was also part of the Deuteronomic Reformer's agenda for affirming the rights of women.

Some biblical scholars, however, are disappointed with the biblical legislation, because it still partakes of the cultural assumptions of its era. Women still are unfortunately subordinate to men in a patriarchal society. For example, women could be cruelly executed for lack of virginity upon marriage (Deut 22:13–21). Married and betrothed women had to defend themselves from complicity in case of rape, or else they would be executed.

If raped in the open country, the woman did not have to prove she was raped, because no one could hear her screams. But if she were raped in the city, and no one heard her scream, then she would be put to death with the man for adultery (Deut 22:23–27). If a man raped an unmarried woman, then he merely had to pay a fine of fifty shekels of silver to the girl's father because he had damaged the father's property (Deut 22:28–29). Naomi Stern questions whether it is appropriate to speak of the Deuteronomic Law Code as a true reform code when such sexual inequities remained.[6] Her observations are appropriate and worthy of response.

To observations such as these we must respond with one of basic theses of this book. Modern Jews and Christians are part of a trajectory created by the biblical literature. We should not glorify the biblical people at those points where their culture and mores conformed to the values of their age. Nor should we take that kind of legislation literally and use it for our modern ethics, as some Christian literalists have done in the past. Rather, we must observe in what directions the biblical authors were attempting to move with their reform legislation. We do not live in a fixed and static universe, nor should our religious values be unchanged and unchanging. We move through evolutionary trajectories in all that we do, and we are heirs of the biblical trajectories. As the biblical scribes generated legislation to improve the rights of poor and oppressed people, especially women, we must continue the same direction, for only then are we truly faithful to the biblical imperatives.

The biblical text comes from a patriarchal age over two thousand years ago, and we should not deny that. Nor should we expect the biblical authors to have been able to reform their society so that it conforms to our modern moral expectations. We must understand how they sought to correct the abuses of their age, and from them take our inspiration. We dare not ossify ourselves in the morality of their social-cultural mode of existence. That would not only be impossible; it would be utterly absurd. We must move forward, enlightened and inspired by the spirit of biblical laws and the imperative to reform human behavior. We are not to imitate the cultural background of the biblical narratives by a flat and literal reading of the text. We must be true to their spirit, not their age.

6. Steinberg, "Deuteronomic Law Code and the Politics of State," 168.

Misuse of Biblical Texts concerning Women

When we discuss the status and rights of women in the Old Testament, we must pay attention also to significant narratives, which too often have been poorly interpreted on the popular level. We may discern this most vividly in the primeval narratives found in the early chapters of Genesis.

In Gen 1:27–28 when God creates the man and the woman, the text clearly states that both the male and the female are created in the image of God, and both are given the commission to "subdue" and have "dominion" over the earth. These are powerful words; Mesopotamians used comparable cognate words to refer to the role of kings. Our biblical text is implying that both the man and the woman are kings and queens in God's world. It is an imperative to rule the world and the animal kingdom responsibly.[7] It is not a command given simply to the man, as some people seem to believe. The text reads,

> 27So God created humankind in his image, in the image of God he created them; male and female he created them. 28God blessed them, and God said to them, "Be fruitful and multiply, and fill the earth and subdue it; and have dominion over the fish of the sea and over the birds of the air and over every living thing that moves upon the earth."

We should note that in v. 27 the word for "humankind" in the Hebrew is 'adam, a word usually translated as "man" and understood by readers to mean "male." But the Hebrew word means (generically) "human," and both male and female are included in the category known as "human." Thus, the New Revised Standard Version uses the term "humankind" to stress for the reader that the blessing and the commission to "rule" are given to men and women, not just men, as so many people think.[8] The implication, of course, is that men and women share equally in the "image of God" and in the imperatives to both reproduce (obviously!) and rule the world. This is an incredibly egalitarian statement to come from the sixth century CE. Yet some Christians deny that the command to responsibly rule the world applies to women.

---

7. Gnuse, *Misunderstood Stories*, 34–40.

8. Otwell, *And Sarah Laughed*, 15–19; Trible, *God and the Rhetoric of Sexuality*, 12–23; Swidler, *Biblical Affirmations of Woman*, 75–77; Westermann, *Genesis 1–11*, 151–61.

From Genesis 2 Christians so often declare that since the "male" was created first and the "female" taken from his rib later, men are superior to women. But the Hebrew text implies something else. The "man" is called 'adam until the woman is created. The word 'adam, again, is a generic reference to "human" as neither male nor female. After the "woman" is taken from his rib, only from that point onward is the original being called "male" (Hebrew: 'ish) in Gen 2:23; 2:24; 3:6. Hence, male and female identities arise simultaneously from the 'adam or the "human" when the woman is created. This accords with Gen 1:27 where the human is created as male and female. Males are not created before females and therefore superior; they are created together.[9] Besides, if priority of creation implies superiority, then all the animals would be superior to the "man" according to the creation sequence in Genesis 1. Some say that woman ('ishshah) is subordinate to the male because she was taken out of the male ('ish), but the "man" ('adam) was taken from the "earth" ('adamah), and no one says that the "man" is subordinate to the "earth."[10]

In Gen 2:18 the woman is said to be a "helper" (the King James Version has "helpmeet") who is suitable for the man. Sometimes readers of the Bible popularly view this as an expression that implies the woman was created to serve the man as his subordinate. However, the Hebrew term, 'ezer, used for "helper" in this passage, elsewhere is used to describe God's actions for people. God is an 'ezer or "helper" for people when they are helpless (Exod 18:4; Deut 33:7, 26, 29; Pss 33:20; 70:5; 115:9–11; 121:2; 124:8; 146:5–6). One would certainly not assume that God acts as the servant or the subordinate to people. Rather, 'ezer is a powerful word used to describe the ability of the newly created woman. She is a powerful helper for the man, certainly an equal partner, and an articulate spokesperson, as the next chapter indicates.[11]

From Genesis 3, Christians so often declare again that woman is inferior to man because the woman is tempted first and then tempts the man in return. Once more the biblical text says something else. Gen 3:6 states that the woman took the fruit and ate, and "she also gave some to her husband, who was with her, and he ate." Notice that the male was with her through

---

9. Trible, *God and the Rhetoric of Sexuality*, 94–105; Swidler, *Biblical Affirmations of Woman*, 76–78; Gnuse, *Misunderstood Stories*, 56, 83–84.

10. Trible, *God and the Rhetoric of Sexuality*, 100–101; Swidler, *Biblical Affirmations of Woman*, 78.

11. Swidler, *Biblical Affirmations of Woman*, 78; Gnuse, *Misunderstood Stories*, 83–84.

this process of dialogue with the snake. He stood by her silently during her discussion with the snake, and he did not disagree, which implies his agreement with her. The male and the woman were tempted simultaneously. The male did not come from work or play somewhere else in the garden (or from the garage) and get surprised by an apple treat from his wife, as we so often portray it. He was a simultaneous participant. When the text says that "the eyes of both were opened" (v.7), it indicates that this is a simultaneous awareness that comes upon them, which means that they must have eaten the fruit at the same time. She took the fruit, gave some to him, and they chomped into the fruit together—rather greedy little children, weren't they?

In east Mediterranean society, where the biblical account arose, when a woman speaks before others in the presence of her husband, it is with the consent and agreement of her husband. In Genesis 3, the man is an approving participant. The fact that the woman speaks is actually a compliment to her, for it implies that she is intelligent and truly a "helper" fit for her husband, because that is what God created her to be.[12] The story actually compliments the woman and all intelligent women—a point we sorely miss in our Sunday school narrations. Instead we try to blame the woman inordinately. A comparable attribution of articulate skill and intelligence will not be found in other ancient Near Eastern literature.

In order to blame the woman more than the man, or give her priority for the sin, some translations omit the expression "he was with her," thus implying that she did this of her own initiative. Translations guilty of omitting this important expression (either deliberately or unconsciously) include the Rheims-Douay Version (1582/1609), the Revised Standard Version (1952) (fortunately the New Revised Standard Version [1993] includes "who was with her"), the New English Bible (1970), the Living Bible (1971), the Good News Bible (1976), and the Revised English Bible (1989). The New World Translation (1984) is very deceptive in saying, "when he was with her," which directly implies that he came along later. The most honest translation is the Contemporary English Version (1995), which says, "Her husband was there with her." It appears that the monotheistic revolution (and its concern with greater equality for women) has not yet made its influence felt upon all the Bible translators in the field.[13]

---

12. Gnuse, *Misunderstood Stories*, 109–11.

13. Ibid., 111.

A New Testament passage affixes blame upon the woman, and this passage often is used to interpret Genesis 3. The author of 1 Tim 2:13–15 says,

> 13For Adam was formed first, then Eve; 14and Adam was not deceived, but the woman was deceived and became a transgressor. 15Yet she will be saved through childbearing.

This passage states that the male was formed before the female, and that the woman and not the man was deceived. We must painfully admit that this New Testament passage misinterprets Genesis 3. As we have seen, the word Hebrew word for "male" is not even used in Genesis 2 until the word for "female" appears. 'Adam does not mean "male." Furthermore, 1 Tim 2:14 literally says that the male was not deceived but the woman was. A simple reading of Genesis 3 will not permit anyone to say that the man was not deceived, for he admits it before God in Gen 3:12, if only to say that the woman deceived him. The author of 1 Tim 2:13–15 has played freely with the text in Genesis.

We must acknowledge that the author of 1 Timothy has a reason for attempting to subordinate women in this text. The later authors of the New Testament, after Paul's death, attempted to slightly subordinate women in order to make Christianity more compatible with Graeco-Roman family values to thus enable Christianity to spread throughout the empire. We must view this as a temporary concession made by the writers of those letters in the late first century CE, but their advice is not meant to be used by Christians forever. Ultimately, when Christianity became the successful religion of the empire, it would have been capable of returning to the more normative rhetoric of Paul in Gal 3:28 wherein he says that the differences between slave and free, male and female, Greek and Judean were abolished in the Christian movement. That is the normative message of Christianity. Galatians 3:28 is the major voice; 1 Tim 2:13–15 is minor voice in the biblical testimony. Christian theologians have often said that "Scripture interprets Scripture," and sometimes Scripture corrects Scripture. Galatians contains the enduring message that is far more congruent with the gospel message of divine love for humanity, while 1 Timothy contains the temporary message for its age. We must wisely see that in the greater message of the Bible, the passage in Galatians is the normative statement for Christian life. The author of 1 Tim 2:13–15 clearly misreads the text in Genesis 2–3 for his own situational needs, but that situation is past. We must have the courage and good sense to make the appropriate interpretation. Unfortunately, too many have allowed 1 Tim 2:13–15 to interpret Genesis 2–3 rather than to let Gal 5:28 interpret 1 Tim 2:13–15.

Thus, some of the truly crucial biblical accounts used to define the status of women must be looked at more closely. These accounts really speak more of the equality and dignity of women, though we have not often interpreted them that way in the past on a popular level. Again, we must remember that these Priestly (Genesis 1) and Yahwist (Genesis 2–3) texts come from the middle of the first millennium BCE. In their age, the attribution of such implied equality to the woman was revolutionary, especially her speaking for the man in Genesis 3, an image not found in other comparable ancient Near Eastern narratives.

Though these narratives do not speak forth directly to laud the rights of women in the ways that we might desire, nonetheless, their respectful treatment of the identity of the primordial woman is truly significant. It betokens the values of an emerging monotheistic belief system in which people are equal before God. These narratives are viewed by critical scholars as taking their final written form in the Babylonian exile, at the time when monotheism was becoming the faith of the Judahite people as a whole.

7

The Dignity of Women in the Jesus Movement

Women in the Gospels

JESUS PROCLAIMED THE RADICAL coming of the kingdom of God, and when that kingdom arrived, people would relate to each other in a new relationship of love. In this new age the poor and the oppressed would be lifted up, and those who were outsiders by virtue of impurity would be included in the kingdom. The poor included sinners, tax collectors, and publicans, according to the rhetoric of Jesus, but from his teachings and his actions we see him enfranchising women, children, sick people rendered impure by their illness, and marginal persons in general. Though Jesus apparently gave greater status to women than his popular culture did, we should not expect him to conform completely to modern expectations, since he functioned in the first-century-CE Palestinian and east Mediterranean context. Nevertheless, what he said and did on behalf of women is impressive for his age.[1] Furthermore, we may underestimate the extent of his proclamation for women, because much of what he said was spoken in behalf of the poor, and women in his age were one of the most significant components of that population that Jesus referred to as "the poor." Speaking out on behalf of the poor meant speaking out for women and their emancipation from the oppressive patriarchal structures of his age. Jesus subverted the authority of the ruling powers and oppressive principles of domination in society by envisioning a lifestyle and a world wherein the principle of relationship

1. Schüssler Fiorenza, *In Memory of Her*, 106–59.

was love and not power. Commentators have pointed out that Jesus (and Paul also) undermined the authority of patriarchal figures and patriarchal assumptions with their strong language of equality before God.[2] People who had the most to gain in such a new age were women. Thus, much of the Jesus tradition speaks directly to the concerns of women in his age. It has been noted that nothing directly negative about women is found in the Gospels, which sets that literature apart from the rest of the literature in the Graeco-Roman world.[3]

In the teachings of Jesus some significant sayings and narrative memories are recorded which recall that Jesus sought to raise the status of women in his ministry in preparation for the coming of the kingdom of God wherein people would be equal before God regardless of race, sex, or status. Most dramatic is Jesus's defense of the woman taken in adultery, a crime that offends and indicts self-righteous men of any age (John 8:1–11). The story does not mention the man with whom she had sexual relations, perhaps indirectly indicting the double standard of any age by showing that the accusing crowd sought to punish the woman but paid no attention to the man. The very fact that they brought the woman to Jesus indicates that they were testing him because they knew him to be a champion of women's rights.[4] Ultimately Jesus spoke to the woman, thus giving her dignity by verbal recognition of her presence, and he directed her to a higher moral standard.

The Gospels testify to wondrous signs accomplished by Jesus, especially healing people. Narratives of healing include those wherein he paid special attention to women. Peter's mother-in-law was healed of a fever (Matt 8:14–15; Mark 1:30–31; Luke 4:38–39). Ancient texts usually do not mention the female family members of teachers and leaders in the religious community, but here Peter's mother-in-law is mentioned. Since she lived in her son's house, she mostly likely was a widow. At Nain Jesus healed a widow's only son, who, of course, was the only person responsible for caring for his mother (Luke 7:11–17), so this story also reflects concern for the poor and marginal people such as widows. A longer narrative recounts how Jesus raised a synagogue leader's daughter from the dead or a deep coma (Matt 9:18–26; Mark 5:21–43; Luke 8:40–56). This is the only story that speaks of Jesus directly touching a corpse, by which he would

2. Ibid., 140–42; Bartchy, "Who Should Be Called Father?"

3. Swidler, *Biblical Affirmations of Woman*, 255.

4. Ibid., 186.

have incurred a great degree of impurity. But Jesus affirmed a dead girl in this regard. Jesus healed a woman with a flow of blood, whose menstrual problems rendered her perpetually unclean (Matt 9:20–22; Mark 5:24–34; Luke 8:42–49). For the gospel tradition to recall the healing of something connected to women's health shows special concern for women in general. By touching the teacher in her unclean condition the woman committed an extreme purity violation. But rather than criticize her for her inappropriate behavior in matters of purity, Jesus praised her. We really fail to appreciate how dramatic this is because we do not share with the original audience deep concern with matters of purity. In another story Jesus healed a crippled woman, probably a victim of severe arthritis (Luke 13:10–13).

In these and other narratives Jesus praised the faith and the moral actions of women, including the widow who gave money from her meager funds (Mark 12:41–44; Luke 21:1–4), and the courageous widow who persisted in addressing a corrupt judge (Luke 18:1–8). In the parable of the bridesmaids he praised the wisdom of the five intelligent ladies who brought sufficient oil for their lamps (Matt 25:1–13). To praise women for their religious virtues stands out in a Graeco-Roman culture that generally disregarded women for any positive standards they might set for people, other than the virtue of absolute obedience to their fathers and husbands. Obviously Jesus set women up as a standard in discourse that was directed to a primarily male audience.

Women were apparently able to approach Jesus and make requests, even poor women. The mother of the sons of Zebedee asked that her sons be made "prime ministers" of Jesus in the coming kingdom, which was a rather courageous move on her part (Matt 20:20–28; Mark 10:35–45). Even the woman who touched Jesus in sneaky fashion received healing (Mark 5:25–34). When she came to him in fear and trembling and apologized for touching him, he praised her by saying, "Daughter, your faith has made your well; go in peace, and be healed of your disease" (v. 34). That she should be praised after doing something rather inappropriate, an impure woman touching a man, is a significant affirmation of women and an equally significant affirmation of their accessibility to Jesus.

One narrative worthy of mention recalls how Jesus particularly praised a Canaanite woman for her faith after their dialogue over the healing of her daughter (Matt 15:21–28, especially v. 28). Not only is the Canaanite or Phoenician woman a female in a male-oriented society, she is a foreigner, a hated member from the Phoenician cities of Tyre and Sidon. When she had the temerity to approach Jesus to request a healing, not only did the disciples of Jesus say, "Send her away, for she keeps shouting after us" (v. 23), Jesus then insulted her three times. First, the text says, "He did not answer her at all" (v. 23). Second, he responded, "I was sent only to the lost sheep of the house of Israel" (v. 24). Third, he crassly said, "It is not fair to take the children's food and throw it to the dogs" (v. 26). This was an egregious statement by Jesus since the word "dog" was also slang for a prostitute. But the woman persisted in her pleas and even responded in somewhat witty fashion, so that finally Jesus declared her faith to be great, and her daughter was healed. In the ancient world women did not approach a male teacher and his male disciples, nor did a teacher address a female. But this woman penetrated the male crowd, threw herself at the feet of Jesus, and made her petition. She also responded cleverly to the statement by Jesus about the "dogs," when she said, "Yes, Lord, yet even the dogs eat the crumbs that fall from their masters' tables" (v. 27). At first glance this appears to be an abjectly humble statement, but it is really a clever retort to what the teacher has just said. She has taken his words and turned them around to justify her continued request for healing. The gospel story portrays her as a clever trickster who has the last word and finally obtains healing for her daughter. The fact that this story was recalled in the oral tradition and ultimately written down in the Gospel of Matthew is, not only testimony to Jesus's attitudes toward women, but also testimony to how the ancient church respectfully regarded her determination and cleverness. Matthew sets her memory forth as an example of faith, persistence, and quick wit. We will not find comparable stories used as moral paradigms elsewhere in the world of Jesus.

Other special stories are those that deal with the anointing of Jesus. The woman at Bethany who anointed him by pouring oil on his head was praised for her actions despite the complaints of the men around Jesus (Matt 26:6–16; Mark 14:3–9). In Luke 7:36–50 and John 12:1–8 the woman anointed Jesus's feet and dried them with her hair. For a woman to touch a man, especially a revered teacher, and to uncover her hair before him was a rather bold and impudent act. But Jesus affirmed her actions.

This anointing was particularly an important image. In the Old Testament, prophets anointed kings to send them forth on their calling as rulers and warriors for the people of God; hence the word for "king," *messiah*, means anointed one. Samuel thus anointed Saul (1 Sam 10:1–8) and David (1 Sam 16:1–13), Elisha sent a prophet to anoint Jehu and send him forth to destroy two kings and become king of Israel (2 Kgs 9:1–13), and Jehoiada anointed Jehoash in a revolution against Athaliah of Judah (2 Kgs 11:4–20). In Mark 14:3–9 and Matt 26:6–16 metaphorically the woman functions as a prophet to anoint and thus send Jesus as the king or the "messiah" forth on his mission to die. Furthermore, the image of a prophetic personage coming into a room quickly and anointing a person to the surprise of the bystanders is the motif that unites the Elisha account and the New Testament accounts: The prophet sent by Elisha barges into the meeting of Jehu and his generals to pull him aside and anoint him king of Israel, just as the woman comes quickly into the room where Jesus is sitting with his disciples. If this connection is deliberate, then the woman in the Markan and Matthean accounts is being portrayed for us in dramatic and almost revolutionary fashion with this strong comparison with the Elisha traditions. But commentators too often fail to make the connection between the gospel stories and the account in 2 Kgs 9:1–13. Jesus, however, has the final word on the woman's actions of anointing, for he declared that what she did for him will be recalled forever.

Women as Disciples

When Jesus taught, both men and women were addressed (Matt 14:21; 15:38). Other teachers in the ancient world would address only men among their followers. Jesus had women disciples whom he taught. This most clearly is demonstrated by the account of Mary and Martha (Luke 10:38–41), wherein Jesus taught Mary and Martha in their home. Mary "sat at Jesus's feet," a rabbinic expression that describes a student learning under a rabbi. It is said that she "listened to his teaching," another clear description of a student. Teaching women in a Palestinian Judean setting was a rather radical action by Jesus. For a teacher to specifically teach two women in their home was an even more dramatic image, and the fact that the later church recalled this account in the Gospels speaks of the value the later church placed upon women disciples.

In John 4:1–42 Jesus has a long dialogue with a woman of Samaria at the well, a place where women should be silent, draw water, and not speak to strangers. This woman was an "outsider" for two reasons: she not only was female, but she was a Samaritan, a group of folk whom Judeans avoided with passion. Furthermore, after talking with him, she went into the city to tell other people about Jesus, and they listened to her. Symbolically the

Gospel of John portrays her as the first apostle, for she is a person going forth to proclaim the message about Jesus, and she is both foreign and female.

Women apparently were included among Jesus's disciples, for they undertook the journeys on foot with the men (Matt 27:55; Luke 23:49–55). We assume that although women were not among the twelve disciples, they were probably to be included among the seventy-two disciples who were sent out on mission (Luke 10:1–12). Jesus's respect for women led the disciples even to speak of the "women of our company" (Luke 24:22). Some are directly recalled by name for later generations in Luke 8:1–3: Mary Magdalene, Joanna, Chuza, and Susanna. Since Luke mentions them specifically, we are tempted to assume that they became well-known and important in later years, perhaps because of their work for the Christian mission.

It is naively said that women were not present at the Last Supper with Jesus and his disciples, but Judean women were present for this important meal celebrating the Passover. The women would light the candles at the beginning of the Passover meal, and, of course, they prepared the food.[5]

The Gospel writers recall that Mary Magdalene, Mary the mother of James and Joses, and Salome followed and served Jesus, and they were direct witnesses of the crucifixion (Matt 27:55–56; Mark 15:40–41; Luke 23:49; John 19:25). They remained close enough to the scene to witness the burial (Matt 27:26; Mark15:40–41; Luke 23:55). In the postresurrection period the disciples engaged in prayer with women, and this is expressly mentioned in Acts 1:14; 5:14. Jesus's movement seems to have been broadly egalitarian, enfranchising many of the poor and marginal people of Galilee and Judea, and women obviously shared in this elevation of status.

It seems to be particularly important that women were recalled as the first witnesses of both the empty tomb (Matt 28:1–8; Mark 16:1–8; Luke 24:1–10; John 20:1) and the resurrected Jesus (Matt 28:9–10; Mark 16:19; John 20:11–18). In a sense, we can say that the women were the first people to proclaim the gospel as they went forth to testify about Jesus's resurrection (Matt 28:8; Mark 16:7, 11; Luke 24:9–11; John 20:18). What is most impressive is that the later biblical traditions recalled that these women indeed were the first witnesses. In that ancient age the testimony of women

---

5. I have heard it publicly said on television that women should not be clergy because they were not present at the Last Supper. Scratch that argument! I have also heard it said that only men can be clergy because the disciples of Jesus were all men. I guess that means that all priests and clergy today must be Judean fishermen also! Why doesn't anyone challenge these statements immediately when they are uttered?

was not recognized as being significant, certainly not in trial situations. To affirm them as the first to testify to the resurrection of Jesus was an incredible thing for the ancient church to recall and for the Gospel writers to record.[6] It indeed reflects that the church valued women far more than contemporary society did. This bears repeating: women were the first to proclaim that Jesus had risen from the dead!

The most dramatic postresurrection appearance of Jesus was the appearance to Mary Magdalene in John 20:11–18, which is a fairly developed account in the biblical text. The later additions to the Gospel of Mark recall that appearance to Mary in shorter form (16:9–11). The early Christians could have forgotten the testimony of the women and very easily remembered only the experiences of the men. In particular, they could have easily wished to forget the memory of the appearance to Mary Magdalene. But the women's experiences were recalled because their presence in the early Christian movement was extremely significant, and their primal testimonies to the risen Jesus are symbolic evidence of their later importance in the church.

Jesus and Divorce

Of importance are the sayings of Jesus on divorce found in Matt 5:31–32; 19:1–12, Mark 10:2–12, and Luke 16:18. Mark adds the reference to women not divorcing their husbands in v. 12 for the sake of the Roman audience: whereas Roman wives could divorce their husbands, Judean wives could not. (Some scholars do observe that women in other parts of the Roman Empire could initiate divorce, and so they locate the composition of Mark outside Rome). With that in mind, we sense that the imperative of Jesus to his original Judean audience forbade men to divorce their wives. What is significant about this is that the men are said to commit adultery against their wives if they remarry (Mark 10:11; Matt 19:9; Luke 16:18; but Matt 5:32 says that the husband forces the woman to commit adultery). This is not logical, for adultery should be possible only before the divorce, and it involves sex with another woman who is also married. One cannot speak of the divorce process as being an act of adultery. Jesus is not giving a guideline about divorce; he is uttering a strong statement in exaggerated rhetoric to address another issue. Jesus is uttering a hyperbolic statement, an impossible saying, to condemn how men so easily could divorce their wives.

6. Swidler, *Biblical Affirmations of Woman*, 204–5.

What Jesus is saying is that men should not divorce their wives in the first place, and he uses radical rhetoric to get this point across to the audience.

In Judean society a man could divorce a woman very easily, despite the fact that the practice of divorcing wives was condemned already by the prophets (Mal 2:14–16). Men perhaps divorced their wives for younger women, and this custom may have been prevalent in Jesus's day. Jesus is speaking less about the issue of divorce and more about the issue of women's rights when he condemns divorce as a form of adultery. Essentially he condemns the men who throw their wives out of their homes to become homeless women in the streets of ancient Palestine. Perhaps a goodly number of the women in the Jesus movement had been older ladies discarded by their husbands. Their fate would have been quite grim except that they were taken in by the followers of Jesus and given new hope. One might sense that the women who went to tomb on that first Easter morning might have included some women who had been discarded by their husbands and saved from a wretched fate by the Jesus movement. Their attempt to attend to the body of Jesus was to be their final act of devotion to a man who had done so much for them.

We have too often looked to these divorce sayings of Jesus for ecclesiastical guidance on the issue of divorce in the modern church, and we have overlooked their powerful statements to defend women in an age when they had very few rights. In so doing, we have diluted the powerful message of equality that may have permeated the Jesus community. By radically attacking the prerogatives of men on the issue of divorce Jesus demonstrated that truly he was a champion of women.[7]

Feminist scholars have pointed out correctly that what Jesus attacked indirectly in the divorce sayings and elsewhere was the assumption of patriarchal rule by men over women in marriage relationships. In the coming kingdom of God those who once were in a position of authority (fathers, husbands, slave owners, rulers) will no longer function with the principle of oppressive domination, but they will relate to those "others" with a deep love and a sense of equality, even if the outward appearance of the relationship continues. In the kingdom no one will want to be great and lord it over others (Matt 23:8–11).[8]

In the Jesus tradition we can point to many items that indicate that Jesus sponsored an egalitarian movement that provided more rights for

7. Ibid., 176.

8. Schüssler Fiorenza, *In Memory of Her*, 143–51.

women than contemporary society had offered them. In this regard Jesus continued the trajectory of social reform inspired by emergent monotheism: he more fully developed egalitarian thought and formed a community in which such equality was to be actualized. Other authors also have seen the teachings of Jesus functioning in this same revolutionary fashion, and we need to continue to actualize this powerful message of Jesus today in the ongoing development of the monotheistic revolution.[9]

9. Theissen, *Biblical Faith*, 83–128.

8

The Dignity of Women
in Paul and the Ancient Church

Paul and Women

PAUL IS OFTEN CONSIDERED misogynistic with many of his supposed observations about women, but too many readers of the biblical text miss his real message. As is so often the case with the biblical tradition, we must focus on the central passages that are thematically foundational before we turn our attention to the more specific texts that arise from particular situations. This is a cardinal rule when doing the theology of Paul. He so often wrote letters with specific advice to individual congregations, and sometimes that advice was meant exclusively for them and not for all the Christians in his mission churches. We must first attend to his programmatic statements before observing his particular bits of advice to specific audiences.

Most significant of all his statements concerning women is the programmatic passage in Gal 3:28, which we quoted previously in regard to slaves,

> There is no longer Jew or Greek, there is no longer slave or free, there is no longer male and female; for all of you are one in Christ Jesus.

When Paul says that all are one in Christ Jesus, he is speaking of the life of believers in the church, and not of how things will be in the afterlife, as some pious Christians have maintained. This is a programmatic statement to describe the new relationships in the Christian community, and they stand in tension with the values of the Graeco-Roman world, with its strong sense of hierarchy and servitude. To say such a thing as Paul did in the Graeco-Roman world was to utter the unthinkable in the minds of many. [1] To declare in public that slaves and free people were equal could bring the death penalty, and to declare the equality of men and women would be to offend most Graeco-Roman men in the extreme. Galatians 3:28 is a powerful statement of human equality, and it reflects the ideological trajectory flowing out of the Old Testament.

Although the earliest Christians were weak and few in number, the days would come when their values would begin to influence society as a whole. Unfortunately, it took Christians too long to realize that these core values and not other teachings were the ones meant to epitomize Christian belief and to have impact on the world! Instead of looking to passages that proclaimed human equality, too often Christians looked to those passages that simply acknowledged the existence of classes and patriarchalism in that age.

Paul's churches in the Hellenistic world were remarkable in that both men and women could worship together. Many state cults and mystery cults separated the men and the women; Paul was revolutionary in bringing the sexes together. Nor did he apparently make the women sit in the back, for women were speaking up in his Corinthian congregation (perhaps a little too much!). We overlook the revolutionary nature of his message when we immediately move to a discussion of how Paul might have subordinated women. In Paul's age it was an egalitarian move to bring the sexes together in a worship setting. It was a hallmark of the ancient church that women, slaves, and children were given a status in the worshiping community that they could not receive in society. Perhaps some of the persecution Christians experienced resulted from the perception that they were overturning the social order by providing this new equality to lesser members of a patriarchal society.

Active Women in Paul's Churches

Paul has been accused of suppressing women as spokespersons or leaders of the faith. This is patently false. In the first generation a number of women

1. Cahill, *Desire of the Everlasting Hills*, 141–42, 147–48, also states boldly that "the primitive Church was the world's first egalitarian society," 148.

were responsible for the missionary spread of Christianity, and they were highly respected by Paul and mentioned by him in his letters.[2] Some of them functioned with male counterparts and others operated alone in their mission work. In 1 Cor 16:16 and 1 Thess 5:12–13 Paul encourages believers to put themselves "at the service of" and to "respect" those who work for the spread of Christianity, and these include female missionaries also.[3]

Special mention is made of several women by Paul. In Rom 16:1 Paul recommends Phoebe of Cenchreae as a deacon to the church, and hers is not a secondary role to male religious leadership. The Greek does not say "deaconess," as though hers were a special office only for women, but it says "deacon," a word used of both men and women. Paul describes himself as a deacon in 1 Cor 3:5 and 2 Cor 3:6, and elsewhere it is a term that refers to the function of preaching and teaching. Thus, Phoebe performs the same clergy function as does Paul. She is performing a ministry that would evolve into an office, the role of later clergy.[4]

A husband-and-wife team, Priscilla (or Prisca) and Aquila, are considered co-workers and preachers, and the two of them are described as having equal status (Acts 18:1–3, 18–19, 24–26; Rom 16:3–5; 1 Cor 16:19; 2 Tim 4:19). Paul mentions her name first, perhaps implying that she is the senior partner.[5]

Andronicus and Junia (Rom 16:7) were in prison with Paul, which implies that they were leaders or preachers, perhaps a team like Prisca and Aquila. Paul says they were prominent among the apostles and Christian before he was, so perhaps they came from the circle of Jerusalem missionaries. The woman Junia in Rom 16:7 is a co-worker among apostles, but later textual versions attempted to change her name to Junius, so that we almost lost the memory of a female clergyperson. The so-called masculine name, Junius, is not attested as a real name in classical sources, so the real

2. Schüssler Fiorenza, *In Memory of Her*, 160–79, provides the best critical discussion of these women; Bristow, *What Paul Really Said about Women*, 54–66; Gerberding, "Women Who Toil in Ministry," 285–91; Hays, *Moral Vision of the New Testament*, 53.

3. Schüssler Fiorenza, *In Memory of Her*, 160–70; Gerberding, "Women Who Toil in Ministry," 288.

4. Gryson, *Ministry of Women in the Early Church*, 3–4, who also points out that the church father Origen of Alexandria in the third century CE recognized her function as such (30); Schüssler Fiorenza, *In Memory of Her*, 170–72; Bristow, *What Paul Really Said about Women*, 56–57; Gerberding, "Women Who Toil in Ministry," 289–90.

5. Bristow, *What Paul Really Said about Women*, 56; Gerberding, "Women Who Toil in Ministry," 287, notes that even John Chrysostom, a fourth-century-CE church father, said this about Priscilla.

name of this person had to be Junia, the name of a woman.[6] The alteration of Junia's name is a tragic example of later Christians trying to suppress the memory of a significant woman leader.

Other women are also mentioned in passing by Paul. In Phil 4:2–3 Euodia and Syntyche are mentioned by Paul as co-workers who "struggled beside in the work of the Lord," which implies comparable ministerial status.[7] In Rom 16:6, 12, Mary, Tryphaena, Tryphosa, and Persis are described as have "worked hard in the Lord," and the term "work hard" is a term elsewhere used by Paul to describe the work of preachers and evangelists, including himself.[8] Lydia of Thyatira (Acts 16:14–15, 40) has a church in her home, which implies, not only that she is a benefactor, but also that she may be the de-facto head of that congregation. Mary, the mother of John Mark and the cousin of Barnabas (Acts 12:12–17; Col 4:10), appears to have been in charge of a house of Hellenists in Jerusalem, and it is significant that the house is said to belong to her and not John Mark.[9] In Col 4:15 we read of Nympha of Laodicea who has a church in her house. Finally, the "elect lady" of 2 John may not simply be the church personified but may be a woman also, who has a church in her home.

The brief or even casual mention of various names connected with Paul in the book of Acts may indicate that these women became well-known leaders in the generation after Paul. Since many of the names are women's names (i.e., Damaris in Acts 17:34), one might suggest that these, too, were significant leaders known to the audience who heard or read the accounts in Acts. If so, we have but the tip of the iceberg in terms of our knowledge about significant female leadership in the first generation of missionary expansion. It is wrong of us to maintain that Paul subordinated women when he spoke so highly of women who functioned as clergy, or at least with a status comparable to his.[10] Considering how little literature we have from Paul and his contemporaries and how poor the status of most women was in the Graeco-Roman world, it is impressive that this number

---

6. Schüssler Fiorenza, *In Memory of Her*, 172; Bristow, *What Paul Really Said about Women*, 57; Gerberding, "Women Who Toil in Ministry," 288–89.

7. Sampley, *Pauline Partnership in Christ*, 63; Schüssler Fiorenza, *In Memory of Her*, 169–70; Bristow, *What Paul Really Said about Women*, 56.

8. Schüssler Fiorenza, *In Memory of Her*, 169; Gerberding, "Women Who Toil in Ministry," 285–87.

9. Schüssler Fiorenza, *In Memory of Her*, 166.

10. Ibid., 160–79; Bristow, *What Paul Really Said about Women*, 54–66.

of women rose to apparent positions of leadership in the first generation of Gentile mission endeavor.

Did Paul Silence Women?

Those who wish to deny to women equal status or a position of authority in the modern church often quote passages of Paul in 1 Corinthians which appear to subordinate women by telling them to be silent (1 Cor 11:1–16; 14:34–35). But these texts appear to be the specific advice of Paul to that congregation for problems that they were facing; this advice does not appear in his other letters as universal encouragement to all the churches. (Over the years several commentators have pointed out the distinct possibility that 1 Cor 14:34–35, the famous "let the woman keep silent" passage, is a later post-Pauline interpolation into the text.[11] If so, the passage, nonetheless, is still part of the canonical book of 1 Corinthians and thus needs to be addressed.)

The Corinthian church appears to have had discord in its religious services due in large part to women. Perhaps the women were speaking charismatically in tongues, a skill they may have learned in the pagan mystery cults that were only for women, in order to put down the men who did not have those skills. Perhaps Paul sensed that this skill was used by a few women to disrupt the services and humiliate the men, so he ordered silence.[12] Paul's telling the women to "prophesy" in church only when they wear a veil in order to indicate their subordination to men (1 Cor 11:2–7) takes away all the women's fun of humiliating the men who lack this charismatic skill, and it thus silences the women without Paul's having to question of the legitimacy and origin of the women's charismatic gift. In addition, the women in the Greek mystery cults and religions venerating oriental deities spoke ecstatically with their hair disheveled and without veils. The Isis cult from Egypt, in particular, had a large following in Corinth, and

---

11. Baird, *1 Corinthians, 2 Corinthians,* 59–60; Fee, *1 Corinthians, 2 Corinthians,* 699–703. Barrett, *Commentary on the First Epistle to the Corinthians,* 330–33, suggests that if these verses really came from Paul, he only might have been telling the women not to chatter during the church assembly, and he was not trying to silence them from speaking meaningfully during worship.

12. Barrett, *Commentary on the First Epistle to the Corinthians,* 333; Baird, *1 Corinthians, 2 Corinthians,* 60, suggest this as an explanation. Fee, *1 Corinthians, 2 Corinthians,* 703–4, discusses this in detail as a possible explanation.

such activities characterized this Asian religion.[13] Paul probably wished for his Christians to distinguish themselves from folks who engaged in those mystery practices in order for Christians to make a better image for Christianity in the Greek world.

The key text in which Paul admonishes women to keep silent (1 Cor 14:34–35) comes in the greater context of his discussion of speaking in tongues (1 Cor 12:1–31; 13:1–13; 14:1–40), and this is no coincidence. Though not all commentators agree that Paul is attempting to silence charismatic women, it would seem to me that the burden of proof lies with those who must somehow discount the literary context of this passage situated in the discussion about speaking in tongues. Perhaps there was a different problem that was the reason for this disruption; we cannot know for sure. But Paul's advice to the women to be silent is a piece of advice given to them in Paul's letter and not to other churches. We should not be using this as a binding moral encouragement in our churches today. We follow the spirit of the imperatives, which call for order and harmony in worship, not the literal message of the imperatives, which was designed only for the Corinthian congregation.

In general, Christians too often have characterized Paul's view of women by an appeal to these passages and by additionally taking these texts out of context. The fuller message of Paul concerning women reveals his strong affirmation of women's dignity, rights, and equality with men, which results from the accomplishments of Jesus. In 1 Cor 7:1–9 Paul speaks of how not only does a husband have rights over his wife's body, but the wife also has rights over her husband's body. That would be an unthinkable utterance among the conservative men of the Greek world for whom the wife was truly the slave of her husband. Thomas Cahill says it so well,

> Paul is actually the New Testament's ultimate democrat; and it is a pathetic irony that the first person in history to exclude consciously all social grades, isms, and biases from his thinking . . . should so often be made to stand at the bar accused of the opposite of what he believed so passionately.[14]

---

13. Schüssler Fiorenza, *In Memory of Her*, 226–36.

14. Cahill, *Desire of the Everlasting Hills*, 156.

Post-Pauline Writers and Submissive Women

Another significant passage worth discussing, because of its misuse by Christians, is Eph 5:21–24, which was probably composed by one of Paul's colleagues after Paul had been executed by Nero. The text reads,

> 21Be subject to one another out of reverence for Christ. 23Wives, be subject to your husbands as you are to the Lord. 23For the husband is the head of the wife just as Christ is the head of the church, the body of which he is the Savior. 24Just as the church is subject to Christ, so also wives ought to be, in everything, to their husbands.

This text is often used to justify male authority over women in modern Christian families. But use of the passage overlooks the historical circumstances of when the letter was written and the actual grammar of the passage. The Deutero-Pauline author is speaking of household and church relationships between Christians in Eph 5:21—6:9. He begins the section with an overarching statement in v. 21, which says, "Be subject to one another out of reverence for Christ." The next verse, v. 22, reads, "Wives, be subject to your husbands as you are to the Lord." People quote this passage very often. What is not mentioned, of course, is that there is no verb in v. 22, so that it reads literally, "Wives so also to your husbands, as to the Lord." The verb form is understood to carry over from the imperative about Christians submitting to each other. But if the verb form carries over from v. 21 to v. 22, so also does the understanding of the verb. Wives are to submit to their husbands in that same way that all Christians submit to one another. This is the submission of equality, not of subordination!

In the Greek world married women were said to be slaves of their husbands, and the appropriate verb form used in much of the literature, as well as in the courts, was *douleo*, "to be a slave." Our biblical author does not use this word but chooses instead the verb form *upotassomenai*, which means "to give allegiance," or "be supportive," and it is a verb form usually spoken of in regard to the freely willed choices made by free, adult Greek males. It is not truly a verb that implies subjection. The word occurs in the active and middle voices throughout the New Testament: in the Gospel of Luke, in Paul's writings, in Hebrews, in James, and in 1 Peter. The subordination suggested by this verb is more of a voluntary submission of a free person. It is a highly respectful way of encouraging women to work respectfully with their husbands. Thus the English translation, "submit," truly loses the nuance of the original Greek text.[15]

Most important and much clearer to readers of the text in Engilsh are the passages that follow v. 22,

> [25]Husbands, love your wives, just as Christ loved the church and gave himself up for her, . . . [28]In the same way, husbands should love their wives as they do their own bodies. He who loves his wife loves himself . . . [33]Each of you should love his wife as himself, and a wife should respect her husband.

These passages define concretely what the wife-husband relationship should be. Husbands are to love their wives in the same way that they love themselves. Even more, husbands are to be willing to die for their wives as Christ died for the church (v. 26), which was a concept that the "good old boys" in Greece could never have accepted.[16] For those of the Greek culture, to whom the author spoke, such nuanced statements would be disdained by those who traditionally viewed the status of women as subordinate. (For that age we might say the Paulinist author was really a feminist.) These passages in Ephesians really deconstruct the "patriarchal notions of marriage" found throughout the Mediterranean world of that age.[17] At any rate, we must see how the language was revolutionary and egalitarian for that time. We have to sense that the author was trying to elevate the status of women, and we should not be critical, if the author does not come up to our modern understandings of sexual equality.

The mere fact that the author of Ephesians is actually addressing women (and slaves) means that he gives them the dignity of being worthy of address in this publicly read letter. In the Graeco-Roman world one would never consider women (or slaves) worthy of such public address; the letter should speak only to men. To address them publicly in this letter is to give them the dignity and value as persons, which their culture denied them. Furthermore, the author calls upon women to freely respect or obey their husbands; he assumes that the women can make this choice. That is incredible. People in the Graeco-Roman world would have assumed that women had no choice in this matter; they were simply slaves of their husbands. We fail to appreciate both of these significant points. The letter

15. O'Grady, "Postmodernism and the Interpretation of Biblical Texts for Behavior," 98–99.

16. Bristow, *What Paul Really Said about Women*, 32–48.

17. Hays, *Moral Vision of the New Testament*, 65.

of Ephesians treats women (and slaves) with incredible respect and dignity. We fail to appreciate the powerful nature of these unspoken assumptions in the letter, because our worldview is so much different than the values of those people in the first century CE. After all, we are the heirs of the biblical text and our values are the result of the trajectory set in motion by them with other passages and concepts in the canon. If we treat their views as less than ours, we have lost sight of how those ancient biblical texts ultimately got us to where we are now in our beliefs.

Other passages in the New Testament contain similar imperatives to women. The text in Ephesians is an elaboration on a similar text in Colossians, for the entire book of Ephesians appears to be an expansion of Colossians. Some commentators believe that Colossians was written by Paul and that Ephesians was written by a colleague of Paul after his death; others (including myself) believe that both letters were written by Paulinists after Paul's death. In Col 3:18–19 we read,

> 18Wives, be subject to your husbands, as is fitting in the Lord.
> 19Husbands, love your wives and never treat them harshly.

Again, the same verb form is used as was used in the Ephesians passage. Furthermore, this text qualifies that imperative in two ways. The particular type of obedience must be one that is "fitting in the Lord," which may imply that absolute submission is inappropriate. The next passage reinforces that idea by telling the husbands that they should not treat their wives harshly. By Graeco-Roman standards this really qualifies the obedience usually expected of women. Men would have considered it to be totally within their rights as husbands to beat their wives.

In 1 Pet 3:1 yet again the same qualified verb appears when it reads, "Wives, in the same way accept the authority of your husbands." Instead of "submit" the English translation reads, "accept," a better translation for all three texts. This passage adds a new insight, however, for the passage continues in v. 1: "so that, even if some of them do not obey the word, they may be won over without a word by their wives' conduct." Non-Christian husbands (who do not hear the word) may become Christians by being impressed by the behavior of their wives. Hence, the obedience is undertaken not simply for the sake of acknowledging patriarchal structures in society but for the sake of conversion. This is another example of strength made perfect in weakness and the Christian strategy of turning the other cheek to win the respect of an adversary. Our biblical author does not partake of the Graeco-Roman values that assume a wife is a slave to her husband in all things; rather, this passage assumes that a wife can have a clever and powerful strategy in relation to her husband. She can convert him. This is truly a high view of women.

A passage often quoted by conservative Christians to maintain that women should not be clergy or teach older children is found in 1 Tim 2:9–12. This text is part of a larger one that portrays itself as a letter written from Paul to Timothy, now that Timothy has become a senior leader in the church. This would have happened only many years after Paul's death, so, again, the letter most likely is written in Paul's name by a later Paulinist writer, perhaps even Timothy himself. The text reads,

> 9Also that the women should dress themselves modestly and de-
> cently in suitable clothing, not with their hair braided, or with gold,
> pearls, or expensive clothes, 10but with good works, as is proper
> for women who profess reverence for God. 11Let a woman learn
> in silence with full submission. 12I permit no woman to teach or
> to have authority over a man; she is to keep silent.

Upon reading this passage, we must remind ourselves of the overall values of the Graeco-Roman world in which this statement was articulated. In the popular cultural assumptions of the age an outspoken woman, especially if she dressed flamboyantly, was suspected of being a prostitute. It should also be noted that the passage refers to teaching, not to preaching or prophesying. In the Graeco-Roman world indeed teaching was exclusively a male prerogative, so also in the Judean tradition. It could be that our passage really only speaks of women teaching but does not exclude women from other clergy functions such as preaching and prophesying, and we have simply read those wider limitations into the passage. Finally, many commentators would point out that this imperative is connected to a guideline that prohibits jewelry for women. The jewelry command really indicates that this passage is encouraging Christians not to conform to some of the social and cultural values of that age. This is an imperative that applies only to the specific Greek audience that receives this letter; it is not a binding imperative for all Christians for all time. The text is saying that women should avoid jewelry and teaching so that they are good cultural examples in the Aegean Greek world of the first century CE. It does not specifically exclude them from other clergy functions (nor does it really prohibit jewelry for women in another age or culture).[18]

18. L. T. Johnson, *1 Timothy, 2 Timothy, Titus*, 68–74.

Another passage that appears to sternly direct women in their life-styles may actually admit the existence of women clergy in the later first century CE. In 1 Tim 3:11 we read that "women likewise must be serious, not slanderers, but temperate, faithful in all things." But if we read the text in its fuller setting, the message may be different. Thus, 1 Tim 3:8–13 reads,

> [8]Deacons likewise must be serious, not double-tongued, not in-dulging in much wine, not greedy for money; [9]they must hold fast to the mystery of the faith with a clear conscience. [10]And let them first be tested; then, if they prove themselves blameless, let them serve as deacons. [11]Women likewise must be serious, not slanderers, but temperate, faithful in all things. [12]Let deacons be married only once, and let them manage their children and their households well; [13]for those who serve well as deacons gain a good standing for themselves and great boldness in the faith that is in Christ Jesus.

The passage that speaks of women is surrounded by directions for the life-style of deacons in general. It seems logical that this passage is a short di-gression specifically on the nature of women deacons, not on all women in the Christian community. Furthermore, the words "faithful in all things" in reference to women appears to be describing their responsibilities in regard to matters of the church community and not just their own personal lives.[19] It is possible that the "deacons" in those early Christian congregations might be under a person called the "overseer" or *episkopos* (1 Tim 3:2), who might be the equivalent of the pastor, in which case the deacons, including the women, are lay assistants. Or perhaps the overseer might be the financial officer of the congregation and the deacons are more like clergy. Ultimately, the office of overseer will evolve into the office of bishop, and deacons will include clergy as well as lay assistants. In these early years of the church, the pastoral responsibilities of both offices were so similar that we would consider both offices to be simply clergy by our standards.[20]

The household codes of the Deutero-Pauline corpus in general call upon women, slaves, and children to be obedient to those in authority over them (Eph 5:21–33; 6:1–9; Col 3:18–25; 4:1–5; 1 Pet 2:11–25; 3:1–9). But we must realize that these imperatives were addressed to a particular

19. Kelly, *Commentary on the Pastoral Epistles*, 83–84; L. T. Johnson, *1 Timothy, 2 Timothy, Titus*, 78.

20. Kelly, *Commentary on the Pastoral Epistles*, 73–85; Dibelius and Conzelmann, *Pastoral Epistles*, 54–57.

social-cultural setting. Christianity admitted such people to their communities and gave them far more status than Graeco-Roman society was wont to offer. Christianity was perceived as a subversive movement that could undermine the traditional family structures and ultimately the state. The Christian authors who articulated those moral imperatives were stressing to their Christian audience that they needed to show others around them that Christians were not trying to undermine society. Christians were to be obedient as an act of love, so that their husbands, masters, and parents could be won over to Christianity by their examples of loving obedience, or so that their superiors could at least respect Christianity and no longer view it as a threat to society. In effect, this literature was commending an ethic of "turn the other cheek" and win your opponents over by a self-sacrificing form of love with obedience. This advice was not primarily commended for life within the Christian community, but rather it contained directions for how to behave before non-Christians in the greater world. Christians were primarily the oppressed segments of society: slaves and women. The masters and husbands often were pagan. Obedience before them might win respect and even converts.[21]

Early Christianity and Women

Christianity advocated many revolutionary ideas for its age; Christians had to fight battles on many ideological fronts. They were called atheists and blasphemers for denying the existence of other gods. The Roman state considered them insidious traitors for failure to recognize the divinity of the emperor, and for this they so often had to die. Judean Christians were rejected increasingly by other Judean movements for their radical messianism and beliefs about Jesus as the fulfillment of messianic hopes, and their refusal to fight in the Judean wars against Rome meant Christians were labeled as traitors among many Judeans. The sharing of goods and the almsgiving practiced by all Christians probably brought criticism from some circles, which was the ancient equivalent of today being accused of Communism in the United States. In general, Greeks found the Christian notions of the resurrection of the body absurd in contrast to more accepted views about complete separation of the good, immortal soul from the evil body at death. The Christian message of egalitarianism was almost too

---

21. Schüssler Fiorenza, *In Memory of Her*, 205–84, esp. 260–70.

much to sustain consistently before the entire pagan world. As Thomas Cahill observed lucidly,

> If, in addition to the wars they were already waging, Christians had followed their ideas to their logical conclusions and taken up cultural crusades against patriarchy and slavery, they would never have survived and we would never have heard of Christianity.[22]

As members of a revolutionary movement, Christians could challenge the Roman state significantly on the issue of slavery, but to challenge the patriarchal familial values would have created too much resistance to the new Christian movement on the grassroots level. So the post-Pauline generation found it necessary to create a compromise ethic and win converts by working within the parameters of some of the traditional values of Graeco-Roman society. In the subsequent generations of the Christian movement there would be slave clergy, but not too many women clergy. Pliny testifies to women slave clergy in Bithynia early in the second century CE in his letter to Emperor Trajan. In the past, scholars read this passage and assumed that Pliny referred to the women as "servants," but his conclusions from their testimony implies that these deacons or "servant" women had significant status. Modern scholars see these women as clergy, perhaps even bishops.[23] But in general, the battle for greater equality for women was placed on a "back-burner" in the ancient church. Perhaps the ancient Christians unconsciously left that agenda for later generations, like ours, to accomplish.

It is worth talking about some of these passages in the Pauline and Deutero-Pauline tradition to make an important observation. Traditional pious Christian interpretation of these texts sees them subordinate women to men; that has almost been the official position of Christianity for centuries. But I maintain that there is a trajectory of development in both the Old Testament and the New Testament that seeks to liberate women and give them dignity and respect equal to men. These passages appear to vitiate that

22. Cahill, *Desire of the Everlasting Hills*, 233. Cahill justly, in my opinion, praises the ideas of Paul as responsible for many latter accomplishments in Christendom: the emergence of monastic sisterhood led by Brigid of Kildare and Hildegard of Bingen, the attempts by St. Patrick of Ireland (inspired by the letter of Philemon) to condemn slavery, the later condemnation of slavery by seventeenth-century Anabaptists and the nineteenth-century Abolitionists, and the ultimate emergence of modern feminist and human rights movements (ibid., 238–39).

23. Schüssler Fiorenza, *In Memory of Her*, 209; Glancy, *Slavery in Early Christianity*, 130.

thesis. That is why these texts must be read more closely. These passages do not suppress women. Often we have not read the biblical text closely, or we have not read biblical texts in their literary context, such as overlooking the greater discussion of charismatic tongues in 1 Corinthians when referring to Paul's admonition for women to be silent. Sometimes the view of women does reflect a certain degree of subordination to men, such as in Eph 5:21–24. But we must remember that we speak of an evolving trajectory of social values that was set in motion by the biblical text and should be continued by us today. We should not expect the biblical texts to conform to our modern ideals of equality. We must see these passages as early stages in the evolutionary process that ultimately gave rise to our modern understandings. The texts do not contradict the notion that monotheistic faith unleashes a sense of egalitarianism. We have to acknowledge that it simply takes time in the social-historical circumstances of the human condition for such ideas to fully emerge. We must also accept that certain ideas must await their proper time before they can emerge in fully developed fashion. The first century CE was not ready for the message of total female equality; that would have been wrenching for them. But the ideas of that age are now meant to come to fruition in our age if we can realize that we are still part of the evolving trajectory of biblically inspired egalitarianism.

Status of Women

When we consider texts that deal with the status of women, we come to realize the importance of the direction in which the legal and moral imperatives of the Old and New Testaments were trying to lead. The context out of which the biblical text arose was one in which women were oppressed by patriarchal assumptions. Too often Christians have read these biblical passages, have observed the subordinate status in which biblical women found themselves, and have thereby assumed that those cultural assumptions are universally binding upon believers in any age.

We should have paid closer attention to what the texts were saying; then we might have noticed that the legal and moral imperatives of the biblical authors often stood in dialectic with the patriarchal assumptions of their age. We might have noticed an evolutionary trajectory in the biblical text that increasingly seeks to liberate women from the bonds of inequality. What we too often did was spiritualize passages that could have been the starting points for speaking of equality. In Gal 3:28 Paul declared that in Christ the differences between the status of women and men were abolished, but in our historical piety we interpreted this to mean that such distinctions would be abolished in heaven or that such equality was valid only in an abstract and ideal way but not in the practical life of the church and certainly not in everyday society. We ignored the plain sense of the text and ran to other passages that implied the subordination of women. Such passages subordinated women, either because they reflected the social values of their age, or because we took them out of context (as we did with the Corinthian imperative for charismatic women to be silent). Too often in the history of Christendom men interpreted the crucial passages, and they consciously or unconsciously interpreted them to the disadvantage of women. We must recognize that biblical texts testify to a reform process that has been initiated in which all people stand before God as equals. We must separate that message from the mere allusions to the patriarchal assumptions of the ancient age.

The recognition of an evolutionary trajectory of reform becomes possible with modern critical study of the Bible. We are able to perceive that the Book of the Covenant in Exodus 21–23 antedates the Deuteronomic laws in Deuteronomy 12–26, and thereby we sense significant social-economic differences between the ages of the two codes, as well as a significant legal-theological development in the latter over against the former. Combined with the modern perception of change and development in human culture, these insights make it possible for us to realize the presence of an evolving trajectory that arises in the biblical text and continues into the modern age.

Ironically, the biblically inspired trajectory that speaks for women's rights has been carried by intellectual and social movements of the post-Enlightenment age—movements that are not connected to the institutional synagogues and churches of the modern age. The biblical text in subtle fashion has influenced the intellectual development of western Europe so that secular movements have proclaimed the message that religious spokespersons should have taught for years. I maintain that in the area of women's rights, as well as on other issues of egalitarianism, the Bible has wrought greater influence among secular reformers than among church leaders over the past three hundred years. The tragedy is that the secular world too often has proclaimed the biblical message unknowingly while the ecclesiastical authorities have stood in the way of that very message. The lesson to be learned is that religionists and religious leaders in the Judeo-Christian tradition must awaken to the message of the biblical tradition. It gives an imperative to continue a process of change and renewal in society that seeks equality and dignity for all people, and especially the equality of male and female.

9

Old Testament Passages
Used to Condemn Homosexuality

The Issue of Homosexuality

THE CHIEF ARGUMENT OF this book has been that there is an evolutionary trajectory set in motion by the biblical tradition that increasingly seeks rights, equality, and dignity for people. This book responds to those intellectuals who have declared that the Bible is an oppressive document by its supposed affirmation of slavery and the subordination of women. I have maintained that we must read the Bible in the context of its age and observe that by comparison to the values of the first millennium BCE and the first-century CE, biblical authors actually regarded slaves and women with greater respect than the values of the contemporary culture did, and furthermore one can observe in the biblical tradition the attempt to give rights and equality to these people increasingly over the years. The Bible is a document of liberation.

Contemporary critics also quickly chide the Bible for its oppressive views on the issue of homosexuality. Conservative preachers adamantly maintain that the Bible clearly condemns male and female homosexual behavior. Advocates of gay rights then accordingly criticize the Bible for articulating these repressive views. To both groups I would say that a closer consideration of the biblical texts might reveal a more complex understanding of the issue of same-sex relationships.

At this point I admit that this topic is different from the discussion of women and slaves. On those two issues I perceive an evolution of values that seeks to advocate more dignity and rights for these oppressed peoples over the years. However, on the issue of homosexuality there is no such trajectory. This is because there are only seven passages that seem to condemn homosexuality, and with such a paucity of texts, one must initially conclude that the biblical tradition really does not care that much about the issue. Since there are only seven texts, one cannot speak about any evolution in the understanding of the issue of homosexuality by biblical authors. But this topic deserves discussion because it is such a hot issue in today's society, and because it is one of those issues for which the Bible is accused of being a retrograde document.

In recent years passionate debates have been carried on within American Christian denominations over the issue of accepting homosexuals as members in good standing within congregations and accepting actively practicing gay men and women as clergy. A number of years ago I offered to address the regional convention of voting lay and clergy delegates in the denomination to which I belong as a clergyperson (the Texas-Louisiana Gulf Coast Synod of the Evangelical Lutheran Church of America [ELCA]) on the topic of what the Bible says about homosexuality. I was told that it would be wise for me not to do so, for although the clergy would understand my presentation, it would cause distress for the laity, especially since I would advocate that individual biblical passages do not directly condemn homosexual relations between two loving, free adults. In the years that followed, several congregations in that synod left the ELCA because of their perception that the ELCA was too tolerant of homosexuals. With my presentation, I probably would have caused those churches to leave even sooner than they did. An issue with such passion connected to it deserves some consideration.

The following chapters contain a discussion of those passages used by Christians to condemn homosexual behavior. I am not addressing how the later Christian tradition interpreted those passages, nor am I discussing significant church pronouncements on the topic, such as Roman Catholic canon law. Nor can I discuss the diverse range of opinions of the many scholars who have commented upon these passages. Either quest would turn this chapter into a large book. What I am presenting here are my observations and some of my own particular theories about these biblical texts.

The seven biblical texts oft quoted by theologians and laity on the theological and the popular levels of discussion to condemn homoerotic behavior of men and women include the story of drunken Noah and his sons; the story of Sodom and Gomorrah, which everyone alludes to with absolute certainty that the men of Sodom are homosexuals; two sentence-long prohibitions in the book of Leviticus that condemn men having sex with each other; two words that describe some form of homoerotic behavior used in two lists of vices in the New Testament; and the condemnation of idolatry and homosexuality by Paul in the book of Romans, the only text that perhaps mentions same-sex activity by both men and women. What we need to do is look at these passages to observe whether they really condemn homosexual behavior between two consenting, free adults, or whether some other form of activity is being described.

Noah and Ham

Some people believe that the sin of Ham in Genesis 9 was a homosexual act perpetrated against Noah, and they refer to the curse on Canaan as being so drastic because the sin was a homosexual act. The text reads as follows in Gen 9:20–27,

> 20Noah, a man of the soil, was the first to plant a vineyard. 21He drank some of the wine and became drunk, and he lay uncovered in his tent. 22And Ham, the father of Canaan, saw the nakedness of his father, and told his two brothers outside. 23Then Shem and Japheth took a garment, laid it on both their shoulders, and walked backward and covered the nakedness of their father; their faces were turned away, and they did not see their father's nakedness. 24When Noah awoke from his wine and knew what his youngest son had done to him, 25he said,
> "Cursed be Canaan;
>   lowest of slaves shall he be to his brothers."
> 26He also said,
> "Blessed by the Lord my God be Shem;
>   and let Canaan be his slave.
> 27May God make space for Japheth,
>   And let him live in the tents of Shem."

A common interpretation of this passage is that Noah became drunk and undressed himself, or perhaps Ham undressed him, then Ham had anal sex with his father to humiliate him and make himself the master in the relationship. According to this interpreation, Ham next either called to his brothers outside the tent or went outside the tent to tell them what he had done to Noah in order to establish his supremacy in the family. When the text says that Noah realized what Ham had done to him, it must imply a physical action, such as rape. The reference to "see the nakedness" of someone can mean to have sex with that person. To "uncover the nakedness of someone" also means to have sex, and even though that expression is not used here, our passage may imply that Ham uncovered Noah and then raped him. Hence, the Jewish and Christian traditions have often assumed that actual sexual intercourse occurred. These interpreters then conclude that we have a homosexual act that leads to the curse on Canaan, the son of Ham.

If Ham actually had sex with Noah, we are talking about rape, an act designed to humiliate and subordinate someone. The same humiliation and subordination occurs in heterosexual rape, but we do not thereby condemn heterosexuality, a point that is overlooked by critics of homoeroticism.[1] Ham's action does not tell us if he is, by our modern definitions, a heterosexual or a homosexual; it tells us that he used sex as an act of power to humiliate his father. Sometimes heterosexuals rape someone of the same sex for the sake of domination, as in prisons, and it does not mean they are homosexuals. In the ancient world those men who are penetrated would be equivalent to what we might call gay, but those who penetrate might be seen as equivalent to what we might call heterosexuals.[2] The latter would have sex with men, women, or animals because they were manly "men" who could express their sexuality in various ways.

Ham also committed an act of incest. Dominating rape and incest are sufficient to warrant the curse that comes upon Canaan; we do not have to conclude that it is homosexuality. Thus, this passage does not address the issue of homosexual love between two free adults, even if it does describe homosexual activity. But it may not actually do even that.

Critical scholars often maintain that Ham did not actually rape his father. When Shem and Japheth came in backwards to avoid looking at Noah, we suspect that inappropriate looking was the actual action of Ham.

1. Pizzuto, "'God Has Made It Plain to Them,'" 165–66.
2. Carden, "Homophobia and Rape in Sodom and Gibeah," 83–96.

If simply covering Noah was the solution to the problem, then the offensive action must have been viewing Noah's nakedness. The use of the verb "to see" in this passage is not the usual way of speaking about sex. More likely we would read, "uncover the nakedness" (Lev 18:6; 20:18) or "lie with" (Lev 20:11–12). So sexual activity may not be the sin. The sin may be two-fold: viewing a close relative naked, which is a purity violation, and failing to help a parent in distress, a social violation, which for a kinship society was an extremely egregious sin.[3] The second-millennium-BCE Aqhat Epic states that it is the responsibility of the son to tend to his father when the old man is drunk: "Who takes him by the hand when he's drunk, Carries him when he's sated with wine."[4] That is what Ham failed to do, and perhaps he even made fun of his father's condition. If this is the case, this passage should not be discussed at all in regard to homosexuality.

I cannot prove this, but I believe that the passage is a double entendre. On the narrative level, Ham simply views his father and fails to help him, but the hint of sexual language with the reference to "lay uncovered" and "saw the nakedness" hints at unbridled sexuality.[5] If that is the case, then the curse on Canaan implies that such unbridled sexuality is typical of Canaanite culture because it goes back to their symbolic ancestor.[6] Such an allusion is sarcastic theological humor by the biblical author, further indicating that we should not use this passage in our debates.

Sodom

In order to understand the story of Sodom and Gomorrah in Genesis 19 we need to read a parallel narrative (Judges 19), an account that too often is overlooked. In Judg 19:15–28 we read about the experience of a Levite, his concubine, and his servant in the Israelite city of Gibeah,

> [15]They turned aside there, to go in and spend the night at Gibeah. He went in and sat down in the open square of the city, but no one took them in to spend the night.

3. Westermann, *Genesis 1–11*, 484, 488–89; Vogels, "Cham découvre les limites de son pére Noé," 554–73; Wenham, *Genesis 1–15*, 198–200; Vervenne, "What Shall We Do with the Drunken Sailor?," 49–50; Embry, "The 'Naked Narrative' from Noah to Leviticus," 417–33.

4. *ANET*, 150.

5. Von Rad, *Genesis*, 137.

6. Vervenne, "What Shall We Do with the Drunken Sailor?," 52–55.

[16]Then at evening there was an old man coming from his work in the field. The man was from the hill country of Ephraim, and he was residing in Gibeah. (The people of the place were Benjaminites.) [17]When the old man looked up and saw the wayfarer in the open square of the city, he said, 'Where are you going and where do you come from?' [18]He answered him, "We are passing from Bethlehem in Judah to the remote part of the hill country of Ephraim, from which I come. I went to Bethlehem in Judah; and I am going to my home. Nobody has offered to take me in. [19]We your servants have straw and fodder for our donkeys, with bread and wine for me and the woman and the young man along with us. We need nothing more." [20]The old man said, "Peace be to you. I will care for all your wants; only do not spend the night in the square." [21]So he brought him into his house, and fed the donkey; they washed their feet, and ate and drank.

[22]While they were enjoying themselves, the men of the city, a perverse lot, surrounded the house, and started pounding on the door. They said to the old man, the master of the house, "Bring out the man who came into your house, so that we may have intercourse with him." [23]And the man, the master of the house, went out to them and said to them, "No, my brothers, do not act so wickedly. Since this man is my guest, do not do this vile thing. [24]Here are my virgin daughter and his concubine; let me bring them out now. Ravish them and do whatever you want to them; but against this man do not do such a vile thing." [25]But the men would not listen to him. So the man seized his concubine, and put her out to them. They wantonly raped her, and abused her all through the night until the morning. And as the dawn began to break, they let her go. [26]As morning appeared, the woman came and fell down at the door of the man's house where her master was, until it was light.

After reading this text, which is part of a much longer and very complicated narrative, we turn our attention to Gen 19:1–11,

[1]The two angels came to Sodom in the evening; and Lot was sitting in the gateway of Sodom. When Lot saw them, he rose to meet them, and bowed down with his face to the ground. [2]He said, "Please, my lords, turn aside to your servant's house and spend the night, and wash your feet; then you can rise early and go on your way." They said, "No; we will spend the night in the square." [3]But he urged them strongly, so they turned aside to him and entered his house; and he made them a feast, and baked unleavened bread,

and they ate. 4But before they lay down, the men of the city, the men of Sodom, both young and old, all the people to the last man, surrounded the house; 5and they called to Lot, "Where are the men who came to you tonight? Bring them out to us, so that we may know them." 6Lot went out of the door to the men, shut the door after him 7and said, "I beg you, my brothers, do not act so wickedly. 8Look, I have two daughters who have not known a man; let me bring them out to you, and do to them as you please; only do nothing to these men, for they have come under the shelter of my roof." 9But they replied, "Stand back!" And they said, "This fellow came here as an alien, and he would play the judge! Now we will deal worse with you than with them." Then they pressed hard against the man Lot, and came near the door to break it down. 10But the men inside reached out their hands and brought Lot into the house with them, and shut the door. 11And they struck with blindness the men who were at the door of the house, both small and great, so that they were unable to find the door.

These two narratives are essentially the same story told in two different versions. The similarities between the two accounts are significant, and they are worthy of detailed listing in order to demonstrate how truly similar the accounts really are:

1. Before even arriving at the city, the travelers receive very hospitable treatment. The Levite is entertained by his father-in-law (Judg 19:3–9); the angels are received graciously by Abraham (Gen 18:1–8).

2. The visitors enter into the city (Judg 19:15; Gen 19:1).

3. They go to either the open square or the city gate, both of which are meeting places for small and large towns respectively (Judg 19:15; Gen 19:1).

4. They are met by the host in the meeting place (Judg 19:16–19; Gen 19:1).

5. The host does not live in that city. In Judges 19 he is an old man from Ephraim (Judg 19:16); in Genesis 19 he is Lot, a pastoralist living among sedentary folk.

6. The host invites them to spend the night in his home (Judg 19:20; Gen 19:2). But both Lot and the old man from Ephraim inappropriately make this offer, for they are not full members of the village community.[7]

7. There is a reference to "spending the night in the square," something that ought not be done (Judg 19:20; Gen 19:2–3).

8. The host takes them into his house (Judg 19:21; Gen 19:3).

9. The host feeds the guests (Judg 19:21: Gen 19:3).

10. The guests intend to spend the night there (Judg 19:21; Gen 19:4).

11. Local men of the city approach the house (Judg 19:22; Gen 19:4).

12. These men are said to "surround the house" (Judg 19:22; Gen 19:4).

13. They seek the attention of those inside. The men of Gibeah pound on the door (Judg 19:22); the men of Sodom call out for Lot (Gen 19:5).

14. The men say, "Bring out the man/men" (Judg 19:22: Gen 19:5).

15. The men clearly indicate that they wish to rape the visitors (Judg 19:22; Gen 19:5). They wish to "know" the men. The same verb, *yada'*, is also used in Gen 4:1, 17, 25; 24:16; 38:26; Judg 11:39; 19:22, 25; 1 Sam 1:19; 1 Kgs 1:4 with the meaning of direct sexual activity. Though few examples out of the 943 usages of the verb refer to sexual activity, the contexts clearly indicate that this is the meaning in those instances where we translate it as such (contra several commentators who believe the Sodom crowd simply wished to talk with the angels).

16. The host goes out to speak to the men (Judg 19:23; Gen 19:6).

17. The host refers to the people in the crowd as "my brothers" (Judg 19:23; Gen 19:7).

18. The host says to the crowd, "Do not act so wickedly" (Judg 19:23; Gen 19:7).

19. The host declares that the men inside are his guests (Judg 19:23–24; Gen 19:8).

20. The host offers two women to the crowd for sex. The man of Ephraim offers his daughter and the Levite's concubine (Judg 19:24); Lot offers his two daughters (Gen 19:8). (It is apparently a bluff with Lot's offer, because the crowd wants the men. Since they become angry and claim

7. Matthews, "Hospitality and Hostility," 3–11.

that he plays the role of "judge" over them, this may imply that they are insulted by his implication that they seek only sex when he offers his daughters, since they really seek to establish their authority over the strangers.)

21. The host says, "Let me bring them out" (Judg 19:24; Gen 19:8).

22. The host says or implies to the crowd that they may do with the women whatever they please (Judg 19:24; Gen 19:8).

23. The crowd rejects his offer (Judg 19:25; Gen 19:9), probably because they want to rape the strangers, and they are being offered women who are local inhabitants. The daughter of the man of Ephraim and both of Lot's daughters are locals, and the crowd wants to rape the strangers to demonstrate their power in the town.

24. The guests move people through the door. The Levite pushes his concubine out to the crowd (Judg 19:25); the two angels pull Lot back into the house (Gen 19:10).

25. Violence occurs outside the house. The concubine of the Levite is raped (Judg 19:25); the men of Sodom are struck blind (Gen 19:11). Claus Westermann continues the comparison of these two narratives into the sections concerning the destruction of Sodom in Genesis 19 and the civil war with Benjamin in Judges 19–21.[8]

I have broken the details down in such extreme fashion, more than any other commentator ever has done, in order to demonstrate clearly that these two are the same account in slightly different guises. Older commentators assumed that Judges 19 imitated the earlier account in Genesis 19 because they often assumed the pentateuchal narratives were older than accounts in the Deuteronomistic History.[9] Others more recently have come to the same conclusion by seeing Judges 19 as a rougher version of Genesis 19 to demonstrate the extent of sin in that age of the judges.[10]

It would appear to me, however, that the account in Judges is older because it is rougher as a narrative and has far greater violence. The Genesis version as a narrative is smoother and far more economical in narrative

8. Westermann, *Genesis 12–36*, 297–98.

9. Wellhausen, *Prolegomena to the History of Ancient Israel*, 235–37; Moore, *Critical and Exegetical Commentary on Judges*, 417–18; Soggin, *Judges*, 282, 288.

10. Lasine, "Guest and Host in Judges 19," 38–41; Brettler, "Book of Judges," 411–12; Matthews, "Hospitality and Hostility," 3–11.

detail, a sign of later development of a literary form. Instead of two women (in Judges 19), one of whom is foreign and the other of whom is local, Genesis 19 has the women paired as the two daughters of Lot. The old man in Judges 19 offers his guest's concubine, and that is quite inhospitable; but Lot offers only his kin. Thus, Genesis has "cleaned up" Lot's actions compared to the old man of Ephraim (contra Stuart Lasine, who believes that Judges 19 "inverts the world" of Genesis 19 by being more violent). In Judg 19:24 the old man invites the crowd to "rape" the women, but Lot simply offers the women, again showing revision in the Genesis 19 version (contra Lasine again). Lot says that the men are his guests once (Gen 19:8), but the man of Ephraim repeats the statement (Judg 19:23–24) so that the Genesis narrative appears to be tighter. In Judg 19:22 it calls the men outside the house "a perverse lot," a select group, but in Gen 19:4 the text generalizes by saying "all the people to the last man," which will ultimately justify the destruction of the entire city by God. In Genesis 19 justice is done when the violent men are struck blind, but in Judges 19 the ending is horrible, and in the ensuing narrative of several chapters the violence is greater and even more revolting. The narrative in Judges 19 is tightly interwoven into the narrative of the Benjaminite civil war of Judges 19–21, whereas the Genesis story is an independent story, somewhat separable from the surrounding narratives in the Abraham cycle.[11] Genesis 19 appears to me to be inspired by Judges 19, and since we now view the pentateuchal narratives (Genesis, Exodus, Leviticus, and Numbers) as later than the Deuteronomistic History (Deuteronomy, Joshua, Judges, Samuel, and Kings), this makes good sense.

If we use the principles of "intertextuality" (that is, if one text has influenced the formation of a second biblical text), we can interpret that second biblical text by reference to the first one. We assume that biblical authors expected their listening audience to do the same thing when the listeners sensed a strong similarity of language between two narratives. If you read Judges 19 after Genesis 19 you could theoretically argue, as some do, that the issue is about homosexuality because the threat of homosexual rape to the two angels in the first story carries over into the second story wherein the rape of a woman then is considered to be less offensive than the potential homosexual rape of a man. (I personally find the argument that the rape of a woman is less offensive than that of a man to be horrible. The

---

11. Westermann, *Genesis 12–36*, 300; Niditch, "'Sodomite' Theme in Judges 19–20," 365–78.

issue is that the host will go to any lengths to defend a guest.) However, if you read Genesis 19 after Judges 19, I believe that it becomes more evident that the issue of rape is the focus of both accounts. In Judges 19 the threatened rape of a man and the actual rape of a woman then leads you to read Genesis 19 as a story of attempted rape of the two angels.

Popular piety has maintained for years that the Sodom narrative is about homosexuality and that the narrative condemns it. However, Genesis 19 is the same account that we read in Judges 19. In Genesis 19 the townsmen try to rape two angels, who are presumably male, but in Judges 19 it is a woman who actually gets raped. If Genesis 19 condemns homosexuality, then Judges 19 condemns heterosexuality. People who love to use Genesis 19 to condemn homosexuals have to avoid Judges 19 because it destroys their argument. Sometimes it is said by sophisticated critics of homosexuality that both passages condemn homosexuality because the men of Gibeah initially sought to rape a man, then settled for a woman. That is illogical. Such a logic of homosexual identity would assume that homosexuals suddenly became heterosexuals. No one seems to make that observation when declaring homosexual activity to be the common denominator of these two stories. That the men of Gibeah ask for a man, then rape a woman, both of whom are strangers to the city, obviously points to the common denominator: they are strangers and targets for rape of subordination. The men of Gibeah rape the concubine of the stranger in order to humiliate him, for he is then unable to protect his woman.[12] That the men of Sodom disdain Lot's offer of women might imply that they want the strangers and not the local girls, or it might imply that they are homosexual. But when they take offense at his offer and claim that he is playing the "judge," it seems to me that they are angry at Lot for assuming their desire is simply for sex when they really wish to demonstrate their power over the strangers.

In both narratives the sin is rape or attempted rape. In particular, it is power rape: that is, sexual violence for the purpose of degrading someone, and the sexual identity of that person is totally irrelevant.[13] A variation on this is provided by some scholars who suggest the crowd wants to rape the visitors and extort information from them because they are perceived to be

12. Bal, "Dealing/With/Women," 328.

13. Wenham, *Genesis 16–50*, 55; Stone, "Gender and Homosexuality in Judges 19," 87–107; Nissinen, *Homoeroticism in the Biblical World*, 47–49; Frymer-Kensky, *Reading the Women of the Bible*, 124–25; Via and Gagnon, *Homosexuality and the Bible*, 5; Siker, "Homosexuality," 882–83; Michaelson, *God vs. Gay?*, 67–72.

spies who have come late at night to search out the city.[14] Genesis 14 tells the story of an attack upon Sodom in which citizens were taken as prisoners and later liberated by Abraham, so that one should expect the citizens to be edgy about strangers. An obvious point to make is that the entire crowd of people around Lot's house cannot all be homosexuals, since the text declares that it is all the men in the city who are present. The entire city cannot be homosexual, or else there would be no population.[15] Homosexual violation, usually by folk we would call heterosexual, in many societies is used to teach subordination to slaves, trespassers, strangers, and newcomers to a community.[16] These stories do not speak of sexual inclination; they are about sexual violence to obtain power over strangers. Conservative commentators who acknowledge that homosexual rape is involved in the story still maintain that thereby all homosexual activity is condemned, but then heterosexual rape in other biblical narratives would require that we condemn all heterosexuality also.

The sin of the men in both cities is compounded by their violation of the customs of hospitality.[17] Strangers who visit a city are to be taken in and given shelter and food, as both the man of Ephraim and Lot did. In fact, by the code of honor in that era, both hosts are duty bound to protect their guests with their lives. Conservative commentators who disdain the argument of hospitality by saying it is too mild a sin to merit the condemnation that Sodom receives fail to appreciate the magnitude of this moral requirement of hospitality in ancient Israel. This obligation to the principles of hospitality means being ready to die to protect your guests, and that is why the hosts in both narratives make the drastic offer of the women to the raging crowd.

I believe that there is an element of bluff here, however. The crowd does not want locals, nor do they particularly want the women. Rather, they want to humiliate the men to make the point that this is their town, they run it, and strangers must recognize their power. Sexual preference is irrelevant. It is all about power rape and the humiliation of strangers. This is the sin that the biblical text condemns in the narration of the events. Added to that would be the Middle Eastern concept that the highest value

14. McDonald, "Hospitality and Hostility," 179–90.

15. White, "Does the Bible Speak about Gays or Same-Sex Orientation?," 14–23.

16. Carden, "Homophobia and Rape in Sodom and Gibeah," 83–96; Gagnon, *Bible and Homosexual Practice*, 77.

17. Fields, *Sodom and Gomorrah*, 54–67; Conon, "Le péché de Sodome," 17–40.

of hospitality to strangers has also been violated. Further, the literary context of Genesis 19 points to this issue of hospitality, for the graciousness of Abraham in providing hospitality for the angelic messengers in Gen 18:1–5 stands in stark contrast to the actions of the citizens of Sodom. Likewise, the literary context of Judges 19 contrasts the hospitality of the Levite's father-in-law with the folk of Gibeah. The citizens of Sodom might also be angry with Lot for offering hospitality to these strangers when he is not really a citizen of the city himself. The account of Sodom has nothing to do with homosexuality between free, consenting adults in a loving relationship.

Sodom Imagery throughout the Bible

Further collaboration for this conclusion may be found by consulting other passages in the Old Testament that refer to Sodom. Consider, for example, Isa 1:9–10, 16–17 which reads,

> 9If the LORD of hosts
>   had not left us a few survivors,
> we would have been like Sodom
>   and become like Gomorrah.
>
> 10Hear the word of the LORD,
>   you rulers of Sodom!
> Listen to the teaching of our God,
>   you people of Gomorrah!
>   . . .
>
> 16Wash yourselves; make yourselves clean;
>   remove the evil of your doings
>   from before my eyes;
> cease to do evil,
>   17learn to do good;
> seek justice,
>   rescue the oppressed,
> defend the orphan,
>   plead for the widow.

In this text the prophet Isaiah compares the nation of Judah to Sodom and Gomorrah, declaring that they almost became like those two destroyed cities because of their sins. When Isaiah tells the folk of Judah what they should be doing, the categories are justice for the oppressed, the orphans, and the widows. By implication, the sins of social injustice in Judah are being attacked by the prophet, and the further implication of the comparison indicates that these were the sins of Sodom.

The prophet Jeremiah likewise implies that the sins of Sodom and Gomorrah may be compared to the sins of Judah, which are described in more general fashion. Jeremiah 23:14 reads,

> But in the prophets of Jerusalem
>   I have seen a more shocking thing:
> they commit adultery and walk in lies;
>   they strengthen the hands of evildoers,
>   so that no one turns from wickedness;
> all of them have become like Sodom to me,
>   and its inhabitants like Gomorrah.

Like the passage in Isaiah, this reference is somewhat vague, but just as the passage in Isaiah makes no connection between Sodom and sexual activity, neither does this passage. Jeremiah 49:18 and 50:40 simply refer to God overthrowing Sodom and Gomorrah.

The prophet Ezekiel provides the clearest description of how the sins of Sodom and Gomorrah were perceived by a later generation. In Ezek 16:48–50 we read,

> 48As I live, says the LORD GOD, your sister Sodom and her daughters have not done as you and your daughters have done. 49This was the guilt of your sister Sodom: she and her daughters had pride, excess of food, and prosperous ease, but did not aid the poor and needy. 50They were haughty, and did abominable things before me; therefore I removed them when I saw it.

This passage clearly identifies the sin of Sodom as failure to help the poor and needy. What the passage in Isaiah seems to imply, this passage in Ezekiel clearly states. In all these passages there is no allusion to sexual sins or sexual inclination. In Ezek 16:53–56 the prophet generically pairs Sodom with Samaria as deserving future disgrace.

The destruction of Sodom, Gomorrah, Admah, and Zeboiim are variously mentioned in brief references elsewhere (Deut 29:22–23; 32:32; Isa

3:9; 13:19; Lam 4:6; Hos 11:8; Amos 4:11; Zeph 2:9). Their destruction is meant as a warning that comparable punishment could come upon Israel and Judah, but no mention of particular sins is given.

The prophets sense that the barbaric behavior of the Sodomites toward strangers indicated their lack of social justice in the rest of their activities. Perhaps the prophets were aware of other traditions about Sodom that we do not have.[18] At any rate, the lack of social justice further reinforces our opinion that the Sodom story is not about homosexuality, at least not in the Old Testament.

In brief allusions in later biblical literature, we read that the sin of Sodom was arrogance. In Sir 16:8 the wisdom teacher says, "He did not spare the neighbors of Lot, whom he loathed on account of their arrogance." Though it does not mention Sodom by name, passages in Wisdom of Solomon 19, which speak of the ungodly, make clear allusions to the account in Genesis 19. We read selected verses of Wis 19:14, 17,

> [14]Others had refused to receive strangers when they came to them,
>
> . . .
>
> [17]They were stricken also with loss of sight—
> just as were those at the door of the righteous man—
> when, surrounded by yawning darkness,
> all of them tried to find the way through their own doors.

This text clearly attributes the sin of inhospitality to strangers as the sin of the citizens of Sodom. A loose allusion is found in Wis 10:6–8, which speaks of a "righteous man" escaping "fire that descended on the Five Cities," which were destroyed because "they passed wisdom by" and thus "left for humankind a reminder of their folly." Arrogance, inhospitality, and folly are mentioned in these texts, but no reference to homoerotic behavior appears.

In the New Testament a number of allusions occur in reference to Sodom. Jesus tells his disciples that those who reject their message will suffer more than the people of Sodom (Matt 10:15; Luke 10:12) and Gomorrah (Matt 10:15). This, again, is the sin of inhospitality, for Jesus is speaking of how some communities will refuse his disciples; he is not speaking of sexual activity. In Matt 11:23–24 Jesus says that had his deeds, which he performed in Capernaum, been seen in Sodom, the Sodomites would have

---

18. Von Rad, *Genesis*, 218.

responded better. In Luke 17:29 Jesus says that the coming judgment will come as quickly as the fire and sulfur came upon Sodom.

Paul refers to Sodom in Rom 9:29 when he is quoting Isa 1:9. However, he says nothing about the sin of Sodom, which we should expect, I suppose, if the passage in Romans 1 were really about some form of homosexual behavior.

In 2 Pet 2:4–18 we read that Sodom and Gomorrah were destroyed due to "the licentiousness of the lawless" (v. 7) and "lawless deeds" (v. 8). The reference in v. 10, "those who indulge their flesh in depraved lust, and who despise authority," may describe the people of Sodom or sinful people in general, for the verses that follow certainly describe sinful human behavior everywhere, not just in Sodom. Thus, one cannot definitely say that the sin of Sodom is portrayed as sexual on the basis of this passage.

In Rev 11:8 Sodom is a symbolic name for the great city in which the two witnesses are killed (Peter and Paul, perhaps), which is most likely Rome.

Only one passage, Jude 7, in the New Testament, refers to the "sexual immorality" and "unnatural lust" of the people in Sodom and Gomorrah, but the text does not specifically identify the sexual depravity as same-sex relationships (though that might be a logical conclusion). It compares their lust with the activity of the "sons of God" or "angels" who came down and had sex with women. This might refer to the text in Gen 6:1–4, where the "sons of god(s)" have sex with the "daughters of men." This is heterosexual activity, or better said, sex between celestial beings and humans. The text in Jude 7 reads,

> 6And the angels who did not keep their own position, but left their proper dwelling, he has kept in eternal chains in deepest darkness for the judgment of the great day. 7Likewise, Sodom and Gomorrah and the surrounding cities, which in the same manner as they, indulged in sexual immorality and pursued unnatural lust, serve as an example by undergoing a punishment of eternal fire.

The important phrase is in v. 7, "in the same manner as they," which indicates that the sin of Sodom and Gomorrah is the same sin as the angels in Gen 6:1–4, whatever that might have been. One would suspect that the sin of the angels was that they came down and had sex with women, as Gen 6:1–4 seems to indicate. If so, the sin that Jude 7 refers to is sex between angels and people in both narratives.

Often for Judeans and Christians "unnatural lust" referred to sex that did not explicitly seek procreation, which could be homosexuality, but it could refer to something else. Perhaps these two passages actually refer to a "transgression of orders" in that the men of Sodom and Gomorrah were seeking sex with angels, which was true, even though the men of Sodom might not have known it. This is the reverse of what the angels had done by coming to earth to obtain human women in Gen 6:1–4.[19] Another author believes that maybe Jude suspected that the women of Sodom desired sex with the angels.[20] Also the possibility exists that the later biblical authors in the New Testament era believed that Sodomites had fertility cult sexual prostitutes (as still existed in their age), and that this was the sin of the city according to the passage in Jude.[21]

When we consider the passages in the Bible, none of them can conclusively be said to declare that the sin of Sodom was homosexuality.[22] In other literature of that age, one Judean pseudepigraphal work refers to anal intercourse (2 Enoch 10:4–5; 34:2) and other pseudepigraphical texts refer to sexual vices in general at Sodom, which might be construed as homosexual references (Jubilees 16:5–9; Testament of Naphtali 3:4–5; 4:1; Testament of Ashur 7:1; Testament of Benjamin 9:1; Testament of Levi 14:6).[23] The equation with homosexuality was made by the Judean philosopher Philo and the Judean historian Josephus, and probably they equated pederasty with homosexuality. On the other hand, in later years some church fathers, such as Origen, Ambrose, and John Cassian, commented upon the sin of Sodom as crass inhospitality to strangers.[24] Not until the fourth century CE did church fathers consistently begin to clearly make the equation with homosexuality.[25] A greater consideration of the testimony of the church fathers takes us beyond the limits of this chapter, however.

19. Bauckham, Jude, 2 Peter, 54; Nissinen, Homoeroticism in the Biblical World, 92–93.

20. Boswell, Christianity, Social Tolerance, and Homosexuality, 97

21. McNeill, Church and the Homosexual, 46–49, 70–71.

22. So also Boswell, Christianity, Social Tolerance, and Homosexuality, 93–96.

23. DeYoung, Homosexuality, 85–109; Esler, "The Sodom Tradition in Romans 1:18–32," 8–9.

24. Boswell, Christianity, Social Tolerance, and Homosexuality, 98, 346.

25. Michaelson, God vs. Gay?, 67

Leviticus 18 and 20

Two passages in the book of Leviticus appear to condemn homosexual behavior. Both these laws appear in what Christians would call the cultic laws of ancient Israel. It is often said that these cultic laws are no longer binding on Christians, so in actuality they are irrelevant for any discussion of homosexuality as a sin. Critical scholars observe that Levitical laws in general condemned activities of the Gentiles; were concerned with Israelite purity issues; and addressed Israel's concept of the created orders of heaven, earth, and seas along with the appropriate activity in those orders. Levitical laws were also concerned with procreation for the underpopulated community of Israel, and they provided an exclusive identity for Israelites and Judahites. For any or all of these reasons it is assumed that the laws are not binding on Christians, who are those Gentiles now in the faith community of the new covenant.[26] But we must admit that numerous laws in Leviticus address criminal activity, so it would be wrong for us to casually dismiss the entire book from the Christian perspective. We must view each law individually to see whether it still articulates a meaningful legal direction for the modern age.

People who condemn homosexual behavior quote Levitical passages on homosexual activity to advance the argument that all homosexuality is sin. They observe that some of the laws in Leviticus describe activities that we today would regard as criminal and sinful, and homosexuality is clearly one of these universal evil acts, in their opinion.

In Leviticus 18 we read a long list of prohibitions against having sex with close relatives, and such lists are found elsewhere in the biblical text. The homosexual prohibition is found among the last three imperatives and reads, in Lev 18:21–24,

> [21]You shall not give any of your offspring to sacrifice them to Molech, and so profane the name of your God: I am the LORD. [22]You shall not lie with a male as with a woman; it is an abomination. [23]You shall not have sexual relations with any animal and defile yourself with it, nor shall any woman give herself to an animal to sexual relations with it: it is perversion. [24]Do not defile yourselves in any of these ways, for by all these practices the nations I am casting out before you have defiled themselves.

---

26. Boswell, *Christianity, Social Tolerance, and Homosexuality*, 100–101; Furnish, "What Does the Bible Say about Homosexuality?," 57–66; White, "Does the Bible Speak about Gays or Same-Sex Orientation?," 14–23.

What is unusual about this placement of the homosexual prohibition is that it is found between two passages that describe behavior attributed to the Canaanites by the Israelites. Sacrificing a child to Molech refers to infant sacrifice, a custom practiced in Phoenicia and later Carthage in North Africa, and perhaps among the Canaanites. The firstborn son of a family was to be offered up as a sacrifice on the eighth day after birth to ensure the continued fertility of the mother. The same was done with the offspring of livestock, and the Israelites performed that ritual. But the theologians of Israel struggled for years to get the Israelites to stop engaging in the sacrifice of human babies. (For instance, they told how Abraham was prevented by God from sacrificing Isaac in Genesis 22.)

The prohibition that follows the injunction against homosexual behavior forbids both men and women from having sex with animals. This too was a reputed custom that supposedly happened in the cultic shrines of other peoples, according to Israelite belief. A devotee might have sex with an animal that particularly represented a specific deity in order to have communion with that deity. The fact that women in particular are mentioned makes it appear that this is cultic activity supposedly done by priestesses. Men working on the farm might have sex with animals to satisfy the male sex drive; the cultural assumptions of that age would not attribute such behavior to women as potentially routine activity. The fact that the prohibition is specifically mentioned in regard to women leads me to suspect that we are describing cultic behavior. Many commentators fail to observe this detail! Whether sex with animals in the Canaanite cult truly occurred is a matter of debate among scholars, but Israelite rhetoric attributed it to them. The point to be made is that the prohibition against homosexuality occurs between two laws describing cultic rituals. Verse 24 then declares that these are the practices of the peoples of the land. The list of kinfolk with whom sex is to be avoided in vv. 6–20 does not necessarily describe the customs of any particular people, but the cultic prohibitions of vv. 21 and 23 do describe activities popularly attributed to Canaanites by the Israelites.

The explicit condemnation of foreign practices in v. 24 would seem to imply cultic activity. Thus, it might appear that those particular cultic activities are the last three activities mentioned in the prohibition list: infant sacrifice, homosexuality, and sex with animals. Furthermore, the word "abomination," which is used in the text at this point, very often describes foreign behavior, especially cultic activity. If "abomination" describes cultic activity in this case, then what is condemned by the prohibition against homosexuality is not general homosexual behavior but cultic homosexual relations in particular, and a strong indication of this comes from the fact that the prohibition against homosexuality follows the prohibition of infant sacrifice and precedes reference to sex with animals by women. The general reference to male homosexual activity might have caused most people in the ancient Near East to think of cultic activity in the first place, and thus many commentators suspect this Levitical command addresses that issue.[27] This is impossible to prove in a totally convincing fashion because we are simply dealing with a list of prohibitions. But the possibility exists that this command describes cultic homosexuality, not general homosexuality.

If it does refer to simple homosexual behavior, then it is in the list because it represents a forbidden form of sexual activity with kinfolk and other sexual actions that do not produce healthy children, according to the beliefs of the author. It is worth pointing out, then, that the prohibition against homosexual behavior in v. 22 follows after a prohibition to avoid having sex with a woman during her menstrual period in v. 19. It is interesting that opponents of homosexual behavior do not make an issue of this particular sexual behavior, which some modern people engage in for the sake of birth control. The Levitical sexual laws, in general, focus on maximalizing the reproductive capacities of the ancient Israelites, because as a people they faced a chronic population shortage. Levitical sexual laws condemn any sexual activity that wastes semen, or any form of sexuality that does not seek procreation.[28] Some authors believe that this renders the homosexual prohibition irrelevant. Furthermore, Levitical laws do not address the question of female homoerotic behavior because such activity did not ultimately affect procreation, nor did it challenge male domination.[29] If same-sex male relations are mentioned and same-sex female relations are not mentioned, perhaps the issue is procreation and loss of semen rather than homosexual relations.

In Leviticus 20 we have another list of prohibitions comparable to the previous list. We read of prohibitions against the Molech offering again (vv. 3–5), against wizards (v. 6), against cursing parents (v. 9), against adultery (v. 10), against sex with close relatives (vv. 11–12, 17, 19–21), against sex

27. Driver, *Critical and Exegetical Commentary on Deuteronomy*, 264; Horner, *Jonathan Loved David*, 73; Boswell, *Christianity, Social Tolerance, and Homosexuality*, 100–101; Nissinen, *Homoeroticism in the Biblical World*, 41–44; Gagnon, *Bible and Homosexual Practice*, 103, 130; Michaelson, *God vs. Gay?*, 61–66.

28. Scroggs, *New Testament and Homosexuality*, 13.

29. Nissinen, *Homoeroticism in the Biblical World*, 43.

with a woman and her daughter (v. 14), against sex with animals (vv. 15–16), against sex with a woman in her menstrual period (v. 18), and then we find the prohibition against homosexual behavior and some other unusual customs in the midst of these other prohibitions. In Lev 20:13 we read,

> If a man lies with a male as with a woman, both of them have committed an abomination; they shall be put to death, their blood is upon them.

The later Jewish tradition held that this law condemned pederasty because the first word is "man," which implies an adult, but the second word is "male," which permits the interpretation that the passive person is a youth or a child.[30] The earlier prohibition in Lev 18:22 would then apply to adults, even though the word used there is "male." However, the word for "male" clearly means a masculine adult person as the use of the word in Gen 1:27 indicates, for there it is paired with "female."[31] So we have to view that Jewish tradition with a critical eye and assume that adults are being described.

However, there is another perspective that I would propose. This passage is immediately followed by the prohibition against having sex with both a mother and her daughter at the same time (v. 14), which some have suspected of being a cultic activity. A comparable Hittite law (OH 191) from the early second millennium BCE permits such a sexual pairing if the two women are in separate parts of the country, but one cannot have sex together with them in the same location.[32] I find it unusual that this activity is accepted in one instance and rejected in the other. I suspect that having sex with the two women at the same time might imply some ritualistic behavior. Hittite laws often were concerned with purity, and they forbade activities that attempted to be divinatory or engage in inappropriate cultic behavior. If the Hittite law accepts such a sexual pairing when the women are separate but rejects such a sexual pairing when the women are together, perhaps the latter instance may actually allude to such cultic practice. Perhaps our biblical prohibition might also condemn some comparable cultic or divinatory behavior.

The following prohibition then condemns sex with animals for men (v. 15) and sex with animals for women (v. 16), which again may be cultic activity. As in Leviticus 18, so here the idea of women having sex with animals

30. Scroggs, *New Testament and Homosexuality*, 72, 78–79.

31. DeYoung, *Homosexuality*, 52; Wold, *Out of Order*, 102–104.

32. Roth, *Law Collections*, 236.

on an everyday basis out on the farm seems very unusual; more likely this passage alludes to a specific ritual in the cult. If someone responds that we have no evidence of such a custom, my response is that there are many things that we do not know about in the ancient world. As it does in the list from Leviticus 18, so here the prohibition against homosexuality occurs with two other prohibitions that may condemn cultic religious behavior.[33] We should be very cautious about using these prohibitions in the modern debate about homosexual behavior.

Some scholars propose a different interpretation. William Stacy Johnson believes that these various sexual commands are directed to the leaders or fathers of extended-family households with the purpose of prohibiting them from taking sexual advantage of people under their authority.[34]

Saul Olyan has provided a significant contribution to the study of both of these texts. He has demonstrated with a philological analysis that the behavior described in these laws is anal intercourse, as indicated by the phrase "lying down with a man as with a woman."[35] Jerome Walsh builds upon Olyan's argument and demonstrates that the law addresses the passive recipient in the sex act, for the person described in the text lies with another man as with a woman, which means that he performs the role of being the woman, or the passive recipient, for the other man. For Walsh, this means that a free adult Israelite male should not perform the role of being a passive recipient, the woman's role.[36] Most people read the text and assume the law is telling the active partner not to use another man as a woman, but Walsh believes that the text is saying that a man should not perform the woman's role. Walsh believes that this is the intended law in Lev 18:22, but that Lev 20:13 implicates both the active and the passive members in the relationship as worthy of death.[37] Though neither Olyan or Walsh suggests that cultic prostitution is involved, I believe that Walsh's argument may imply it. The passive partner condemned in Lev 18:22 is the cultic prostitute, and this might be the earlier version of the law. The later law in Lev 20:13 then condemns both the cultic prostitute and the devotee by decreeing that both should die. That the earlier law condemned only

33. McNeill, *Church and the Homosexual*, 57.

34. W. S. Johnson, *Time to Embrace*, 124–29; W. S. Johnson, "Empire and Order," 172.

35. Olyan, "'And with a Male You Shall Not Lie the Lying Down of a Woman,'" 179–206.

36. Walsh, "Leviticus 18:22 and 20:13," 205–7.

37. Ibid., 208.

the passive partner implies that something is especially blameworthy about this role, and not simply that it is demeaning for a free male to assume this role. I believe the especially blameworthy nature of this passive sexual role in Lev 18:22 is that it is a form of cultic prostitution, and that this is why the earlier form of the law condemned the passive recipient and not the person who undertook the active penetration. The later law, which condemns both partners to death, is a stern attempt to destroy this cultic religious activity altogether.

It is worth pointing out that the action described in both of these passages is called a *to'eba*, an "abomination." "Abomination" is a term that can apply to many actions, both criminal and cultic in the books of Leviticus and Deuteronomy (child sacrifice, sorcery, adultery, cross-dressing, murder, false oaths, oppressing the poor, charging interest). It was considered to be a very serious violation of divinely given guidelines, and we today would consider some of these to be serious crimes.[38] But "abomination" is typically used to describe those actions that bring impurity upon Israelites and destroy the identity of the Israelite as a chosen member of God's people. Though Christians may appropriate some of the moral guidelines of the book of Leviticus, we do not use all the purity guidelines, which were designed to make Israel an exclusive people. This creates a debate as to whether the homosexuality guidelines in Leviticus are purity guidelines that are no longer relevant for us.[39] That this activity in Leviticus 18 is called an abomination is irrelevant, even though so many authors spend much verbiage on the issue (too much, in fact), because the real question is what the text really condemns, whether it is all homosexual behavior or cultic homosexual behavior. If cultic homosexual behavior is condemned, then we should not use this passage in the modern debates about homosexuality.

Cultic Prostitutes

As a final point in regard to Old Testament texts, appeals have been made to a number of passages because the texts appear to condemn the presence of homosexual male priests in the temple of Jerusalem. These are Deut 23:17–18; 1 Kgs 14:24; 15:12; 22:46; 2 Kgs 23:7. Deuteronomy 23:17–18 declares that neither men nor women of Israel can be "temple prostitutes," and

---

38. Wold, *Out of Order*, 110–14, 121–36, sees the laws in Leviticus 18 forbidding the transgression of kinship, gender, and species lines; DeYoung, *Homosexuality*, 65–68.

39. Via and Gagnon, *Homosexuality and the Bible*, 5–11.

the fee or the wages of prostitutes may not be used in payment for a vow. First Kings 14:24 refers to "male temple prostitutes" in the land of Judah. First Kings 15:12 states that King Asa of Judah "put away the male temple prostitutes" from Judah. First Kings 22:46 tells us that King Jehoshaphat of Judah "exterminated" the remnant of "male temple prostitutes" that his father, Asa, did not remove. Finally, 2 Kgs 23:7 says that Josiah, king of Judah, "broke down the houses of the male temple prostitutes." First of all, it should be noted that a number of scholars suspect that "temple prostitutes" may be an incorrect translation for the Hebrew word, *qedeshim*. The word may really denote simple priests devoted to some particular deity in the worship cult, and perhaps their offensive identity is due to the fact that they are devoted to a deity other than Yahweh. Some scholars suggest that we have no real solid evidence that such male prostitutes existed in either Mesopotamia or Israel. These scholars suggest that rather we do have evidence that the accusation of male prostitution was a rhetorical insult hurled at one's perceived opponents.[40] Other scholars, including myself, believe that there actually were temple prostitutes. James DeYoung and Robert Gagnon provide excellent arguments that they are male prostitutes, which we need not rehearse here.[41] Whatever these individuals are, they are clearly cultic prostitutes, and their behavior is condemned because they are cultic prostitutes, not homosexuals in general.[42] Female temple prostitutes dedicated to the goddess Asherah are also condemned, and no one concludes from this that heterosexuality is being condemned. Conservative critics often overlook that point, and that is a very significant point. The sin is prostitution, not sexual identity, and the sin of prostitution is made abhorrent in the mind of the biblical author because it is done as a cultic activity, a form of worship, be it to Yahweh or a foreign deity.

It is worth responding to Robert Gagnon's extremely detailed work at this point. His writings are cited by conservative Protestant denominations to justify their condemnation of homosexuality. In his thorough evaluation of the homosexual texts in the Old Testament, he concludes that the cultural and intellectual assumptions behind those passages, especially the Levitical laws, is one which avers that all male homosexual activity is evil.

40. Oden, *Bible without Theology*, 131–53; Bird, "End of the Male Cult Prostitute," 37–80; and Bird, "Bible in Christian Ethical Deliberation concerning Homosexuality," 146–61, 170–73.

41. DeYoung, *Homosexuality*, 40–43; Gagnon, *Bible and Homosexual Practice*, 100–110.

42. Scroggs, *New Testament and Homosexuality*, 71.

The condemnation of cultic male homosexuality is thus the condemnation of all homosexuality.[43] Gagnon probably is correct about the cultural assumptions of that age and maybe even about the attitudes of the biblical authors. However, we theologize from of the texts, not from the cultural assumptions of the age or from something the biblical authors may have thought but did not write down. In the Old Testament there are laws that seek to obtain rights for slaves and women, but the cultural assumptions of the age would denigrate the value of slaves and women. We see where the texts lead us, not where the cultural assumptions of the authors stood. Biblical texts often lead us beyond the values of the age in which they were written. That is obvious with passages concerning women and slaves. The homosexual texts are few in number, so it is not so obvious that we should ignore the greater cultural assumptions of the age. The homosexual texts, and the laws in particular, do not lead us anywhere; they simply prohibit certain forms of activity. But the bottom line is that we theologize from the texts, not from our scholarly reconstruction of the cultural values of the authors. The texts appear to condemn rape and cultic prostitution, not generic homosexuality; we should not therefore conclude all homosexual behavior is condemned.[44]

Thus, we might conclude that the passages in the Old Testament that speak of same-sex activity generally refer to rape or cultic prostitution. To use them to condemn modern forms of homoerotic love is inappropriate. Critics of homosexual behavior, however, might respond that it is more important to see what the New Testament passages about homosexuality say. We thus turn to those passages in the next chapter.

43. Gagnon, *Bible and Homosexual Practice*, 43–157, esp. 130–31.

44. Stiebert, and Walsh, "Does the Hebrew Bible Have Anything to Say about Homosexuality?," 119–52.

10

New Testament Passages
Used to Condemn Homosexuality

Mission of Jesus

FOR CHRISTIANS THE NEW Testament becomes the significant portion of the Bible on the issue of homosexuality, for herein we find the specific words of Paul in particular, who appears to condemn homosexual behavior. But a closer look at these texts will provide us with different perspectives.

When we first turn to the New Testament an important observation to make is that the Jesus tradition provides no negative reference to homosexual behavior, even though the sayings address so many ethical aspects of life. Though commentators point that out, sometimes they direct our attention to two passages that might have a subtle allusion to homosexual behavior without any judgmental nuance. The reference in Matt 19:12 to those in the kingdom of God who are "eunuchs from birth" may describe people of homosexual orientation, and the allusion is somewhat positive in affirming their avoidance of marriage. When Jesus heals the Roman centurion's servant (Matt 4:5–13; Luke 7:1–10), the servant is described as a "young boy," which may imply that the servant was the boy lover of the Roman soldier. Jesus's healing of that boy could be seen as acceptance, much as Jesus also accepted sinners, tax collectors, and publicans. Of course, Jesus also called upon people in these categories to change their behavior.[1]

---

1. Michaelson, *God vs. Gay?*, 73–77.

However, most commentators do not believe that the Roman soldier's boy is his lover.[2] Use of these two passages in the debate over homosexuality is highly speculative.

New Testament Vice Lists

In the New Testament two "vice lists" contain words that supposedly mean "homosexual." Vice lists and virtue lists are rhetorical devices used by New Testament authors to give moral advice to Christians by characterizing the bad behavior of unbelievers or the vices that Christian converts have left behind, or the vices that sometimes Christians still might have, or the virtues to which Christians should aspire.[3] Vice lists in particular are sometimes an interesting mix of really horrid activities, such as murder and slave trading, and the everyday vices most people have, such as greed, envy, and gossip. I suspect that many of the New Testament vice lists serve the purpose of condemning the everyday, common vices by including them in lists with very sinful activities. The horrid vices would then be a foil for the author to really imply that Christians should seek to overcome greed, gossip, and envy.

Thus, in Paul's letters, for example, Rom 1:29–30 lists the following vices: wickedness, evil, covetousness, malice, *envy*,[4] murder, strife, deceit, craftiness, *gossip*, slander, hatred of God, insolence, *haughtiness*, *boasting*, inventing evil, rebelliousness toward parents, foolishness, faithlessness, heartlessness, and ruthlessness. Rom 13:13 lists reveling, drunkenness, debauchery, licentiousness, quarreling, and *jealousy*; Gal 5:19–21 lists fornication, impurity, licentiousness, idolatry, sorcery, enmities, strife, *jealousy*, *anger*, quarrels, dissensions, factions, *envy*, drunkenness, and carousing. First Corinthians 5:10 lists the following vicious people: the *greedy*, robbers, and idolaters; and 1 Cor 5:11 lists the sexually immoral, the *greedy*, the idolater, the reviler, the drunkard, and the robber. In other New Testament literature, Mark 7:21–22 lists fornication, theft, murder, adultery, avarice, wickedness, deceit, licentiousness, *envy*, *slander*, *pride*, and folly; and Rev 21:8 lists the following types of people: the cowardly, the faithless, the polluted, murderers, fornicators, sorcerers, idolaters, and *liars*. In regard to the

2. Loader, *Sexuality in the New Testament*, 33.

3. J. H. Elliott, "No Kingdom of God for Softies?," 21–23; Lopez, "Does the Vice List in 1 Corinthians 6:9–10 Describe Believers or Unbelievers?," 59–73.

4. The italicized words in this list and in following lists potentially describe everyone.

two lists under consideration for their possible mention of homosexuality, 1 Cor 6:9–10 lists fornicators, idolaters, adulterers, male prostitutes, sodomites, thieves, the *greedy*, drunkards, revilers, and robbers; and 1 Tim 1:9–10 lists the following kinds of people: lawless, disobedient, godless, *sinful*, unholy, and profane. The same list in 1 Timothy has murderers of father or mother, murderers (in general), fornicators, sodomites, slave traders, *liars*, and perjurers. Words like *envious, haughty, gossipy, boastful, jealous, angry, greedy, sinful, slanderous, prideful*, and *lying* describe everyone. A vice list can sometimes use extreme examples of evil behavior to condemn the common sinful activities of everyone in order to declare that all sin is significant and requires repentance, forgiveness, and commitment to good behavior. Some vice lists may be designed to really condemn the common vices we all share. The two lists that include homosexual behavior appear to belong to this category. I believe it is theologically inappropriate to rely heavily for an important moral debate on passages that list single words for rhetorical effect.

The words that supposedly mean "homosexual" in these lists may actually mean something else, and this makes the use of these texts in the homosexual debate among Christians today very tenuous. The two passages in question are 1 Cor 6:9–10 and 1 Tim 1:10. The text in 1 Cor 6:9–10 reads as follows,

> 9Do you not know that wrongdoers will not inherit the kingdom of God? Do not be deceived! Fornicators, idolaters, adulterers, male prostitutes, sodomites, 10thieves, the greedy, drunkards, revilers, robbers—none of these will inherit the kingdom of God.

The first thing to notice is the unevenness of the list. As noted above, the vice of greed is thrown in with some serious activities to get the audience to pay attention to their own greed, and the other serious vices are listed for effect.

The two Greek words that have been translated as "male prostitutes" and "sodomites" in the New Revised Standard Version have been understood in the past to refer to homosexuals in general. But this translation seeks to indicate that the words may have a more specialized meaning and do not refer to all homosexual behavior.

Past English translations have produced a range of meanings. The old King James Version (1611) reads, "nor effeminate, nor abusers of themselves with mankind"; the New American Standard Bible (1960) reads, "nor effeminate, nor homosexuals"; the Jerusalem Bible (1966) reads, "catamites, sodomites"; the New International Version (1973) reads, "nor homosexuals, nor sodomites"; the New King James Version (1982) reads, "nor homosexuals, nor sodomites"; the New Jerusalem Bible (1985) reads, "the self-indulgent, sodomites"; and the New American Bible (1986) reads, "nor boy prostitutes" for the first word. The last two English translations, like the New Revised Standard Version, acknowledge that the text may not be describing generic homosexuality.

The word for "male prostitute" in Greek is *malakoi*, a word that literally means "soft person" or "passive one." It may refer to the receptive, penetrated partner in sexual relations between men. Literally the biblical word simply means "soft," and it is often used with that simple meaning, as in "soft" clothing (Matt 11:8; Luke 7:25). In some literature of the Graeco-Roman era it refers to those who wore makeup, dressed as women, shaved their bodies, and indeed took a passive role in sex. The word refers to men and boys who allowed themselves to be used sexually as the passive partner in a homosexual relationship, usually for money, hence the translation of "male prostitute." It could also mean a slave who is used by his master as the passive recipient in a sexual relationship. However, in some Greek literature *malakoi* can mean general moral laxity, licentiousness, or wanton behavior, with no explicit reference to homosexual acts.[5] In the most general terms, *malakoi* means "softness" (as in soft clothing, rich food, a gentle breeze, laziness, weakness, moral laxity); it can describe a person who was effeminate, physically soft, or a sissy; it can denote someone who does not appreciate education or warfare, or someone who has too much sex with women (how ironic!).[6] Perhaps the word was used as slang to describe an effeminate person, such as a boy prostitute or a boy slave who would offer his services to clients, perhaps older men.[7] In this passage *malakoi* might specify a young teen-age boy used for sexual purposes who might be "kept" by an older man in some form of servitude.[8] Or perhaps, at the other end

5. Boswell, *Christianity, Social Tolerance, and Homosexuality*, 106–7, 339–41; Fee, *First Epistle to the Corinthians*, 243–44; McNeill, *Church and the Homosexual*, 52; J. H. Elliott, "No Kingdom of God for Softies?," 23–28, provides the most detailed analysis; Michaelson, *God vs. Gay?*, 88.

6. Martin, "*Arsenokoites* and *Malakos*," 124–26; Via and Gagnon, *Homosexuality and the Bible*, 11–12; J. H. Elliott, "No Kingdom of God for Softies?," 23–28.

7. Scroggs, *New Testament and Homosexuality*, 42, 62–65, 106–9; Snyder, *First Corinthians*, 73; Murphy-O'Connor, *1 Corinthians*, 49; J. H. Elliott, "No Kingdom of God for Softies?," 27; W. S. Johnson, "Empire and Order," 167.

8. Fee, *First Epistle to the Corinthians*, 243–44; Waetjen, "Same-Sex Sexual Relations

of the spectrum, in this passage *malakoi* simply may mean, "debauched individual."[9] Ultimately, none of these possibilities describe a sexual relationships in which love is present.

The word for "sodomites" is the Greek word *arsenokoitai*, which literally means "men who go to bed." This word does not occur prior to Paul in Greek literature; after Paul Christian authors occasionally use the term to describe general sexual activity.[10] John Boswell surveyed Christian authors and observes that this word is hardly ever used to describe homosexual behavior.[11] In Rom 13:13 Paul uses the term *koitai* by itself to simply mean excessive sexual activity, so we might wish to be a little cautious in attributing specific meanings to the mind of Paul in regard to the word *arsenokoitai*.[12]

If we consider the word by itself, we may note that the two words *arseno* ("man") and *koiten* ("intercourse") occur as separate words in the commands of Lev 18:22 and 20:13 in the Greek translation of the Old Testament, the Septuagint. We might assume that Judeans, or perhaps even Paul, created the Greek word *arsenokoitai*, inspired by the Greek text of Lev 18:22 and 20:13.[13] However, some scholars reject this idea.[14] Paul may have coined the term, but its quick use in a list of vices implies that he believed his audience was familiar with it, so the term probably arose in Greek-speaking Judean circles.[15]

Since the word means the active male partner in the text of Lev 18:22, according to Jewish interpretation, we could assume that the word has the same meaning for Paul. If *arsenokoitai* refers to the active partners in sexual relationships (which "sodomite" historically did), then it may be a word used to describe older men who have sex with young boys.[16] It could

in Antiquity," 109–10; Richie, "Argument against the Use of the Word 'Homosexual.'"

9. McNeil, *Church and the Homosexual*, 56.

10. Ibid., 52–53; Scroggs, *New Testament and Homosexuality*, 107; Gagnon, *Bible and Homosexual Practice*, 314.

11. Boswell, *Christianity, Social Tolerance, and Christianity*, 342–50.

12. McNeill, *Church and the Homosexual*, 53; Nissinen, *Homoeroticism in the Biblical World*, 114–16.

13. Wright, "Homosexuals or Prostitutes?," 125–53; Scroggs, *New Testament and Homosexuality*, 83, 107–8; Waetjen, "Same-Sex Sexual Relations in Antiquity," 109–10; Wold, *Out of Order*, 189–94; DeYoung, *Homosexuality*, 195–99; Gagnon, *Bible and Homosexual Practice*, 315; Via and Gagnon, *Homosexuality and the Bible*, 12–13.

14. Nissinen, *Homoeroticism in the Biblical World*, 116.

15. Frederickson, "Natural and Unnatural Use in Romans 1:24–27," 220.

16. McNeill, *Church and the Homosexual*, 52; Scroggs, *New Testament and*

additionally mean a sexually rapacious individual.[17] Dale Martin argues cogently that in some second-century-CE Christian texts[18] the word denotes someone who victimizes a poor person (such as a slave or a young boy) in a sexual fashion.[19] In our understanding, this word would mean "pederast" regardless of who is correct in the discussion.

We sense that the young boy in the Graeco–Roman world, either a free male attached to an older male, or a young slave boy being sexually abused by his master, is characterized by the term *malakoi*. Other scholars, however, believe the word refers to men who were freed slaves, who now offered their bodies for money as male prostitutes rather than being forced to submit to sex, as happened when they formerly were slaves, so that the word would mean "male prostitutes."[20] Whichever definition we use, it certainly would not describe a person in a loving relationship with another free, adult male.

When we put both words together, *arsenokoitai* and *malakoi*, we have the two words that describe the homosexual relationships that would have been observed most frequently by Paul. These were the master, old man, abusive sexual partner, or pederast on the one hand, and the slave, young boy, or victim on the other hand. That is why Paul pairs them in this sentence; they may be euphemisms for the active and the passive participants in a sexual relationship.[21] Ultimately, I believe both words describe abusive sexual relationships, not loving relationships.

The other vice list, which critics of homosexuality like to quote, is located in 1 Tim 1:9–10, and it reads as follows,

> 9This means understanding that the law is laid down not for the
> innocent but for the lawless and disobedient, for the godless and

Homosexuality, 72, 107–9; Siker, "Homosexuality," 883; Richie, "Argument against the Use of the Word 'Homosexual'" 723–29.

17. Michaelson, *God vs. Gay?*, 92.

18. See *Sibylline Oracle*, 2.70–77 and *Acts of John*, section 36, where the term is listed with forms of economic oppression and not sexuality.

19. Martin, "*Arsenokoites* and *Malakos*," 120–23.

20. Boswell, *Christianity, Social Tolerance, and Homosexuality*, 107, 341–44; W. S. Johnson, "Empire and Order," 167.

21. Barrett, *A Commentary on the First Epistle to the Corinthians*, 140; Horner, *Sex in the Bible*, 89–90; Conzelmann, *1 Corinthians*, 108; Talbert, *Reading Corinthians*, 23; J. H. Elliott, "No Kingdom of God for Softies?," 32, 34, especially pairs them; Siker, "Homosexuality," 883; Gagnon, *Bible and Homosexual Practice*, 316; Pizzuto, "'God Has Made It Plain to Them,'" 167; Loader, *Sexuality in the New Testament*, 30–32.

sinful, for the unholy and profane for those who kill their father or
mother, for murderers, ¹⁰fornicators, sodomites, slave traders, liars, perjurers, and whatever else is contrary to the sound teaching.

Notice again, the word "liars," a common sin, is found in the list to catch the
attention of the listener or the reader of this text. The word used in this passage, so often quoted to condemn homosexuality, is "sodomites." The Greek
word is once more *arsenokoitai*, a word that might mean "pederast." So,
again, this vice probably does not describe general homosexual behavior.
The word used prior to *arsenokoitai* is "fornicators," a word commonly used
in the Greek world for prostitutes. In this particular text, there might be a
connection in that the *arsenokoitai* are the people who use the prostitutes
for sexual pleasures. The word that follows both of these words is "slave
traders," and "slave traders" are the people who kidnap and sell young boys
as "prostitutes" to the *arsenokoitai*. Perhaps there is a connection between
all three words to describe the sexual phenomena of the Graeco-Roman
world.²² Homosexual love between two free, adult males or females may
not be described here either.

The New Revised Standard Version translates these two words in both
passages as "male prostitutes" and "sodomites" respectively, giving them a
specialized meaning. The New King James Version and the New American
Bible translate these words likewise. However, the old King James Version
and the New International Version translate the words as "homosexuals,"
so that readers of those translations will quote their bibles emphatically to
condemn homosexuality.

It is also worth pointing out that the ancient world did not have our
understanding of *homosexual* and *heterosexual*. In fact, the term *homosexual* originated only in the nineteenth century. Our understanding of
homosexual would be somewhat related to the ancient understanding of the
passive male partner in a sexual relationship with another male, and great
disdain was shown for such a person. The ancient understanding of the
active partner in a male same-sex relationship would be more equivalent to
our definition of *heterosexual*.²³ Graeco-Romans believed that a powerful
sexual male would have sex with both men and women, and animals too,
if the situation arose. Thus, both in the Assyrian armies of the eighth and
seventh centuries BCE and in the Roman armies of the New Testament
era, the soldiers would routinely rape male prisoners from armies they had

22. Scroggs, *New Testament and Homosexuality*, 119–20.

23. Carden, "Homophobia and Rape in Sodom and Gibeah," 83–96.

defeated in battle. This was a political statement of victory and total power over the defeated enemy.[24] These armies did not recruit only gay men. This was power rape, and it did not define a soldier as homosexual in our sense of the word. The ancient equivalent definitions of *homosexual* and *heterosexual*, if they even had anything like these notions, were altogether different from our own. This difference between first-century notions and our contemporary notions makes our use of these New Testament passages inappropriate. The New Testament is condemning the violent use of sex to degrade and humiliate people, not sexual inclinations.

Romans 1

A conservative critic of homosexual behavior once said to me, "If all those other passages can be shown to be irrelevant to the homosexual debate, at least I have one certain biblical text that clearly condemns homosexuality." He, of course, was referring to Rom 1:26–27. I will reproduce Rom 1:22–27, for I believe we need the entire context to see what Paul is really saying. Rom 1:22–27 reads,

> [22]Claiming to be wise, they became fools; [23]and they exchanged the glory of the immortal God for images resembling a moral human being or birds or four-footed animals or reptiles.
>
> [24]Therefore God gave them up in the lusts of their hearts to impurity, to the degrading of their bodies among themselves, [25]because they exchanged the truth about God for a lie and worshiped and served the creature rather than the Creator, who is blessed forever! Amen.
>
> [26]For this reason God gave them up to degrading passions. Their women exchanged natural intercourse for unnatural, [27]and in the same way also the men, giving up natural intercourse with women, were consumed with passion for one another. Men committed shameless acts with men and received in their own persons the due penalty for their error.

The opponent of homosexuality quotes the last two verses and declares that here we have a clear condemnation of both male and female homosexuality. I would respond by saying we must observe how v. 26 begins. The words are "for this reason." That initial statement means that the homosexual behavior is the result of the idolatry described in the previous verses. In other

---

24. W. S. Johnson, "Empire and Order," 163.

words, the idolatry and the homosexual behavior go together and describe the same people. Sophisticated critics of homosexual behavior do indeed observe this also. They observe that Paul believed idolatry in general to be the root sin that could lead to sexual perversions, including homosexuality, and their discussion ends there. But the point I wish to make is that Paul is not speaking about all homosexuals; he is speaking about a specific group of homosexuals who engage in a particular form of idolatrous worship, not just general idolatry.

The idolatry that is described is the theriomorphic representation of God or the gods. *Theriomorphic* means "representing something in the form of an animal." Paul says that this group of people portrays God or their gods as animals: as birds, four-footed animals, or reptiles in v. 23. Paul repeats the notion again in v. 25 when he says that they worship the creature. Then in v. 26 Paul says that because of this worship activity these people are given over to homoerotic behavior. In particular, he notes that the men "give up" natural heterosexual love for homosexual love. Who is Paul describing?

The only group of people in the Mediterranean area who portrayed their gods as animals were the Egyptians. In Rome the significant imported Egyptian cult was the worship of the goddess Isis. Isis was portrayed as a human female, but her son Horus was portrayed as a falcon. Other accompanying Egyptian deities were portrayed as an ibis (Thoth), a cow (Hathor sometimes), a lioness (Tefnut), a ram (Khnum), a hippopotamus (Tawaret and Seth sometimes), a cat (Bastet), a jackal or dog (Anubis), a crocodile (Sobek), a beetle (Khepri), and so forth. Isis was called the "queen of heaven," and she was portrayed as a gracious mother to Horus and a deity who loved humanity. In this list we might notice Paul's references to a human figure (Isis), a bird (Horus), and a four-footed animal (Hathor), three deities most popular in the Isis cult.

In the public and very flamboyant cultic processions at Rome, Isis priests carried images of animal-faced gods and other unusual objects, including a golden urn with sacred water from the Nile. Lucius Apuleius, in his classical work, *The Golden Ass*, observed Anubis portrayed as a dog and another deity (probably Hathor) in the image of a cow in a colorful Isis parade.[25]

Devotees in these parades frequently stopped at altars along the roads with their sumptuous and magnificent displays, thus making quite

25. Apuleius, *Golden Ass*, 556–57.

an impression on common Romans.[26] Lucius Apuleius provides at length a vivid description of his supernatural vision of Isis and the actual spectacular Isis parade he witnessed.[27] The parade would feature (1) masked persons; (2) women in white gowns; (3) *stolistes* waving the garments of the goddess Isis; (4) *dadophori* with torches; (5) *hymnodes*, singers with flutes and brass instruments; (6) initiates; and (7) priests with shaven heads and linen robes, who carried images of animal-faced gods and strange symbols, such as the urn with Nile water.[28] The average Roman would have been familiar with the theriomorphic imagery for the gods to which Paul alludes, and Paul's Roman audience would immediately have thought of them when he alludes to animals in his initial statements. Romans were "fascinated by the languishing songs and intoxicating melodies" sung by the singers and overall by the "pomp of their festivities and the magnificence of their processions."[29]

I must ask myself what would Paul's Roman audience have heard in their imagination as this letter was read publicly to them? As Romans, the animal references would have made them think of the Isis cult, and the following language by Paul would continue to be joined to the Isis cult in their minds as they connected it to the Isis priestesses and priests. I will not ask, what did Paul think of homosexuality? I will ask, what did his audience hear when he wrote what he did? They would have thought of the Isis cult. Furthermore, I am sure that Paul intended for them to think of the Isis cult.

Commentators generally pay little attention to Paul's references to animals. Bernadette Brooten notes that Paul's allusions most likely were inspired by the Egyptian deities. She also draws a parallel between the author of the Wisdom of Solomon (15:18–19) and the Judean philosopher Judaeus Philo (*On the Decalogue* 76–80), who both condemned the use of animals as the images for God.[30] Brooten, however, does not draw the conclusion that Paul may have been describing in particular the Isis cult in Rome. Both Philo and the author of Wisdom of Solomon lived in Egypt and so were quite familiar with theriomorphic images. The text in Wis 15:18 says that the foolish "worship even the most hated animals, which are worse than all others." Paul might have shared the invective of Wisdom of Solomon and

26. Cumont, *Oriental Religions in Roman Paganism*, 97.

27. Apuleius, *Golden Ass*, 543–67.

28. Cumont, *Oriental Religions in Roman Paganism*, 97.

29. Ibid., 29.

30. Brooten, *Love between Women*, 231–32.

Philo on this matter, for he was apparently familiar at least with the former work, as commentators have noted in the past.

In the Isis cult, male priests had to abstain from sexual activity during ceremonies and festivals, and there were virgin priestesses. Lucius Apuleius in his ancient literary work implied that the male priests permanently practiced chastity, and for him that was too great a burden to bear, so he could not become an Isis priest after his dramatic conversion.[31] Perpetual sexual abstinence by men would not have been viewed favorably in the moral climate of Rome, where so much emphasis was placed upon the family. Paul's reference in Rom 1:27 to men who give up their sexuality might describe sexually abstinent priests (who then presumably can love only each other, according to the popular gossip of Romans), and Paul's snide comment in Rom 1:26 about the women loving each other might be a reference to the priestesses, who were supposed to be virgins.

Notice, however, that Paul does not say that the women directly loved other women; we assume that. What he says is that women gave up natural love for unnatural love, which could mean unusual sexual behavior with men or some other form of sexual behavior that does not procreate. We do not know for sure what he means. Some critical scholars have made a good argument that Paul is condemning noncoital heterosexual activity by these women.[32] He may be condemning sexual activity between the priestesses and the male priests that might have involved use of an artificial phallus by the female on the male, for that is what Clement of Alexandria seems to be condemning around 200 CE when he speaks of these cults.[33]

Significantly, lesbians are mentioned nowhere else in the Bible, presumably because female same-sex interactions did not offend. They did not involve penetration; did not humiliate a man—whether a slave, prisoner of war, or a youth; and did not ultimately affect procreation. Thus, female same-sex relationships did not affect male pride. Why does Paul even mention it here? Why does he mention it before male homoerotic behavior? I believe Paul is thinking of mystery-cult priestesses, and in particular of the priestesses of Isis, who were very visible in Rome during their Isis celebrations. A critique of the Isis cult would begin with them. The fact that Paul mentions women before men in Rom 1:22–27 is important, I believe. Some

31. Apuleius, *Golden Ass*, 570–71.

32. Miller, "Practices of Romans 1:26," 1–11; Debel, "Admonition on Sexual Affairs," 39–64.

33. Townsley, "Paul, the Goddess Religions, and Queer Sects," 725–26.

scholars might counter my argument by pointing out that traditional Roman piety particularly despised female homoeroticism, and Paul may be speaking to female homosexuality in general.[34] But this traditional Roman attitude might have further encouraged Paul to imply that Isis priestesses were engaging in behavior that offended traditional Roman piety.

Romans in general did not like the cult of Isis. Its ethics often encouraged greater sexual freedom among devotees (even though abstinence for priests during festivals was advocated), and this sexual license offended many Romans. It was said that young men went to Isis temples to have sexual adventures.[35] Both Caesars Augustus and Tiberius expelled the Egyptian gods from Rome on the charge of immorality and opposition to the social order because the new religion stressed the inner spiritual life over public interests.[36] Under Caesar Tiberius (15–37 CE) in particular the Isis priests in Rome were arrested and crucified, the temple of Isis was dismantled, and followers were expelled from the city in 19 CE.[37] Already in the early years of its presence in Rome, the Roman senate ordered Serapis (the Greek version of Osiris) and Isis shrines destroyed in 59, 58, 53, and 48 BCE due to corrupting influences engendered by the religion, loose morality, and the emotional piety connected to the cult. Caligula (37–41 CE) gave the Isis movement a protected status, however, and the movement began to rebound in the next generation.[38] During the revival of the Isis cult, Paul went to Rome. Roman women in particular were attracted to the emotional aspects of the Isis cult, and to an equal degree, the Cybele cult as well.[39]

Paul's letter to the Romans was written at a time when the Isis cult was growing in popularity despite the hostility of many Romans. Thus, if Paul wrote this letter to the Romans, a group of folk he had not yet visited, it would have been politic for him to condemn something as a form of immoral behavior that he knew most Romans did not like in the first place. That would be wise rhetoric on his part. Paul himself might have despised the Isis cult for its similarity to Christianity, for it spoke of a god, Osiris or Serapis, who died and was yet alive; it spoke of the forgiveness of sins provided by Isis; it spoke of the compassionate love of Isis and of devotees who

34. Jewett, "Social Context and Implications," 231–32.

35. Cumont, *Oriental Religions in Roman Paganism*, 91.

36. Ibid., 39.

37. Angus, *Mystery-Religions and Christianity*, 38; Danker, "Isis," 3:95.

38. Cumont, *Oriental Religions in Roman Paganism*, 81.

39. Ibid., 44.

would experience immortality with Osiris in the afterlife. Thus, I believe that Paul is not condemning homosexuality in general. He is condemning the Isis cult. I know that I cannot convince many scholars with this argument, but I offer it as a thought-provoking suggestion.

Some scholars suggest that in Romans 1 Paul may be loosely condemning a wide range of goddess cults of the ancient Mediterranean world, all of which had followers in Rome. Goddesses such as Cybele from Asia Minor (with dramatically castrated priests who carried their testicles in their hands), Diana from Ephesus, Aphrodite (from Greece) and Venus (from Rome) had eunuch priests and virgin priestesses as votaries in their service. Romans, in general, were critical of these cults.

The existence of such temple servants can be found in Sumerian texts from the third millennium BCE. These texts describe *gala* priests and *assinu* priests who engaged in anal sex with worshipers who came to the temples. The word *assinu* combines the Sumerian symbols for dog and woman, which probably gave rise to the slang in both Hebrew and Greek that called a male prostitute a "dog." The *assinu* priest may have been castrated. The male prostitute might have assumed the posture of a dog in the sexual act, hence the insulting nickname in the ancient world and in the Bible.

In Greece the priests were called *galli* priests, and, in particular, the cult of Cybele in Turkey had such priests. Apuleius refers to such eunuch priests and attributes homoerotic desires and behavior to them.[40] Apuleius makes fun of them by portraying them in one of his narratives as oversexed and desirous of sex with a young boy but disappointed when they discover that their partner for sex is a donkey.[41] Cybele was assimilated to Atargatis, a mother goddess in Syria, who was virtually identical to Ishtar, so there is continuity in all these traditions with the various female deities.[42]

The *galli* priests were known for their extreme behavior. They flagellated themselves, and the neophytes would use a sharp stone to castrate themselves.[43] Self-castration would occur in a state of ecstasy, probably aided by the influence of drugs. (It would have to be!) These *galli* priests believed that their self-castration enabled them to become more like their gods, an idea that particularly would have horrified Paul. His references in Rom 1:27 to men giving up desire for women might allude to the self-

40. Townsley, "Paul, the Goddess Religions, and Queer Sects," 724–25.

41. Apuleius, *Golden Ass*, 387–89.

42. Nissinen, *Homoeroticism in the Biblical World*, 31–32.

43. Cumont, *Oriental Religions in Roman Paganism*, 56–67.

castration practiced in some cults, such as in those of Attis and Cybele. After self-castration the priests carried their recently severed testicles in their hands displaying them door-to-door in the community as a demonstration of piety. Since devotees of Attis and Cybele were found in Galatia, Paul might readily recall this folk from his mission work there. In Gal 5:12 he desires that his opponents from Jerusalem "castrate" themselves," and this might have been a sarcastic allusion to the Attis priests, which the Galatian audience would have appreciated. Perhaps Paul is throwing in a loose allusion to Attis priests in a freewheeling condemnation of the Isis cult in Romans 1, or perhaps Isis priests at times were castrated. Would this be why Apuleius chose not to become an Isis priest, even though he did not mention it? Perhaps Paul alludes to self-castration when he says they "received in their own persons the due penalty for their error" (Rom 1:27). Most commentators usually suggest that this simply refers to anal and penile damage that results from homosexual behavior.[44]

The cultic activity connected to Isis devotion as well as to other goddesses proliferated in the Mediterranean world between the fourth century BCE and the third century CE. Thus, Paul's diatribe in Rom 1:18–32 may be about such idolatrous religions in general, and vv. 26–27 attack the sex practices connected to worship. What Paul would find offensive about this cultic behavior, besides the obvious worship of other gods, is that the sexual behavior did not bring about procreation, and that is what makes it "unnatural."

Paul has a broad definition for "unnatural," for in Rom 4:18 he speaks of how God grafts the wild olive branch onto the domestic grapevine, describing this as "unnatural." So Paul's use of the word is not exclusively in sexual categories.[45] However, conservative commentators have analyzed in great detail how Paul uses the concept of "unnatural" and have observed that he very often uses it for serious moral offenses, including sexual activity.[46] These commentators then assume that Paul is describing homosexuality as "unnatural." However, Paul certainly would have viewed the activity of the Isis devotees in general to be most "unnatural," so his reference might not be exclusively to homosexual behavior. Paul's description of what is "unnatural" could include some bizarre female sexual activity. Jeramy Townsley also believes that Paul is condemning the sexual actions of the mystery reli-

44. Loader, *Sexuality in the New Testament*, 20.

45. McNeill, *The Church and the Homosexual*, 53.

46. Wold, *Out of Order*, 177–86; DeYoung, *Homosexuality*, 142–64.

gions in general with this concept, not any form of sexual orientation, for in Paul's age people did not think in terms of sexual orientations (heterosexual or homosexual); they thought in terms of actions.[47] Paul would have seen the activities in so many of these mystery cults as "unnatural." It has also been observed that Paul may have been guilty of a category mistake; he may have confused "unnatural" activities with what were really merely the "customs" of his age.[48] Ultimately, I believe too much energy is spent on trying to understand what Paul meant by "unnatural" in regard to the modern homosexuality debate, because the more important question is, what is he actually describing in Romans 1? If Paul is speaking of cultic sexuality, then this passage is irrelevant for the modern debate concerning the sinfulness of homosexual behavior. This is especially true if the allusion to the women is actually referring to "unnatural" heterosexual activity.

Robert Gagnon's comprehensive evaluation of this text demands a short response. He believes that Paul is speaking generally of all same-sex activity. One of his arguments suggests that in Romans 1 Paul subtly alludes to Gen 1:27, where heterosexual marriage is instituted. When Paul speaks of birds, four-footed animals and reptiles in Rom 1:23, the two Greek words that he uses for "birds" and reptiles" are the same words that the Greek Septuagint uses in Gen 1:26; and the words that he uses for "females" and "males" are the same words in the Greek translation of Gen 1:27,[49] which is a foundational text for marriage and heterosexual union. Gagnon believes that by alluding to Genesis 1 and its clear description of the heterosexual relationship between the man and the woman, Paul thereby condemns any homoerotic behavior. In response, I note that to say Paul was inspired by Genesis 1 is a good observation. I believe that Paul might have drawn upon the animal language of Genesis for two of the words in his invective against the Isis cult. I would respond to Gagnon that all three words used by Paul, "birds," "four-footed animals," and "reptiles," more directly correspond to animals revered as theriomorphic images of the Egyptian gods in the Isis cult, especially Horus and Hathor. The words for "male" and "female" used by Paul would be normal words used to describe people. That the language in Romans 1 is similar to Genesis 1 I do not doubt, but I believe the real correspondence is between this language and the cult of Isis in Rome.

47. Townsley, "Paul, the Goddess Religions, and Queer Sects," 707–28.

48. Phipps, "Paul on 'Unnatural' Sex," 128–31.

49. Gagnon, *Bible and Homosexual Practice*, 290–91; so also Loader, *Sexuality in the New Testament*, 27.

Gagnon mounts a convincing argument that Judeans in Paul's day would have condemned all forms of homosexuality; this is especially demonstrated in the very extensive writings of Philo and Josephus, and Gagnon firmly believes that Paul shared those convictions. Martti Nissinen also observes the same values in the writings of Philo, Josephus, and other Judean authors in this era.[50] As Gagnon reads Romans 1, he extrapolates Paul's condemnation of the particular activity described in this text to conclude that Paul used this language to condemn all same-sex activities.[51] Even if Gagnon is correct in understanding that Paul would condemn all homosexual behavior, as stated earlier, we theologize from the biblical texts, not from the reconstructed intellectual and religious values of the biblical culture or of an individual biblical author. Sometimes such scholarly speculation is helpful on particular issues, and it can inspire preachers in their sermonizing, but we cannot routinely theologize for significant church positions using our scholarly conclusions about the probable beliefs of biblical authors.

I creatively suggest what the thinking of biblical authors might have been in my biblical commentaries and writings frequently, but I would not wish for my views to be enshrined as official theology for any denomination. They are scholarly opinions, and scholarly opinions change over the years. Would we theologize from the general understandings of biblical authors about slavery, women, and war, or would we rather see what the texts in particular say about those issues? Often the biblical texts lead us to look beyond the mere cultural assumptions of the age when they were articulated. Would we ask Paul or extrapolate from his culturally conditioned beliefs what he felt about using medicine, flying in airplanes, or how the universe was constructed? Would we ask Paul his opinion about having sex with our wives in their nonfertile period? (Many Christians do that as a form of birth control.) I mention that last example because conservative critics often say that we can bracket Paul's scientific views as part of the learning of his age but that matters of sexuality have eternal value and should not be dismissed as culturally conditioned. But in reality, we do believe differently from the biblical authors on certain moral issues because of the great cultural chasm between us and their age. The church and individual denominations should craft official theology from the biblical

50. Nissinen, *Homoeroticism in the Biblical World*, 89–102.

51. Gagnon, *Bible and Homosexual Practice*, 159–83, 229–303; so also Smith, "Ancient Bisexuality," 223–56.

texts, not from our scholarly reconstructions of their thought. Of course, for many Christians, theology is also crafted based on natural knowledge, the reigning philosophical paradigm, human existential need, and inner spiritual insight. All the more should theologians be cautious about making biblical texts say more than they actually do!

Finally, there are other ways of interpreting these verses in Romans 1. Some scholars suggest that Paul is describing homosexual behavior outside the cult. Others suggest that Paul is describing the rich and powerful Romans of his age who engaged in degenerate sexual activity and forced slaves to do their sexual bidding. According to this view, what is being described is slave sex and sexual abuse of slaves and young children, and that abuse of people is what makes it so evil. Idolatry permits that kind of immoral behavior. Many of the Christians in Paul's Roman audience were probably male slaves forced into submissive sex by their masters as a statement of the superior status the master held. The Christian slaves would resonate strongly with Paul's angry language.[52] Others believe that Paul's audience would have immediately thought of pederasty when they heard these lines, because that was so common and so abusive.[53] It has also been suggested that Paul is describing homosexual behavior in this passage as an example of Gentile "uncleanness" but not necessarily of sin; in this view, homosexual behavior is an impurity resulting from idol worship.[54] (I do not find that argument too convincing.) It has been hypothesized that Paul condemns not so much homosexual behavior as the unbridled lust that occurs in such contexts.[55] Perhaps Paul simply modeled his discourse after the popular understanding of the Sodom story in his age in order to talk about Gentile sin in general.[56] (I find this argument rather odd, since he still is speaking of something that he finds offensive.) Many ideas have been suggested in regard to these passages.

The conservative who sees Rom 1:26–27 as a condemnation of homosexual behavior sometimes will maintain that Paul is really pointing out two different forms of immoral behavior, idolatry and homosexuality in

52. Furnish, *Moral Teaching of Paul*, 52–83; Scroggs, *New Testament and Homosexuality*, 115–18; Hultgren, "Being Faithful to the Scriptures," 315–25; Jewett, "Social Context and Implications," 238–40.

53. Miller, "Pederasty and Romans 1:27," 861–66.

54. Countryman, *Dirt, Greed, and Sex*, 104–23; Kalin, "Roman 1:26–27 and Homosexuality," 423–32.

55. Frederickson, "Natural and Unnatural Use in Romans 1:24–27," 177–222.

56. Esler, "Sodom Tradition in Romans 1:18–32," 4–16.

this chapter. I point adamantly, however, to the expression "for this reason" in v. 26, which connects the idolatry and the homosexuality by implying that the idolatry leads to the homosexual behavior. We must think in terms of the idolatry that Paul may be describing and connect it to the sexual activity he criticizes. Too often folks who quote Rom 1:26–27 simply speak of idolatry in general and move quickly to the sexual characterizations.

We need to pay attention to the theriomorphic imagery connected to the worship of other gods. If Paul is making a significant statement with his references to animals, then the Isis cult comes immediately to mind. Furthermore, Paul is correct in making the connection between the idolatry of animal imagery and the sexual activity. The Isis religion with its theriomorphic imagery, as well as the other goddess religions, indeed did mandate that sometimes male priests had to be castrated and that the priestesses had to be perpetually virgin. That Paul was referring to either the Isis religion or one of the other goddess cults is borne out by the testimony of the third-century-CE church father Hippolytus, who links the references in Rom 1:26–27 with castrated priests in these other religions, which he still observed in his own age.[57] My thesis is not unique; Hippolytus beat me to it eighteen centuries ago. Hippolytus (*Refutation of all Heresies*, book 5, chap 2) characterized the beliefs of a group of people known as the Naassenes, who combined Christianity with ideas from the cult of Attis and Cybele. According to Hippolytus, the Naassenes quoted Romans 1 to affirm their belief that the castrated Attis passes over into a new world where he becomes a "new creature, a new man," a hermaphrodite by virtue of his self-castration. Hippolytus believed that Paul's statements actually rejected their beliefs in particular, even though the Naassenes quoted the passage to support their views.[58]

In these verses of Romans 1 I believe that Paul's description of idolatry is very closely connected to the sexual practices he condemns. He is condemning the Isis cult and perhaps related mystery religions, not general homosexuality.

57. Townsley, "Paul, the Goddess Religions, and Queer Sects," 723.

58. Hippolytus, *Refutation of All Heresies*, bk. 5, in Roberts and Donaldson, *Ante-Nicene Fathers*, 5:49.

Conclusion

In conclusion, I believe that there is no passage in the biblical text that truly condemns a loving relationship between two free adults who truly love each other. This, of course, does not settle the debate, for there still remain the views found in the history of the Christian tradition, the official pronouncements of church bodies, and the scientific discussion of gender identity. I cannot discuss those issues. But I would maintain that the biblical texts should not be called forth in the condemnation of gay and lesbian people in our society today.

Some voices today, especially among my college students and among intelligentsia in general, declare that the Bible is an oppressive book because it supported slavery, and it still suppresses women and condemns gays. I say that this is not true whenever I have the opportunity; I try to teach the students otherwise. That is one of the reasons for writing this book. Maybe I am defending the Bible against its critics as much as I am defending the rights of gay and lesbian individuals.

11

Conclusion

I HAVE ATTEMPTED TO sail between the Scylla and Charybdis of two very different attitudes toward the biblical text. One approach to the Bible appropriates the text literally and maintains that women must be subordinate in society and obedient to their husbands, and that homosexuality is an egregious sin against God and must be condemned. I deal with such views in the ecclesiastical circles in which I sometimes move. Two centuries ago people with these views would have strongly supported the institution of slavery. The other approach to the Bible evaluates the text critically and maintains that it is an oppressive document and must be radically depatriarchalized or interpreted in such a way that its oppressive structures may be unveiled and rejected. Even though these critical advocates still maintain that it is a valuable document for religious life, this approach somehow loses the text as a theological authority for the church and for religious people in general. The Bible essentially is the only source that all Christians use in common for theology and ethics, so that to lose it would give Christians ultimately a great sense of anomie and loss of identity.

I seek to maintain the value of the Bible as a religious document that can speak authoritatively to the life of the institutional church and to believers in general. But in order for this to happen in a way that does not oppress people, the Bible must be understood in its historical context. We must understand that it comes from an age when slavery was an accepted institution, when women lived in a patriarchal society, and when sexual values were complex and different from our own. We must then see where the Bible stands in relationship to the values of that contemporary age, especially on the issues of slavery, debt-slavery, and the status of women. If we observe what were the values of that society and how the biblical narratives reflect the harsh realities of its age, we might see that the biblical authors attempted to transcend their age and their culture.

The authors of the biblical text may best be understood in the light of the legislation they proposed and in the light of how the narratives they relate often painfully reflect the harshness of their age. Biblical laws sought to elevate the rights and dignity of slaves, of the poor, and of women. If you do not believe in the inspiration of the biblical text, at least admit that the authors were intelligentsia who intellectually were ahead of their time. Of course, their values do not rise to the level of our modern egalitarian values, but that is because the biblical authors lived two thousand years ago. Recognize that what we believe today is in part an outcome of their beliefs and teachings, which have evolved over the years.

I have repeatedly appealed to the idea of evolution in this volume, I have spoken of a trajectory of values. When we see the teachings of the biblical authors, we do not ossify their beliefs and teachings as they articulated them. Rather, we should see that as they attempted to transcend the repression of their culture, the biblical authors set in motion an evolutionary advance that has continued up into our own day. They strove to advocate the rights and dignity of poor people and women; we should continue to engage in the same activity, and we should further develop the standards they set for us. In part, we have done that. They sought to provide rights for slaves; in modern era we sought abolitionism. Many abolitionists two centuries ago were motivated and inspired by passages in the biblical text. The biblical authors elevated the rights and dignity of women; in the modern age we have seen the emergence of women's suffrage and more recently the call for women's ordination in the churches. We are faithful to the biblical text when we seek to bring to fruition the movements of thought they initiated.

I have written this book primarily for college students. For most students the Bible is an outdated and meaningless work, and even in denominational schools that attitude is now prevalent among the majority of students. To them I say the Bible is a book of liberation; it set in motion ideas that would lead to abolitionism and women's rights in the modern era. Do not condemn it as a work that justifies slavery and women's subordination. Understand the Bible in its historical context and see where it was attempting to lead.

There is another type of student, not as common as the first type just mentioned. This person has been nurtured in very conservative Roman Catholic or Protestant circles and has been taught that women are meant to be submissive to men, that homosexuality is a great sin, and that the scientific theory of evolution is completely wrong. This student has received other teachings as well that reflect the conservative values of our age, especially from where I write, here in the southern United States. This person has been taught that the Bible adamantly teaches all of these things. As a college professor I have strained mightily for years to teach students otherwise, to teach students that the Bible is a testimony to egalitarianism and liberation, that all people, regardless of race or sex, are equal. (The issue for which I have been most criticized in the greater community of New Orleans is that I teach the compatibility of the Bible and the theory of evolution.)

This book is also written for other people. I would like to think it has value for clergy, who may find themselves confronting the same folks I describe: those who call themselves born-again or Bible-believing Christians as well as those who view themselves and intellectuals and who view the Bible as a regressive book. Perhaps this volume will provide these intellectuals with points to counter those who use the Bible to subordinate women and attack homosexuals. However, such debates often prove fruitless. Perhaps this volume can provide intellectuals with reassurance that their beliefs about human equality, women's rights, and gay rights can be substantiated by recourse to the biblical text. At least I hope that this volume can provide some readers with a meaningful exercise in an intellectual quest through the biblical text.

This is a textbook, not a scholarly work. Critical readers will observe that I summarize what many scholars and commentators have said over the years. But too often their words do not filter down to general audiences. This book tries to speak to a broader audience, or at least a college crowd, perhaps religious-studies majors. Footnotes abound in the work, though not in profuse number, in order to demonstrate that the arguments presented here are based on substantive scholarship from the guild. They also provide direction for further reading and research, if a person is so-minded to move in that direction.

In terms of originality, I have again pursued my paradigm of "emergent monotheism," which I have discussed in previous works over the past thirty years. I believe that monotheistic faith is always developing, and it has been developing for the past two thousand years or more. Monotheism brings with it specific values about human dignity and equality, and these values develop more as the years pass. Ultimately, monotheism carries with it many implications, but for society to truly hear and incorporate totally those implications takes time. As I have said throughout the book, society must be ready to hear the message of the great intellectuals who crafted the biblical text before the implications of their message can be fully implemented.

Along the way, I have proposed some creative ideas. Perhaps to some they might be persuasive. The most significant of these might be my suggestion that Paul is describing the Isis cult in Romans 1. You may or may not be convinced by the presentation. It is difficult to convincingly prove any new great argument in biblical studies. If it were possible to marshal an argument for some grand new insight, rest assured that some German scholar probably mentioned it briefly in a late nineteenth- or early twentieth-century commentary. The obvious has already been exposited; what remains, I believe, are suggestive arguments. Paul's condemnation of the Isis cult is a suggestive or probative argument. My detailed comparison of the Gibeah (Judges 19) and Sodom (Genesis 19) story is distinctive. So are my detailed arguments for cultic prostitution in Leviticus 18 and 20 and the use of New Testament vice lists to highlight the sins of average Christians. Otherwise the analysis of biblical texts connected to slaves, debt-slaves, land restoration, and women's rights in both testaments, and the commentary on passages in Genesis 1–3 all generally summarize what other great commentators have said about the texts in question.

I hope that this volume speaks to you as a reader in a meaningful fashion. To those of you who are pedagogues, I hope it gives you ideas for your educational discourse in either church or academy. Perhaps you might even find use for this volume as a textbook. But, above all, I hope that the message of this book has made an impression: The Bible is a volume that speaks of human liberation, dignity, and equality. Few today seem to understand that; the message must be proclaimed.

Bibliography

Albertz, Rainer. *A History of Israelite Religion in the Old Testament Period.* Translated by John Bowden. 2 vols. OTL. Louisville: Westminster John Knox, 1994.

Alter, Robert. *The Art of Biblical Narrative.* New York: Basic Books, 1981.

Amit, Yairah. "The Jubilee Law—an Attempt at Instituting Social Justice." In *Justice and Righteousness: Biblical Themes and Their Influence*, edited by Henning Graf Reventlow and Yair Hoffman, 47–59. JSOTSup 137. Sheffield: JSOT Press, 1992.

Angus, Samuel. *The Mystery-Religions and Christianity.* London: Murray, 1928.

Apuleius. *The Golden Ass: Being the Metamorphoses of Lucius Apuleius.* Translated by W. Adlington. Revised by S. Gaselee. Loeb Classical Library. Cambridge: Harvard University Press, 1965 (orig. ed. 1915).

Arneth, Martin. "Der Exodus der Sklaven." *Kerygma und Dogma* 59 (2013) 109–24.

Baird, William. *1 Corinthians, 2 Corinthians.* Knox Preaching Guides. Atlanta: John Knox, 1980.

Bal, Mieke. "Dealing/With/Women: Daughters in the Book of Judges." In *Women in the Hebrew Bible*, edited by Alice Bach, 317–33. New York: Routledge, 1999.

Balch, David L., ed. *Homosexuality, Science, and the "Plain Sense" of Scripture.* 2000. Reprinted, Eugene, OR: Wipf & Stock, 2007.

Barrett, C. K. *A Commentary on the First Epistle to the Corinthians.* Harper's New Testament Commentaries. New York: Harper & Row, 1968.

Bartchy, S. Scott. *MALLON CHRESAI: First-Century Slavery and 1 Corinthians 7:21.* SBLDS 11. 1973. Reprinted, Eugene, OR: Wipf & Stock, 2003.

———. "Philemon, Epistle to." In *The Anchor Bible Dictionary*, edited by David Noel Freedman, 6:305–10. 6 vols. New York: Doubleday, 1992.

———. "Slavery (Graeco-Roman)." In *The Anchor Bible Dictionary*, edited by David Noel Freedman, 5:65–72. 6 vols. New York: Doubleday, 1992.

———. "Who Should Be Called Father? Paul of Tarsus between the Jesus Tradition and Patria Potestas." *BTB* 33 (2003) 135–47.

Bauckham, Richard. *Jude, 2 Peter.* WBC 50. Waco, TX: Word, 1983.

Berman, Joshua. "The History of Legal Theory and the Study of Biblical Law." *CBQ* 76 (2014) 19–39.

Bird, Phyllis. "The Bible in Christian Ethical Deliberation concerning Homosexuality: Old Testament Contributions." In *Homosexuality, Science and the "Plain Sense" of Scripture*, edited by David L. Balch 142–76. 2000. Reprinted, Eugene, OR: Wipf & Stock, 2007.

———. "The End of the Male Cult Prostitute." In *Congress Volume: Cambridge 1995; Fifteenth Congress of the International Organization for the Study of the Old Testament,* edited by J. A. Emerton, 37–80. Vetus Testamentum Supplements 66. Leiden: Brill, 1997.

Boswell, John. *Christianity, Social Tolerance, and Homosexuality: Gay People in Western Europe from the Beginning of the Christian Era to the Fourteenth Century.* Chicago: University of Chicago Press, 1980.

Bottéro, Jean. "Le 'Code' de Hammurabi." *Annali della Scuola Normale Superiore di Pisa classe di lettere e filosophia* 12 (1982) 409–44.

Brawley, Robert L., ed. *Biblical Ethics & Homosexuality: Listening to Scripture.* Louisville: Westminster John Knox, 1996.

Braxton, Brad Ronnell. *The Tyranny of Resolution: 1 Corinthians 7:17–24.* SBLDS 181. Atlanta: Society of Biblical Literature, 2000.

Brettler, Marc. "The Book of Judges: Literature as Politics." *JBL* 108 (1989) 395–418.

Briggs, Sheila. "Paul on Bondage and Freedom in Imperial Roman Society." In *Paul and Politics: Ekklesia, Israel, Imperium, Interpretation,* edited by Richard A. Horsley, 110–23. Harrisburg, PA: Trinity, 2000.

Bristow, John. *What Paul Really Said about Women.* San Francisco: HarperSanFrancisco, 1991.

Brooten, Bernadette J. *Love between Women: Early Christian Responses to Female Homoeroticism.* Chicago Series on Sexuality, History, and Society. Chicago: University of Chicago Press, 1996.

Bruce, F. F. *The Epistles to the Colossians, to Philemon, and to the Ephesians.* New International Commentary of the New Testament. Grand Rapids: Eerdmans, 1984.

Brueggemann, Walter. *Old Testament Theology: Essays on Structure, Theme, and Text.* Edited by Patrick Miller. Minneapolis: Fortress, 1992.

———. *The Prophetic Imagination.* 2nd ed. Minneapolis: Fortress, 2001.

Cahill, Thomas. *Desire of the Everlasting Hills: The World before and after Jesus.* New York: Doubleday, 1999.

Carden, Michael. "Homophobia and Rape in Sodom and Gibeah: A Response to Ken Stone." *JSOT* 82 (1999) 83–96.

Carmichael, Calum. "The Three Laws on the Release of Slaves (Ex 21,2–11; Dtn 15,12–18; Lev 25,39–46." *ZAW* 112 (2000) 509–25.

Chaney, Marvin L. "Debt Easement in Israelite History and Tradition." In *The Bible and the Politics of Exegesis: Essays in Honor of Norman K. Gottwald on His Sixty-fifth Birthday,* edited by David Jobling et al., 172–39. Cleveland: Pilgrim, 1991.

Charpin, Dominique. "Les Decrets Royaux á l'Epoque Paleo-babylonienne, á Propos d'un Ouvrage Recent." *Archiv für Orientforshung* 34 (1987) 36–44.

Chirichigno, Gregory C. *Debt-Slavery in Israel and the Ancient Near East.* JSOTSup 141. Sheffield: Sheffield Academic, 1993.

Cobb, John B. *Christ in a Pluralistic Age.* Philadelphia: Westminster, 1975.

Comblin, Joseph. "Monotheism and Popular Religion." Translated by Dinah Livingstone. In *Monotheism,* edited by Claude Geffré et al., 91–99. Concilium 177. Edinburgh: T. & T. Clark, 1985.

Conon, Gérald. "Le péché de Sodome: Exégése et herméneutique." *Theoforum* 38 (2007) 17–40.

Conzelmann, Hans. *1 Corinthians.* Translated by James W. Leitch. Hermeneia. Philadelphia: Fortress, 1976.

Coogan, Michael, ed. *The New Oxford Annotated Bible: New Revised Standard Version*. 3rd ed. New York: Oxford University Press, 2001.

Countryman, L. William. *Dirt, Greed, and Sex: Sexual Ethics in the New Testament and Their Implications for Today*. 2nd ed. Minneapolis: Fortress, 2007.

Cousar, Charles B. *Galatians*. Interpretation. Atlanta: John Knox, 1982.

Craigie, Peter C. *The Book of Deuteronomy*. New International Commentary on the Old Testament. Grand Rapids: Eerdmans, 1976.

Croatto, Severino J. *Exodus: A Hermeneutics of Freedom*. Translated by Salvator Attanasio. Maryknoll, NY: Orbis, 1981.

Crüsemann, Frank. *The Torah: The Theology and History of Old Testament Law*. Translated by Allan W. Mahnke. Minneapolis: Fortress, 1996.

Cumont, Franz. *The Oriental Religions in Roman Paganism*. New York: Dover, 1956 (orig. ed. 1911).

Danker, Frederick. "Isis." In *New Interpreter's Dictionary of the Bible*, edited by Katharine Doob Sackenfeld, 3:95–96. 5 vols. Nashville: Abingdon, 2006–2009.

Davies, Philip R. *Scribes and Schools: The Canonization of the Hebrew Scriptures*. Library of Ancient Israel. Louisville: Westminster John Knox, 1998.

Dawes, Gregory W. "'But If You Can Gain Your Freedom' (1 Corinthians 7:17–24)." *CBQ* 52 (1990) 681–97.

Debel, Hans. "An Admonition on Sexual Affairs: A Reconsideration of Rom 1:26–27." *Louvain Studies* 34 (2009–10) 39–64.

Dever, William G. "How Was Ancient Israel Different?" In *The Breakout: The Origins of Civilization*, edited by Martha Lambert-Karlovsky, 62–67. Peabody Museum Monographs 9. Cambridge: Peabody Museum of Archaeology and Ethnology, Harvard University, 2000.

DeYoung, James B. *Homosexuality: Contemporary Claims Examined in Light of the Bible and Other Ancient Literature and Law*. Grand Rapids: Kregel, 2000.

Dibelius, Martin, and Hans Conzelmann. *The Pastoral Epistles*. Translated by Philip Buttolph and Adela Yarbro. Hermeneia. Philadelphia: Fortress, 1972.

Dietrich, Walter. "Über Werden und Wesen des biblischen Monotheismus." In *Ein Gott allein? JHWH-Verehrung und biblischer Monotheismus im Kontext der israelitischen und altorientalischen Religionsgeschichte*, edited by Walter Dietrich and Martin Klopfenstein 13–30. Orbis biblicus et orientalis 139. Göttingen: Vandenhoeck & Ruprecht, 1994.

Driver, Samuel. *Deuteronomy*. 3rd ed. International Critical Commentary. Edinburgh: T. & T. Clark, 1902.

Dunn, James D. G. *The Epistles to the Colossians and to Philemon*. The New International Greek Testament Commentary. Grand Rapids: Eerdmans, 1996.

Edwards, Chilperic. *The Hammurabi Code, and Sinaitic Legislation*. Port Washington, NY: Kennikat, 1904.

Elliott, John H. "No Kingdom of God for Softies? Or, What Was Paul Really Saying? Corinthians 6:9–10 in Context." *BTB* 34 (2004) 17–40.

Elliott, Neil. *Liberating Paul: The Justice of God and the Politics of the Apostle*. Bible and Liberation. Maryknoll, NY: Orbis, 1994.

Embry, Brad. "The 'Naked Narrative' from Noah to Leviticus: Reassessing Voyeurism in the Account of Noah's Nakedness in Genesis 9:22–24." *JSOT* 35 (2011) 417–33.

Esler, Philip F. "The Sodom Tradition in Romans 1:18–32." *BTB* 34 (2004) 4–16.

Fager, Jeffrey. "Land Tenure in the Biblical Jubilee: A Moral World View." *Hebrew Annual Review* 11 (1987) 59–68.

Fee, Gordon D. *The First Epistle to the Corinthians*. New International Commentary on the New Testament. Grand Rapids: Eerdmans, 1987.

Fensham, F. Charles. "Widow, Orphan, and the Poor in Ancient Near Eastern Legal Literature." *Journal for Near Eastern Studies* 21 (1962) 161–71.

Fields, Weston W. *Sodom and Gomorrah: History and Motif in Biblical Narrative*. JSOTSup 231. Sheffield: Sheffield Academic, 1997.

Fishbane, Michael. *Biblical Interpretation in Ancient Israel*. Oxford: Clarendon, 1985.

Fitzmyer, Joseph A. *The Letter to Philemon*. Anchor Bible 34C. New York: Doubleday, 2000.

Fitzpatrick-McKinley, Anne. *The Transformation of Torah from Scribal Advice to Law*. JSOTSup 287. Sheffield: Sheffield Academic, 1999.

Fowden, Garth. *Empire to Commonwealth: Consequences of Monotheism in Late Antiquity*. Princeton: Princeton University Press, 1993.

Frederickson, David E. "Natural and Unnatural Use in Romans 1:24–27: Paul and the Philosophic Critique of Eros." In *Homosexuality, Science and the "Plain Sense" of Scripture*, edited by David L. Balch, 197–222. 2000. Reprinted, Eugene, OR: Wipf & Stock, 2007.

Freedman, David Noel, ed. *The Anchor Bible Dictionary*. 6 vols. New York: Doubleday, 1992.

Frymer-Kensky, Tikva. *Reading the Women of the Bible: A New Interpretation of Their Stories*. New York: Schocken, 2002.

Furnish, Victor Paul. *The Moral Teaching of Paul*. Nashville: Abingdon, 1979.

———. "What Does the Bible Say about Homosexuality?" In *Caught in the Crossfire: Helping Christians Debate Homosexuality*, edited by Sally B. Geis and Donald E. Messer, 57–66. Nashville: Abingdon, 1994.

Gagnon, Robert A. J. *The Bible and Homosexual Practice: Texts and Hermeneutics*. Nashville: Abingdon, 2001.

Gamoran, Hillel. "The Biblical Law against Interest on Loans." *Journal of Near Eastern Studies* 30 (1971) 125–35.

Gerberding, Keith. "Women Who Toil in Ministry, Even as Paul." *CTM* 18 (1991) 285–91.

Gerstenberger, Erhard S. "In der Schuldenfalle: Zwangsvollstreckung? Insolvenzregelungen in Lev 25 und ihre theologischen Folgen." *Bibel und Kirche* 62 (2007) 16–21.

———. *Yahweh—the Patriarch: Ancient Images of God and Feminist Theology*. Translated by Frederick J. Gaiser. Minneapolis: Fortress, 1996.

Getty, Mary Ann. *Philippians and Philemon*. New Testament Message 14. Wilmington, DE: Glazier, 1980.

Gimbutas, Marija. *The Gods and Goddesses of Old Europe, 7000–3500 B.C., Myths and Legends*. London: Thames & Hudson, 1974.

Glancy, Jennifer A. *Slavery in Early Christianity*. Oxford: Oxford University Press, 2002.

Glass, Zipporah. "Land, Slave Labor and Law: Engaging Ancient Israel's Economy." *Journal for the Study of the Old Testament* 91 (2000) 27–39.

Gnuse, Robert Karl. "Breakthrough or Tyranny: Monotheism's Contested Implications." *Horizons* 34 (2007) 78–95.

———. "Jubilee Legislation in Leviticus: Israel's Vision of Social Reform." *BTB* 15 (1985) 43–48.

————. *Misunderstood Stories: Theological Commentary on Genesis 1–11*. Eugene, OR: Cascade Books, 2014.

————. *No Other Gods: Emergent Monotheism in Israel*. JSOTSup 241. Sheffield: Sheffield Academic, 1997.

————. *No Tolerance for Tyrants: The Biblical Assault on Kings and Kingship*. Collegeville, MN: Liturgical, 2011.

————. *The Old Testament and Process Theology*. St. Louis: Chalice, 2000.

————. "Seven Gay Texts: Biblical Passages Used to Condemn Homosexuality." *BTB* 45 (2015) 68–87.

————. *You Shall Not Steal: Community and Property in the Biblical Tradition*. 1985. Reprinted, Eugene, OR: Wipf & Stock, 2011.

Goldenberg, Robert. *The Nations That Know Thee Not: Ancient Jewish Attitudes towards Other Religions*. Reappraisals of the Jews' Social and Intellectual History. New York: New York University Press, 1998.

Gowan, Donald. "Wealth and Poverty in the Old Testament: The Case of the Widow, the Orphan, and the Sojourner." *Interpretation* 41 (1987) 354–67.

Grayson, A. K. *Assyrian Rulers of the Third and Second Millennium B.C.* The Royal Inscriptions of Mesopotamia. Assyrian Periods 1. Toronto: University of Toronto Press, 1987.

Greengus, Samuel. "Legal and Social Institutions of Ancient Mesopotamia." In *Civilizations of the Ancient Near East*, edited by Jack Sasson, 1:469–84. 4 vols. 1995. Reprinted, Peabody, MA: Hendrickson, 2000.

Gross, Rita. "Religious Diversity: Some Implications for Monotheism." *Cross Currents* 49 (1999) 349–66.

Gryson, Roger. *The Ministry of Women in the Early Church*. Translated by Jean Laporte and Mary Louise Hall. Collegeville, MN: Liturgical, 1976.

Habel, Norman C. "The Future of Social Justice Research in the Hebrew Scriptures: Questions of Authority and Relevance." In *Old Testament Interpretation: Past, Present, and Future*, edited by James Luther Mays et al., 277–91. Nashville: Abingdon, 1995.

Hamilton, Jeffries M. *Social Justice and Deuteronomy*. Society of Biblical Literature Dissertation Series 136. Atlanta: Scholars, 1992.

Harrill, J. Albert. "Paul and Slavery: The Problem of 1 Corinthians 7:21." *Biblical Research* 39 (1994) 5–28.

Harris, Roberta L. *The World of the Bible*. London: Thames & Hudson, 1995.

Hays, Richard B. *The Moral Vision of the New Testament*. San Francisco: HarperSanFrancisco, 1996.

Hopkins, David C. *The Highlands of Canaan: Agricultural Life in the Early Iron Age*. The Social World of Biblical Antiquity Series 3. Sheffield: Almond, 1985.

Hippolytus. *The Refutation of All Heresies*, book 5. Translated by J. H. MacMahon. In *The Ante-Nicene Fathers*, edited by Alexander Roberts and James Donaldson, 5: Grand Rapids: Eerdmans, 1978.

Horner, Tom. *Jonathan Loved David: :Homosexuality in Biblical Times*. Philadelphia: Westminster, 1978.

————. *Sex in the Bible*. Rutland, VT: Tuttle, 1974.

Hudson, Michael. "Proclaim Liberty throughout the Land: The Economic Roots of Jubilee." *Bible Review* 15/1 (1999) 26–33.

Hultgren, Arland J. "Being Faithful to the Scriptures: Romans 1:26–27 as a Case in Point." *Word & World* 14 (1994) 315–25.

Hyatt, J. Philip. *Commentary on Exodus*. New Century Bible. London: Oliphants, 1971.

Jackson, Bernard S. "Ideas of Law and Legal Administration: A Semiotic Approach." In *The World of Ancient Israel: Sociological, Anthropological, and Political Perspectives*, edited by R. E. Clements, 185–202. Cambridge: Cambridge University Press, 1989.

Jacobsen, Thorkild, ed. and trans. *The Harps That Once—Sumerian Poetry in Translation*. New Haven: Yale University Press, 1987.

Jewett, Robert. "The Social Context and Implications of Homoerotic References in Romans 1:24–27." In *Homosexuality, Science and the "Plain Sense" of Scripture*, edited by David L. Balch, 223–41. 2000. Reprinted, Eugene, OR: Wipf & Stock, 2007.

Johnson, Luke Timothy. *1 Timothy, 2 Timothy, Titus*. Knox Preaching Guides. Atlanta: John Knox, 1987.

Johnson, William Stacy. "Empire and Order: The Gospel and Same-Gender Relationships." *BTB* 37 (2007) 161–73.

———. *A Time to Embrace: Same-Gender Relationships in Religion, Law, and Politics*. Grand Rapids: Eerdmans, 2006.

Kalin, Everett R. "Romans 1:26–27 and Homosexuality." *CTM* 30 (2003) 423–32.

Kelly, J. N. D. *A Commentary on the Pastoral Epistles: Timothy I & II, and Titus*. Harper's New Testament Commentaries. San Francisco: Harper & Row, 1960.

Kessler, Rainer. "Das Erlassjahrgesetz Dtn 15,1–11: Ein Gebot und seine Umsetzung." *Theologie und Glaube* 100 (2010) 15–30.

Kilchör, Benjamin. "Frei aber arm? Soziale Sicherheit als Schlüssel zum Verhältnis der Sklaven freilassungsgesetze im Pentateuch." *Vetus Testamentum* 62 (2012) 381–97.

Knight, Douglas A. *Law, Power, and Justice in Ancient Israel*. Library of Ancient Israel. Louisville: Westminster John Knox, 2011.

Knohl, Israel. *The Sanctuary of Silence: The Priestly Torah and the Holiness School*. Minneapolis: Fortress, 1995.

Lamberg-Karlovsky, C. C. "The Near Eastern 'Breakout' and the Mesopotamian Social Contract." In *The Breakout: The Origins of Civilization*, edited by Martha Lamberg-Karlovsky, 12–23. Peabody Museum Monographs 9. Cambridge: Peabody Museum of Archaeology and Ethnology, Harvard University, 2000.

Lamberg-Karlovsky, Martha, ed. *The Breakout: The Origins of Civilization*. Peabody Museum Monographs 9. Cambridge: Peabody Museum of Archaeology and Ethnology, Harvard University, 2000.

Lambert, Maurice. "Les 'Reforms' d'Urukagina." *Revue d'assyriologie et d'archéologie orientale* 50 (1956)169–84.

Lang, Bernard. *Monotheism and the Prophetic Minority: An Essay in Biblical History and Sociology*. The Social World of Biblical Antiquity Series 1. Sheffield: Almond, 1983.

Lasine, Stuart. "Guest and Host in Judges 19: Lot's Hospitality in an Inverted World." *JSOT* 29 (1984) 37–59.

Lehner, Mark. "Absolutism and Reciprocity in Ancient Egypt." In *The Breakout: The Origins of Civilization,* edited by Martha Lamberg-Karlovsky, 84–87. Cambridge: Peabody Museum of Archaeology and Ethnology, Harvard University, 2000.

Lerner, Gerda. *The Creation of Patriarchy*. Women and History 1. New York: Oxford University Press, 1986.

Leuchter, Mark. "The Manumission Laws in Leviticus and Deuteronomy: The Jeremiah Connection." *JBL* 127 (2008) 635–53.

Loader, William. *Sexuality in the New Testament: Understanding the Key Texts*. Louisville: Westminster John Knox, 2010.

Loewenstamm, Samuel E. "Law." In *The Judges*, edited by Benjamin Mazar, 231–67. The History of the Jewish People: Ancient Times (1st ser.) 3. New Brunswick, NJ: Rutgers University Press, 1971.

———. "*Neshek* and *m/tarbith*." *JBL* 88 (1969) 78–80.

Lohse, Eduard. *Colossians and Philemon*. Translated by William Poehlmann and Robert Karris. Hermeneia. Philadelphia: Fortress, 1971.

Lopez, René A. "Does the Vice List in 1 Corinthians 6:9–10 Describe Believers or Unbelievers?" *Bibliotheca Sacra* 164 (2007) 59–73.

Lowery, Richard H. *Sabbath and Jubilee*. Understanding Biblical Themes. St. Louis: Chalice, 2000.

Lutz, Donald. "The Relative Influence of European Writers on Late Eighteenth Century American Political Thought." *American Political Science Review* 78 (1984) 189–97.

Malchow, Bruce V. *Social Justice in the Hebrew Bible: What's New and What's Old*. Collegeville, MN: Liturgical, 1996.

Maloney, Robert P. "Usury and Restrictions on Interest-Taking in the Ancient Near East." *CBQ* 36 (1974) 1–20.

Marquard, Odo. "Lob des Polytheismus: über Monomythie und Polymythie." In *Philosophie und Mythos*, edited by Hans Poser, 40–58. Berlin: de Gruyter, 1979.

Marshall, Jay W. *Israel and the Book of the Covenant: An Anthropological Approach to Biblical Law*. SBLDS 140. Atlanta: Scholars, 1993.

Martin, Dale B. "*Arsenokoites* and *Malakos*: Meanings and Consequences." In *Biblical Ethics & Homosexuality: Listening to Scripture*, edited by Robert L. Brawley, 117–36. Louisville: Westminster John Knox, 1996.

———. *Slavery as Salvation: The Metaphor of Slavery in Pauline Christianity*. New Haven: Yale University Press, 1990.

Matthews, Victor H. "Hospitality and Hostility in Genesis 19 and Judges 19." *BTB* 22 (1992) 3–11.

McDonald, Nathan. "Hospitality and Hostility: Reading Genesis 19 in Light of 2 Samuel 10 (and Vice Versa)." In *Universalism and Particularism in Sodom and Gomorrah: Essays in Memory of Ron Pirson*, edited by Diana Lipton, 179–90. Society of Biblical Literature: Ancient Israel and Its Literature 11. Atlanta: Society of Biblical Literature, 2012.

McNeill, John J. *The Church and the Homosexual*. Rev. ed. Boston: Beacon, 1988.

Mendelsohn, Isaac. *Slavery in the Ancient Near East*. New York: Oxford University Press, 1949.

———. "Slavery in the Old Testament." In *Interpreter's Dictionary of the Bible*, edited by George Buttrick, 4:383–91. 4 vols. New York: Abingdon, 1962.

Meyers, Carol L. *Households and Holiness*. Facets. Minneapolis: Fortress, 2005.

Michaels, Axel. "Monotheismus und Fundamentalismus. Eine These und ihre Gegenthese." In *Ein Gott allein? JHWH-Verehrung und biblischer Monotheismus im Kontext der israelitischen und altorientalischen Religionsgeschichte*, edited by Walter Dietrich and Martin Klopfenstein, 51–57. Orbis biblicus et orientalis 139. Göttingen: Vandenhoeck und Ruprecht, 1994.

Michaelson, Jay. *God vs. Gay?: The Religious Case for Equality*. Queer Action / Queer Ideas. Boston: Beacon, 2011.

Milgrom, Jacob. "Sweet Land and Liberty." *Bible Review* 9/4 (1993) 8, 54.

Miller, J. E. "Pederasty and Romans 1:27: A Response to Mark Smith." *Journal of the American Academy of Religion* 65 (1997) 861–66.

————. "The Practices of Romans 1:26: Homosexual or Heterosexual?" *Novum Testamentum* 37 (1995) 1–11.

Mitchell, Hinckley G. T. *Ethics of the Old Testament*. Chicago: University of Chicago Press, 1912.

Moore, George F. *A Critical and Exegetical Commentary on Judges*. The International Critical Commentary. Edinburgh: T. & T. Clark, 1895.

Morgenstern, Julian. "Sabbatical Year." In *Interpreter's Dictionary of the Bible*, edited by George A. Buttrick, 4:142. 4 vols. New York: Abingdon, 1962.

Murphy-O'Connor, J. *1 Corinthians*. Doubleday Bible Commentary. New York: Doubleday, 1998.

Neufeld, E. "The Prohibitions against Loans at Interest in Ancient Hebrew Law." *Hebrew Union College Annual* 226 (1955) 355–412.

Nicholson, Ernst. "Deuteronomy's Vision of Israel." In *Storia e tradizioni di Israele*, edited by D. Garrone and F. Israele, 191–204. Brescia: Paideia, 1991.

Niditch, Susan. "The 'Sodomite' Theme in Judges 19–20: Family, Community, and Social Disintegration." *CBQ* 44 (1982) 365–78.

Nissinen, Martti. *Homoeroticism in the Biblical World: A Historical Perspective*. Translated by Kirsi Stjerna. Minneapolis: Fortress, 1998.

Nolland, John. "Romans 1:26–27 and the Homosexuality Debate." *Horizons in Biblical Theology* 22 (2000) 32–57.

North, Robert Grady. *Sociology of the Biblical Jubilee*. Analecta Biblica 4. Rome: Pontifical Biblical Institute, 1954.

Oden, Robert A. *The Bible Without Theology: The Theological Tradition and Alternatives to It*. New Voices in Biblical Studies. San Francisco: Harper & Row, 1987.

O'Grady, John E. "Postmodernism and the Interpretation of Biblical Texts for Behavior." *BTB* 33 (2003) 95–103.

Olyan, Saul M. "'And with a Male You Shall Not Lie the Lying Down of a Woman': On the Meaning and Significance of Leviticus 18:22 and 20:13." *Journal of the History of Sexuality* 5 (1994) 179–206.

Otto, Eckart. "False Weights in the Scales of Biblical Justice." In *Gender and Law in the Hebrew Bible and the Ancient Near East*, edited by Victor H. Matthews et al., 128–46. JSOTSup 262. Sheffield: Shef-field Academic, 1998.

Otwell, John H. *And Sarah Laughed: The Status of Woman in the Old Testament*. Philadelphia: Westminster, 1977.

Patrick, Dale. *Old Testament Law*. 1985. Reprinted, Eugene, OR: Wipf & Stock, 2011.

Petersen, David L. "Israel and Monotheism: The Unfinished Agenda." In *Canon, Theology, and Old Testament Interpretation: Essays in Honor of Brevard S. Childs*, edited by Gene Tucker et al., 92–107. Philadelphia: Fortress, 1988.

Petersen, Norman R. *Rediscovering Paul: Philemon and the Sociology of Paul's Narrative World*. 1985. Reprinted, Eugene, OR: Wipf & Stock, 2008.

Phillips, Anthony. *Ancient Israel's Criminal Law: A New Approach to the Decalogue*. Oxford: Blackwell, 1970.

————. *Deuteronomy*. Cambridge Bible Commentary. Cambridge: Cambridge University Press, 1973.

Phipps, William E. "Paul on 'Unnatural' Sex." *CTM* 29 (2002) 128–31.

Pizzuto, Vincent. "'God Has Made It Plain to Them': An Indictment of Rome's Hermeneutic Homophobia." *BTB* 38 (2008) 163–83.

Porter, J. R. *Leviticus.* Cambridge Bible Commentary. Cambridge: Cambridge University Press, 1976.

Pritchard, James B., ed. *Ancient Near Eastern Texts Relating to the Old Testament.* 3rd ed. Princeton: Princeton University Press, 1969.

Pruitt, Brad A. "The Sabbatical Year of Release: The Social Location and Practice of *Semittah* in Deuteronomy 15:1–18." *Restoration Quarterly* 52 (2010) 81–92.

Rad, Gerhard von. *Genesis.* Rev. ed. Translated by John H. Marks. OTL. Philadelphia: Westminster, 1972.

Rankin, O. S. *Israel's Wisdom Literature: Its Bearing on Theology and the History of Religion.* 1936. Reprinted, New York: Schocken, 1969.

Richie, Cristina. "An Argument against the Use of the Word 'Homosexual' in English Translations of the Bible." *Heythrop Journal* 51 (2010) 723–29.

Roth, Martha, ed. *Law Collections from Mesopotamia and Asia Minor.* 2nd ed. Society of Biblical Literature Writings from the Ancient World 6. Atlanta: Scholars, 1997.

Saggs, H. W. F. *Babylonians.* Peoples of the Past 1. Norman: University of Oklahoma Press, 1995.

Sampley, J. Paul. *Pauline Partnership in Christ: Christian Community and Commitment in Light of Roman Law.* Philadelphia: Fortress, 1980.

Sanders, James A. *The Monotheistic Process.* Eugene, OR: Cascade Books, 2014.

Schüssler Fiorenza, Elisabeth. *In Memory of Her: A Feminist Theological Reconstruction of Christian Origins.* New York: Crossroad, 1983.

Schwartz, Regina M. *The Curse of Cain: The Violent Legacy of Monotheism.* Chicago: University of Chicago Press, 1997.

Scroggs, Robin. *The New Testament and Homosexuality: Contextual Background for Contemporary Debate.* Philadelphia: Fortress, 1983.

Siker, Jeffrey S. "Homosexuality." In *New Interpreter's Dictionary of the Bible,* edited by Katharine Doob Sackenfeld, 2:882–84. 5 vols. Nashville: Abingdon, 2006–2009.

Smith, Mark D. "Ancient Bisexuality and the Interpretation of Romans 1:26–27." *Journal of the American Academy of Religion* 64 (1996) 223–56.

Smith, Mark S. *The Early History of God: Yahweh and the Other Deities in Ancient Israel.* 2nd ed. Biblical Resource Series. Grand Rapids: Eerdmans, 2002.

———. *Memoirs of God: History, Memory, and the Experience of the Divine in Ancient Israel.* Minneapolis: Fortress, 2004.

———. *The Origins of Biblical Monotheism.* Oxford: Oxford University Press, 2000.

Snaith, Norman H. *Leviticus and Numbers.* Century Bible. London: Nelson, 1967.

Snyder, Graydon F. *First Corinthians: A Faith Community Commentary.* Macon, GA: Mercer University Press, 1992.

Soggin, J. Alberto. *Judges: A Commentary.* Translated by John Bowden. OTL. Philadelphia: Westminster, 1981.

Sperling, S. David. *The Original Torah: The Political Intent of the Bible's Writers.* Reappraisals in Jewish Social and Intellectual History. New York: New York University Press, 1998.

Stackert, Jeffry. "The Sabbath of the Land in the Holiness Legislation: Combining Priestly and Non-Priestly Perspectives." *CBQ* 73 (2011) 239–50.

Stein, Siegfried. "The Laws on Interest in the Old Testament." *Journal of Theological Studies* 4 (1953) 161–70.

Steinberg, Naomi. "The Deuteronomic Law Code and the Politics of State." In *The Bible and the Politics of Exegesis: Essays in Honor of Norman K. Gottwald on His Sixty-fifth Birthday,* edited by David Jobling et al., 161–70. Cleveland: Pilgrim, 1991.

Stiebert, J., and J. T. Walsh. "Does the Hebrew Bible Have Anything to Say about Homosexuality?" *Old Testament Essays* 14 (2001) 119–52.

Stone, Ken. "Gender and Homosexuality in Judges 19: Subject-Honor, Object-Shame?" *JSOT* 67 (1995) 87–107.

Swidler, Leonard J. *Biblical Affirmations of Woman*. Philadelphia: Westminster, 1979.

Talbert, Charles H. *Reading Corinthians: A Literary and Theological Commentary on 1 and 2 Corinthians*. Reading the New Testament Series. New York: Crossroad, 1989.

Theissen, Gerd. *Biblical Faith: An Evolutionary Approach*. Translated by John Bowden. Philadelphia: Fortress, 1985.

Townsley, Jeramy. "Paul, the Goddess Religions, and Queer Sects: Romans 1:23–28." *JBL* 130 (2014) 707–28.

Trible, Phyllis. *God and the Rhetoric of Sexuality*. Overtures to Biblical Theology. Philadelphia: Fortress, 1978.

———. *Texts of Terror: Literary-Feminist Readings of Biblical Narratives*. Overtures to Bib-lical Theology. Philadelphia: Fortress, 1984.

Van Seters, John. *A Law Book for the Diaspora: Revision in the Study of the Covenant Code*. Oxford: Oxford University Press, 2003.

———. "The Law of the Hebrew Slave." *ZAW* 108 (1996) 534–46.

———. "The Law of the Hebrew Slave: A Continuing Debate." *ZAW* 119 (2007) 169–83.

Varso, Miroslave. "Interest (Usury) and Its Variations in the Biblical Law Codices." *Communio Viatorum* 50 (2008) 323–38.

Vaux, Roland de. *Ancient Israel: Its Life and Institutions*. Translated by John McHugh. New York: McGraw Hill, 1961.

Vervenne, Marc. "What Shall We Do with the Drunken Sailor? A Critical Re-Examination of Genesis 9:20–27." *JSOT* 68 (1995) 33–55.

Veyne, Paul. *The Roman Empire*. In *From Pagan Rome to Byzantium*, 5–233. Translated by Arthur Goldhammer. A History of the Private Life 1. Cambridge: Belknap, 1987.

Via, Dan O., and Robert A. J. Gagnon. *Homosexuality and the Bible: Two Views*. Minneapolis: Fortress, 2003.

Vogels, Walter. "Cham découvre les limites de son pére Noé." *Nouvelle Revue Théologique* 109 (1987) 554–73.

Wacholder, Ben Zion. "The Calendar of Sabbatical Cycles during the Second Temple and Early Rabbinic Period." *Hebrew Union College Annual* 44 (1973) 153–96.

———. "Sabbatical Year." In *Interpreter's Dictionary of the Bible Supplementary Volume*, edited by Keith Crim, 762–63. Nashville: Abingdon, 1976.

Waetjen, Herman C. "Same-Sex Sexual Relations in Antiquity and Sexuality and Sexual Identity in Contemporary American Society." In *Biblical Ethics & Homosexuality: Listening to Scripture*, edited by Robert L. Brawley, 103–16. Louisville: Westminster John Knox, 1996.

Waldow, Hans Eberhard von. "Social Responsibility and Social Structure in Early Israel." *CBQ* 32 (1970) 184–204.

Wall, Robert W. *Colossians & Philemon*. IVP New Testament Commentary Series 12. Downer's Grove, IL: InterVarsity, 1993.

Walsh, Jerome T. "Leviticus 18:22 and 20:13: Who is Doing What to Whom?" *JBL* 120 (2001) 201–9.

Watson, Alan. *The Evolution of Law*. Oxford: Blackwell, 1985.

Weber, Max. *Ancient Judaism*. Translated and edited by Hans Gerth and Don Martindale. Glencoe, IL: Free Press, 1952 (orig. ed. 1917–19).

Weinfeld, Moshe. *Social Justice in Ancient Israel and in the Ancient Near East*. Minneapolis: Fortress, 1995.

Wellhausen, Julius. *Prolegomena to the History of Ancient Israel*. Translated by Robertson Smith. Meridian Library 6. New York: Meridian, 1957.

Wenham, Gordon J. *Genesis 1–15*. WBC 1. Waco, TX: Word, 1987.

———. *Genesis 16–50*. WBC 2. Nashville: Nelson, 1994.

Westermann, Claus. *Genesis 1–11*. Translated by John J. Scullion. Continental Commentaries. Minneapolis: Augsburg, 1984.

———. *Genesis 12–36*. Translated by John J. Scullion. Continental Commentaries Minneapolis: Augsburg, 1985.

White, Leland J. "Does the Bible Speak about Gays or Same-Sex Orientation? A Test Case in Biblical Ethics: Part I." *BTB* 25 (1995) 14–23.

Willey, Gordon R. "Ancient Chinese, New World, and Near Eastern Ideological Traditions." In *The Breakout: The Origins of Civilization*, edited by Martha Lamberg-Karlovsky, 25–38. Cambridge: Peabody Museum of Archaeology and Ethnology, Harvard University, 2000.

Wold, Donald J. *Out of Order: Homosexuality in the Bible and the Ancient Near East*. Grand Rapids: Baker Academic, 1998.

Wright, Christopher J. H. *Deuteronomy*. New International Biblical Commentary: Old Testament Series 4. Peabody, MA: Hendrickson, 1996.

Wright, D. E. "Homosexuals or Prostitutes? The Meaning of *Arsenokoitai* (1 Cor. 6:9, 1 Tim 1:10)." *Vigiliae Christianae* 38 (1984) 125–53.

Scripture Index

Subject Index

Name Index

Alexander the Great, 50
Ambrose, 133
Amenemope, wisdom literature
    collections of, 30
Amenenhet, wisdom literature
    collections of, 30
Ammi-saduqa (1646–1626 BCE), 31
Ammi-saduqa (1646–1626), Edit
    of, 29
Andronicus, 103
Aphrodite, 154
Apollos, 65
Artargatis, 154
Asa, king of Judah, 140
Asherah, 15
    female temple prostitutes
        dedicated to, 140
Athaliah of Judah, 96
Augustus, Egyptian gods expelled
    from Rome by, 153

Boswell, John, 146
Brigid of Kildare, 113*n*
Brooten, Bernadette, 151

Cahill, Thomas, 106, 113
Caligula (37–41 CE), and Isis
    movement, 153
Canaan, curse on, 119
zzClement of Alexandria, 152
Constantine the Great, 9, 12
Cousar, Charles, 75
Crüsemann, Frank, 19

Darius I of Persia, 23
David, 95
de Vaux, Roland, 52
DeYoung, James, 140
Diana, 154

Elisha, 95, 96
Enmetana of Lagash (2404–2375
    BCE), 29, 30
Eshnnunna, Amorite law code from,
    31
Euodia, 104
Ezra, 11

Frymer-Kensky, Tikva, 10–11

Gagnon, Robert, 140–41, 156
Gerstenberger, Erhard S., 16
Gimbutas, Marija, 14
Goldenberg, Robert, 8–9
Gudea of Lagash (2404–2375 BCE),
    30

Ham, 119–21
Hamilton, Jeffries, 44
Hammurabi (1792–1750 BCE), 32
    Amorite law code from, 31
    justice and, 29
    Law Code, 25–26, 46
    laws on women as property,
        15–16
    misharum and *anduraru*
        proclamations, 44

Lightning Source UK Ltd.
Milton Keynes UK
UKOW04f1358150216

268396UK00002B/162/P